DEPARTMENT OF THE ARMY
WASHINGTON 25, D. C.

IN REPLY REFER TO:

CMH

SUBJECT: Distribution of Manuscript

TO : Addressee

    The inclosed manuscript is forwarded for your use and retention.

    FOR THE CHIEF OF MILITARY HISTORY:

1 Incl
  as

                  JOEL F. THOMASON
                  Colonel Artillery
                  Executive

Preface

Through Instructions No. 126 to the Japanese Government, 12 October 1945, subject: Institution for War Records Investigation, steps were initiated to exploit military historical records and official reports of the Japanese War Ministry and Japanese General Staff. Upon dissolution of the War Ministry and the Japanese General Staff, and the transfer of their former functions to the Demobilization Bureau, research and compilation continued and developed into a series of historical monographs.

The paucity of original orders, plans and unit journals, which are normally essential in the preparation of this type of record, most of which were lost or destroyed during field operations or bombing raids, rendered the task of compilation most difficult; particularly distressing has been the complete lack of official strength reports, normal in AG or G3 records. However, while many of the important orders, plans and estimates have been reconstructed from memory and therefore are not textually identical with the originals, they are believed to be generally accurate and reliable.

Under the supervision of the Demobilization Bureau, the basic material contained in this monograph was compiled and written in Japanese by former officers, on duty in command and staff units within major units during the period of operations. Translation was effected through the facilities of Military Intelligence Service Group, G2, Headquarters, Far East Command.

This Japanese Operational Monograph was rewritten in English by the Japanese Research Division, Military History Section, Headquarters, Army Forces Far East and is based on the translation of the Japanese original.

FOREWORD

This monograph deals with military operations in North China from the time of the outbreak of the China Incident in July 1937 to the outbreak of the Pacific War in December 1941.

As the basic Japanese document from which this monograph was written was prepared by Lieutenant General Takuma Shimoyama, former staff officer of the North China Area Army, Lieutenant General Gun Hashimoto, former chief of staff of the First Army and Lieutenant Colonel Heizo Ishiwari, former chief of the Military History Division, Army General Staff largely from memory, it was necessary for the Military History Section, HQ AFFE, to conduct extensive research in order to evaluate the information, check and correct facts and dates and, where necessary, to add further pertinent data and/or explanatory footnotes for clarity.

The writer was assisted in the research by Hachiro Tokunaga, formerly a lieutenant colonel in the Intelligence Section of Imperial General Headquarters.

The spelling of place names is that used in AMS 5301.

Additional monographs covering the operations of the Japanese Armed Forces in the China area are:

Title	Period	Mono No
China Area Operations Record, Vol. I	Jul 37 - Nov 41	70*
China Area Operations Record, Vol. II	Dec 41 - Dec 43	71
China Area Operations Record, Vol. III	Jan 44 - Aug 45	72
China Area Operations Record: Command of China Expeditionary Army	Aug 43 - Aug 45	129*
China Area Operations Record: Sixth Area Army Operations	May 44 - Aug 45	130*
Central China Area Operations Record, Vol. I	1937 - 1941	179
South China Area Operations Record, Vol. I	1937 - 1941	180
Operations in the Kun-lun-kuan Area	Dec 39 - Feb 40	74*
Ch'ang-sha Operations, 1st to 4th Period	Sep 38 - Aug 44	75

China Area Air Operations Record:
  China Incident and Greater East
  Asia War   Jul 37 - Aug 44   76

China Incident Naval Air Operations   Jul 37 - Nov 37   166

* Indicates: Edited and forwarded to OCMH

                                               21 January 1955

TABLE OF CONTENTS

	Page
CHAPTER I – From the Outbreak of the China Incident to the Yangchu Operation	
Outbreak and Spread of the China Incident	15
The Lukouchiao (Marco Polo Bridge) Incident	15
Langfang and Kuanganmen Incidents	19
Reinforcement and Disposition of the Forces in North China	24
Organization of the North China Area Army	27
Preparations for Combat by North China Area Army	28
Chahar Operation	31
Chohsien – Chingyuan Operation	37
Operations in the Vicinity of Shihchiachuang and Fuyang Ho	75
Preparations for Combat by the 1st Army	75
Actual Combat	80
Yangchu Operation	85
CHAPTER II – Hopeh, Tungshan and Wuchang – Hankou Operations	
General Situation Prior to the Hopeh Operation	105
Operational Plan of the 1st Army	114
Honan Province Operation North of the Huang Ho	119
Operation of the 14th Division	119

Movement of the 16th Division	122
Southern Shansi Province Operation	122
Operation of the 108th Division	122
Operation of the 20th Division	126
Operation of the 109th Division	127
Pursuit Operation in Southern Shansi Province	128
Air Operations During the Hopeh Operation	131
Situation after the Campaign	137
Tungshan Operation	139
General Situation Prior to and During the Battle in the vicinity of Taierhchuang	139
Mopping up Operations in the 2d Army Sector	140
The 2d Army's Attack in the Vicinity of Tayun Ho	141
Air support of the 2d Army in the Vicinity of Tayun Ho	144
Sakamoto Detachment's Battle near Taierhchuang	144
Co-operation of the Provisional Air Corps at Taierhchuang	146
Tactical Command by Imperial General Headquarters	150
Operational Command of the North China Area Army	154
Operational Command of the Central China Expeditionary Army	156

Air Operational Areas	157
Operation by the North China Area Army	158
2d Army Operation to Contain the Main Force of the Enemy	158
Disposition of the North China Area Army for the Battle of Tungshan	161
Outline of the Operational Progress of the 2d Army	162
Outline of the Operational Progress of the 1st Army	164
Cooperation of the Provisional Air Corps	166
Operation by the Central China Expeditionary Army	166
Cooperation of the 3d Air Brigade	172
Pursuit by the North China Area Army	174
Pursuit by the Central China Expeditionary Army	180
Garrisoning of Occupied Areas	184
Situation in the North China Area During the Wuchang - Hankou - Hanyang - Operation	188
General Situation After the Tungshan Operation	188
Imperial General Headquarters Orders Relative to the Drive Against the Wuchang - Hankou - Hanyang Area	190
North China Area Army's Support of the Drive on the Wuchang - Hankou - Hanyang Area	191
Air Operations in North China Area During the Wuchang - Hankou - Hanyang Area Campaign	192

CHAPTER III - Operations During 1939

    Estimate of the Situation   199

    Measures taken During 1939   200

    Summary of Mopping-up Operations   207

    Security Measures   218

    Mopping-up Operation in Shansi Province Area   221

        Mopping-up Operation Against the Southern Shansi Army   221

        Mopping-up Operation Against the Northern Shansi Army   222

    Wutaishan Operation   224

        Situation Before the Operation   224

        Tactical Command   226

        The First Phase (Mopping up of Taihuaichen and vicinity)   226

        The Second Phase (mopping up of Western Wutaishan)   228

        The Third Phase (Mopping up of Lungchuankuan and Vicinity)   231

        The Fourth Phase (Mopping up Hungchiachai and Vicinity)   235

    Eastern Shansi Province Operation   243

        Situation Prior to the Operation   243

        Tactical Command   243

        Outline of the Operation   249

        Changchih Area Operation   262

Operations on the Mongolian Border	263
Spring Counterattack Operation	263
Enemy's Winter Offensive and Japanese Counterattack	267
The Northern Kiangsu Province Operation	275
Situation Prior to the Operation	275
Summary of Operational Progress	277
Southern Shantung Province Operation	283
Summary of Operational Progress	284
Western Shantung Province Operation	285
Realignment of Troop Strength in China	286

CHAPTER IV - Mopping-Up Operations During 1940

Mongolian Border Area Operation	293
Southern Shansi Province Operation	299
Hsiangning Operation	308
Repulsing Operation in Southern Shansi Province	315
Central Shansi Province Operation	316
Disposition of Chinese Forces in Hopeh, Shantung and Northern Kiangsu Province areas	320

CHAPTER V - Mopping-Up Operations in the Shansi Province Area During 1941

Western Shansi Province Operation	325
Tactical Command	328
Summary of Operational Progress by 1st Army	337

	Summary of the Progress of Operation by Forces Directly Attached to the Area Army	340
	Containing Operation in Central China	344
	Summary of Operational Progress	345

CHARTS

No 1	Table of Troop Distribution of 1st Army	115
No 2	Summary of 1st Army's Operational Plan for Mopping up the Wutaishan Mountainous District	227
No 3	Plan for Disposition of 12th Army troops, Northern Kiangsu Province Operation	277

MAPS

No 1	Disposition of China Garrison Army 26 July 1937	21
No 2	Chahar Operation mid-August - mid-October 1937	35
No 3	Chohsien - Chingyuan Operation Phase I 14 - 17 September 1937	39
No 4	Chohsien-Chingyuan Operation Phase II 17 - 20 September 1937	53
No 5	Chohsien - Chingyuan Operation Phase III 21 - 24 September 1937	65
No 6	Chohsien-Chingyuan Operation Phase IV 24 - 27 September 1937	73
No 7	Disposition of North China Area 27 September 1937	77
No 8	Combat in the Vicinity of Shihchiachuang Fuyang Ho October 1937	87
No 9	Yangchu Operation 14 October - 16 November 1937	99

No 10	Chinese War Sectors July 1937 - September 1945	111
No 11	1st Army Operational Boundaries 11 February 1938	117
No 12	Honan Province Operation North of Huang Ho 7 - 27 February 1938	123
No 13	Southern Shansi Province Operation 11 February - 8 March 1938	133
No 14	Taierhchuang Operation 20 February - 9 April 1938	147
No 15	North China Area Army Operation 18 April - 19 May 1938	159
No 16	Central China Expeditionary Army Operation 23 April - 20 May 1938	167
No 17	Pursuit by The North China Area Army 18 May - 12 June 1938	175
No 18	Pursuit by The Central China Expeditionary Army 18 - 24 May 1938	181
No 19	Wutaishan Operation First Phase 8 - 15 May 1939	229
No 20	Wutaishan Operation Second Phase 18 - 21 May 1939	233
No 21	Wutaishan Operation Third Phase 4 - 8 June 1939	237
No 22	Wutaishan Operation Fourth Phase 19 - 22 June 1939	241
No 23	Eastern Shansi Province Operation 3 July - 21 August 1939	255
No 24	Mopping-Up Actions After Eastern Shansi Province Operation 6 August - 9 September 1939	259

No 25	Changchih Area Operation 7 - 10 October 1939	265
No 26	Mongolian Border Operation 10 April - 31 May 1939	269
No 27	Mongolian Border Operation 11 December 1939 - mid January 1940	273
No 28	Northern Kiangsu Province Operation 24 February - 13 March 1939	281
No 29	First Houtao Operation 28 January - 1 March 1940	297
No 30	Second Houtao Operation 21 - 29 March 1940	301
No 31	Southern Shansi Province Operation 17 April - Early May 1940	309
No 32	Hsiangning Operation 10 - 20 May 1940	313
No 33	Chungyuan Operation 7 May - 15 June 1941	341
No 34	Chungyuan Containing Operation 5 - 22 May 1941	347

APPENDIX

Appendix No 1	North China Area Army Order of Battle, 31 August 1937	349

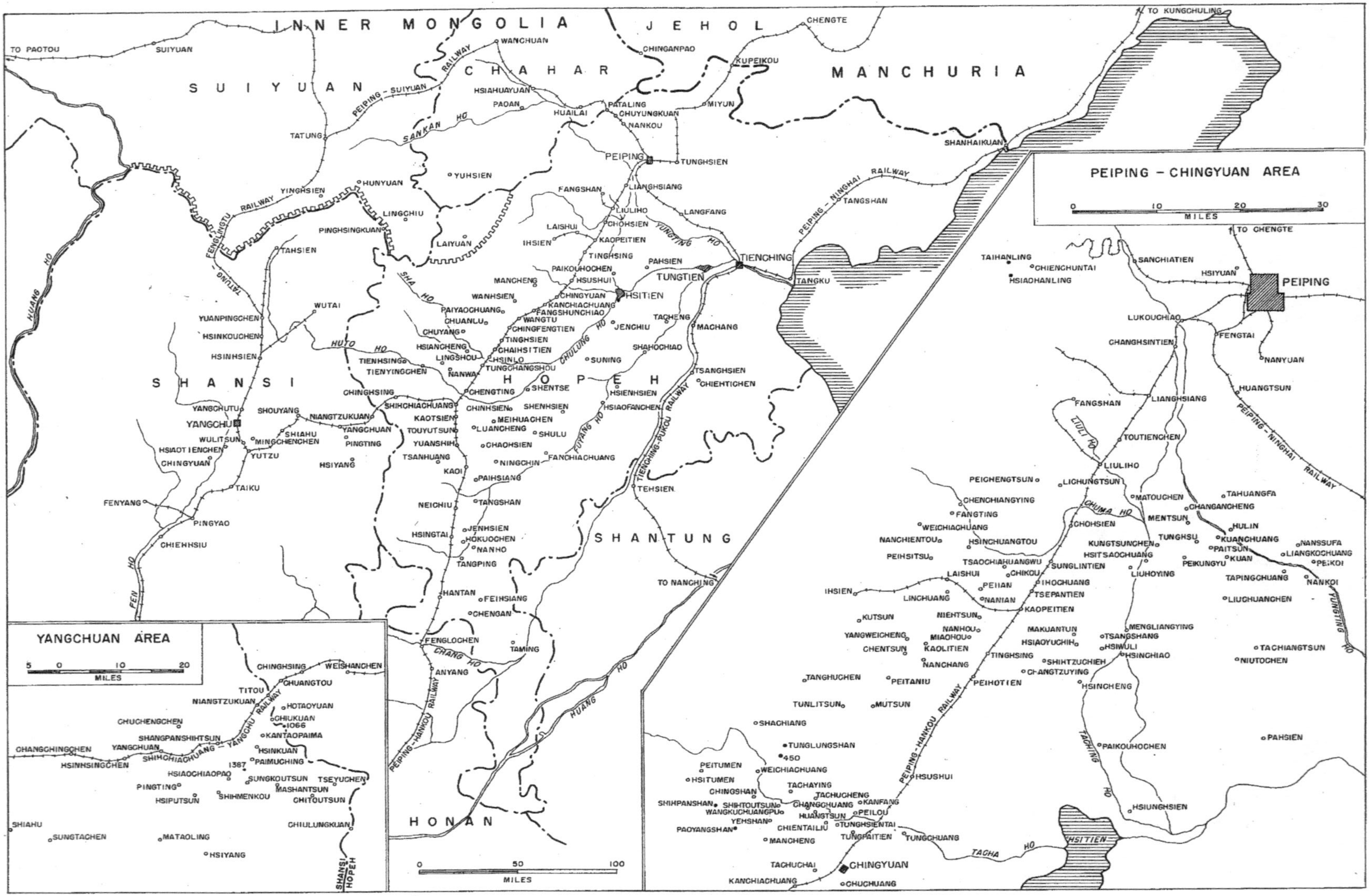
INNER MONGOLIA
JEHOL
MANCHURIA
SUIYUAN
CHAHAR
SHANSI
HOPEH
SHANTUNG
HONAN
TO PAOTOU
SUIYUAN
WANCHUAN
CHENGTE
CHINGANPAO
KUPEIKOU
MIYUN
SHANHAIKUAN
TO KUNGCHULING
PEIPING - SUIYUAN RAILWAY
HSIAHUAYUAN
PAOAN
HUAILAI
PATALING
CHUYUNGKUAN
NANKOU
TATUNG
SANKAN HO
PEIPING
TUNGHSIEN
YUHSIEN
HUNYUAN
YINGHSIEN
RAILWAY
FENGLINGTU
TATUNG
LINGCHIU
PINGHSINGKUAN
LAIYUAN
TAHSIEN
FANGSHAN
LIANGHSIANG
LIULIHO
CHOHSIEN
LANGFANG
LAISHUI
IHSIEN
KAOPEITIEN
YUNGTING HO
TINGHSING
PAIKOUHOCHEN
PAHSIEN
TUNGTIEN
TIENCHING
TANGKU
PEIPING - NINGHAI RAILWAY
TANGSHAN
MANCHENG
HSUSHUI
HSITIEN
WANHSIEN
CHINGYUAN
KANCHIACHUANG
FANGSHUNCHIAO
PAIYAOCHUANG
CHUANLU
WANGTU
CHINGFENGTIEN
TINGHSIEN
CHAIHSITIEN
HSINLO
TUNGCHANGSHOU
CHUYANG
HSIANCHENG
LINGSHOU
NANWA
CHULUNG HO
JENCHIU
TACHENG
MACHANG
SHAHOCHIAO
SUNING
TSANGHSIEN
CHIEHTICHEN
SHA HO
HUTO HO
WUTAI
YUANPINGCHEN
HSINKOUCHEN
HSINHSIEN
TIENHSING
TIENYINGCHEN
CHINGHSING
CHENGTING
SHENTSE
HSIENHSIEN
HSIAOFANCHEN
SHIHCHIACHUANG
CHINHSIEN
SHENHSIEN
KAOTSIEN
MEIHUACHEN
TOUYUTSUN
LUANCHENG
SHULU
YUANSHIH
CHAOHSIEN
FUYANG HO
TIENCHING - PUKOU RAILWAY
TSANHUANG
NINGCHIN
FANCHIACHUANG
KAOI
PAIHSIANG
TEHSIEN
YANGCHUTU
SHOUYANG
NIANGTZUKUAN
YANGCHU
SHIAHU
YANGCHUAN
WULITSUN
MINGCHIENCHEN
PINGTING
HSIAOTIENCHEN
YUTZU
CHINGYUAN
HSIYANG
TAIKU
FENYANG
PINGYAO
CHIEHHSIU
FEN HO
HUANG HO
NEICHIU
TANGSHAN
HSINGTAI
JENHSIEN
HOKUOCHEN
NANHO
TANGPING
TO NANCHING
HANTAN
FEIHSIANG
CHENGAN
FENGLOCHEN
TAMING
CHANG HO
ANYANG
PEIPING - HANKOU RAILWAY
HUANG HO
0 50 100
MILES
YANGCHUAN AREA
5 0 10 20
MILES
CHINGHSING
WEISHANCHEN
TITOU
CHUANGTOU
NIANGTZUKUAN
HOTAOYUAN
CHIUKUAN
1066
CHUCHENGCHEN
KANTAOPAIMA
SHANGPANSHIHTSUN
CHANGCHINGCHEN
YANGCHUAN
SHIHCHIACHUANG - YANGCHU RAILWAY
HSINKUAN
HSINHSINGCHEN
1387
PAIMUCHING
HSIAOCHIAOPAO
SUNGKOUTSUN
TSEYUCHEN
PINGTING
MASHANTSUN
HSIPUTSUN
SHIHMENKOU
CHITOUTSUN
SHIAHU
CHIULUNGKUAN
SUNGTACHEN
MATAOLING
HSIYANG
SHANSI
HOPEH
PEIPING - CHINGYUAN AREA
0 10 20 30
MILES
TO CHENGTE
TAIHANLING
CHIENCHUNTAI
HSIAOHANLING
SANCHIATIEN
HSIYUAN
PEIPING
LUKOUCHIAO
FENGTAI
CHANGHSINTIEN
NANYUAN
HUANGTSUN
PEIPING - NINGHAI RAILWAY
FANGSHAN
LIANGHSIANG
LIULI HO
TOUTIENCHEN
LIULIHO
PEICHENGTSUN
LICHUNGTSUN
MATOUCHEN
TAHUANGFA
CHANGANCHENG
CHENCHIANGYING
FANGTING
CHUMA HO
MENTSUN
HULIN
WEICHIACHUANG
CHOHSIEN
TUNGHSU
KUANCHUANG
NANSSUFA
NANCHIENTOU
HSINCHUANGTOU
KUNGTSUNCHEN
PAITSUN
LIANGKOCHUANG
HSITSAOCHUANG
KUAN
PEIKOI
PEIHSITSU
TSAOCHIAHUANGWU
SUNGLINTIEN
PEIKUNGYU
LAISHUI
CHIKOU
LIUHOYING
TAPINGCHUANG
NANKOI
PEIIAN
IHOCHUANG
IHSIEN
LINCHUANG
NANIAN
TSEPANTIEN
LIUCHUANCHEN
YUNGTING HO
KAOPEITIEN
KUTSUN
NIEHTSUN
MAKUANTUN
MENGLIANGYING
YANGWEICHENG
NANHOU
MIAOHOU
HSIAOYUCHIH
TSANGSHANG
HSIWULI
TACHIANGTSUN
CHENTSUN
KAOLITIEN
TINGHSING
HSINGHIAO
NIUTOCHEN
NANCHANG
SHIHTZUCHIEH
CHANGTZUYING
TANGHUCHEN
PEITANIU
PEIHOTIEN
HSINCHENG
TUNLITSUN
MUTSUN
PEIPING - HANKOU RAILWAY
SHACHIANG
PAHSIEN
TUNGLUNGSHAN
450
TACHING HO
PAIKOUHOCHEN
PEITUMEN
WEICHIACHUANG
HSUSHUI
HSITUMEN
CHINGSHAN
TACHAYING
TACHUCHENG
SHIHPANSHAN
SHIHTOUTSUN
CHANGCHUANG
KANFANG
WANGKUCHUANGPU
HSIUNGHSIEN
YEHSHAN
HUANGTSUN
PEILOU
PAOYANGSHAN
CHIENTAILIU
TUNGHSIENTAI
MANCHENG
TUNGPAITIEN
TUNGCHUANG
TACHA HO
HSITIEN
TACHUCHAI
CHINGYUAN
KANCHIACHUANG
CHUCHUANG

CHAPTER I

From the Outbreak of the China Incident to the
Yangchu Operation

Outbreak and Spread of the China Incident

The Lukouchiao (Marco Polo Bridge) Incident

On the night of 7 July 1937, while a company of the Japanese 3d Battalion, 1st Infantry Regiment, stationed at Fengtai, was on night maneuvers at the drill ground north of Lukouchiao (Marco Polo Bridge), it was fired upon from the direction of the embankment of the Yungting Ho. The remaining companies of the 3d Battalion hastened to the scene, and, in self-defense, returned the fire of the hostile unit, which belonged to Sung Cheyuan's 29th Army. Both sides suffered some casualties during the engagement. This was the beginning of the China Incident.

At that time, Japan, in accordance with the terms of the Boxer Protocol of 1901, maintained a garrison in North China to protect the rights of its nationals living there and to guard lines of communications between Peiping and the harbors of North China. The strength of this garrison was approximately 3,000 men and was disposed as follows:

Headquarters, China Garrison Army   Tienching
    (Commander: Lt Gen Tashiro)[1]

---

1. Due to illness, General Tashiro was recalled to Tokyo on 11 July 1937. He died in Tienching on his way home. He was replaced, as commander of the China Garrison Army, by Lt. Gen Kiyoshi Katsuki.

Headquarters, Infantry Brigade	Peiping
1st Infantry Regiment	
Main Force	Peiping
One Battalion	Fengtai
One Battalion	Tienching
2d Infantry Regiment	
Main Force	Tienching
An element	Between Tienching and Shanhaikuan
Artillery Regiment	Tienching
Tank Unit	"
Cavalry Unit	"
Engineer Unit	"
Signal Unit	"

The Chinese strength comprised four divisions, two independent brigades, two cavalry divisions and one cavalry brigade. These units were placed under the 29th Army, commanded by Sung Cheyuan, a war lord from Chahar and Hopeh Provinces, and disposed as follows: the 37th Division under the command of Feng Chih-an, Governor of Hopeh Province, was stationed between Peiping and Chingyuan; the 38th Division, under the command of Chang Tzu-chung, mayor of Tienching, was stationed between Peiping and Tienching; the 132d Division, under the command of Chaotengyu was stationed in the southern part of Hopeh Province, and the 143d Division, under the command of Liu Juming, Governor of Chahar Province, was stationed in the Province of Chahar.[2]

At that time, even though Sung Cheyuan claimed to support the

---

2. Although all available Japanese sources have been explored, disposition of the two independent brigades, two cavalry divisions and one cavalry brigade is unknown.

same pro-Japanese principles as his predecessor, Feng Yu-hsiang,[3] he was strongly influenced by the Nanching Government and the anti-Japanese sentiment which was fast gaining strength throughout China.[4] Feng Chih-an, commander of the 37th Division, was strongly anti-Japanese.

The Japanese Government instructed the China Garrison Army to endeavor to settle the incident amicably and to do everything possible to prevent its spreading to other parts of China. At the same time, in order to be prepared should negotiations fail, the Central Authorities[5] in Japan ordered the Kwantung Army to send

---

3. Feng Yu-hsiang, well known for his pro-Japanese principles, was appointed Vice Chief of the National Defense Council by Chiang Kaishek in 1935. On 17 July 1937 he was appointed Commander in Chief of the Chinese North China Area Army.
4. Although Sung Cheyuan had been appointed war lord of Chahar and Hopeh Provinces by Chiang Kaishek, his native home was in Leling in Shantung Province. Unwilling to participate in the cease fire negotiations with the Japanese, fearing loss of face, he went to Leling and allowed his subordinates to carry on the negotiations. At the request of his officers he returned and met with Lt Gen Katsuki, Japanese Army commander, in Tienching on the afternoon of 18 July. Sung admitted that the incident had been incited by Chinese acts and offered apologies, promising, at the same time, that he would punish the responsible officers. He also promised to fulfil Japanese demands in regard to the incident, the principal demand being the withdrawal of the 37th Division. The following day, 19 July, Sung returned to Peiping but was unable to control his subordinate officers and further incidents ensued.
5. Prior to 17 November 1937, when Imperial General Headquarters was established in Tokyo to cope with the situation in China, Central Authorities comprised the Army and Navy General Staffs and the War and Navy Ministries.

immediately to north China the 11th Independent Infantry Brigade, commanded by Maj Gen Shigeyasu Suzuki, which was stationed at Chengte, the 1st Independent Mixed Brigade, commanded by Maj Gen Koji Sakai, a motorized unit stationed at Kungchuling and one temporarily organized air unit.[6] All units were instructed to retain their peacetime organization. The 20th Division, which was stationed in Korea under the command of Lt Gen Bunzaburo Kawagishi, also was ordered to north China.

With the exception of the disposition of the air unit at Tienching airfield and the movement of the main strength of the China Garrison Army to Tunghsien and Fengtai, all other troops were stationed some distance from Peiping and Tienching in an endeavor to prevent aggravation of the incident. In an effort to alleviate the situation, the Japanese Army requested the withdrawal of the China 37th Division from the area, but the Chinese refused to comply with this request and small units of both the Japanese and Chinese armies set up camps opposite each other north of Yuanping (Lukouchiao). There was a nightly exchange of fire caused by wanton firing by the Chinese troops. This

---

6. This air unit was composed of six squadrons, including reconnaissance, fighter and bomber squadrons and was commanded by Colonel Kamijyo. These squadrons were drawn from air units in Manchuria, under the command of the Kwantung Army.

eventually led to the Langfang and Kuanganmen Incidents.

Langfang and Kuanganmen Incidents

On 25 July, while a Japanese signal unit was repairing communication wires at the Langfang station, a Chinese unit belonging to the 38th Division, which was camped near the station, launched a surprise attack against the signal unit. An infantry company of the China Garrison Army stationed nearby to protect the railway successfully defended the station throughout the night but suffered severe casualties.

On 26 July, the China Garrison Army lodged a protest with the Chinese in regard to this incident and, at the same time, reiterated their demand that the 37th Division be withdrawn from the Lukouchiao area within 24 hours. In spite of this, on the same day (26 July), Chinese troops perpetrated another unprovoked attack. An infantry battalion of the China Garrison Army, which had been stationed near Fengtai, was returning to Peiping, according to orders, to protect Japanese nationals within the walled city. This move had been agreed to by the Chinese. About sunset, when about half the battalion had passed through the Kuanganmen Gate, the Chinese suddenly closed the gate and began firing on the Japanese troops from on top of the wall, inflicting heavy casualties.

By this time, anti-Japanese feeling had reached such a pitch in Peiping that the China Garrison Army found it difficult to protect

its nationals and maintain lines of communication. Therefore, on
the evening of 26 July, the China Garrison Army commander decided
that the situation had become so critical that it would be necessary
to drive the 29th Chinese Army from the Peiping - Tienching area.
The Central Authorities in Tokyo approved this decision.[7]

The Chinese 29th Army, which opposed the Japanese forces, had,
in addition to its peacetime organization, the 132d Division and a
cavalry division which had previously been stationed in the southern
part of Hopeh Province. These forces had advanced northward and were
concentrated at Nanyuan, the main camp of the 38th Division, which
also included an airfield. The 37th Division was concentrated at
Hsiyuan and in and around the walled city of Peiping. In addition,
there were other troops not directly affiliated with the 29th Army
in the northern part of Peiping.

In order to sweep this enemy force from the area, the commander
of the China Garrison Army decided to direct the main attack against
Nanyuan, where the main body of the enemy force was concentrated.
He, therefore, issued an order late on the night of the 26th to attack Nanyuan at dawn of the 28th. According to the order, the 20th
Division was to attack from the south, the Kawabe Group (commanded by
Maj Gen Kawabe and composed of 2 infantry regiments, 1 cavalry unit,
1 tank unit, 1 engineer unit and 1 signal unit) from the west, and

---

7. The disposition of the China Garrison Army as of 26 July 1937
is shown on Map 1.

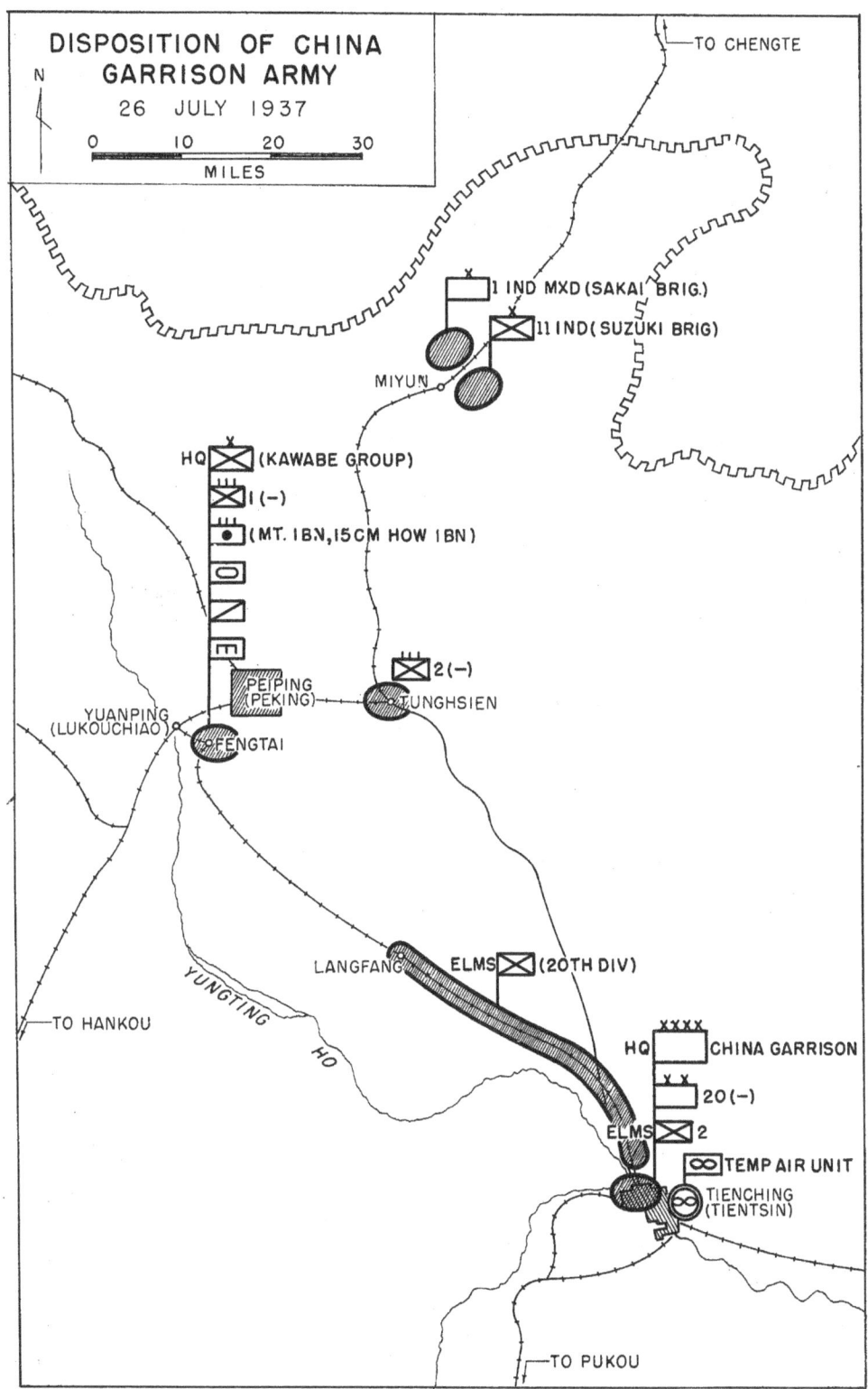

the main force of the 2d Infantry Regiment of the China Garrison Army from the east. The air unit was to give support wherever necessary. The order also provided that the Sakai and Suzuki Brigades would attack the enemy in the northern and western sectors of Peiping. No attack was contemplated against the enemy in the walled city of Peiping as it was considered that the walls would enable the enemy to resist. Also, an attack on the city might endanger the lives of Japanese nationals there and the maintenance of law and order would be affected by fighting within the city. Further measures were to be taken to induce the enemy to evacuate of their own accord through the good offices of the Minkai.[8]

The air unit used the Tienching airfield. The reconnaissance unit was engaged mainly in reconnoitering the situation in regard to the Chinese Kuomintang Army, which was advancing northward along the Peiping - Hankou railway.

In the early morning of 28 July, the attack on the Nanyuan sector was begun. Just before sunset, the enemy showed signs of wavering after a day-long fierce battle, and the tank unit of the Kawabe Group advanced to the northern part of Nanyuan, thus severing their retreat route. At sunset the enemy fled in confusion, leaving many dead, including the commander of the 132d Division.

---

8. A citizens' council composed of influential persons in Peiping.

The 1st Independent Mixed Brigade (Sakai Brigade with a strength of approximately 4,000 men) and the 11th Independent Infantry Brigade (Suzuki Brigade with a strength of approximately 3,000 men) attacked enemy units based in the villages north of Peiping, and, by evening, the Sakai Brigade had occupied Hsiyuan, and the Suzuki Brigade had reached a point near the northwest corner of the walled city of Peiping. On 29 July, the Sakai Brigade continued its pursuit of the enemy in the area north of Peiping, crossed Yungting Ho and captured a hill near Changhsintien. On 30 July, the 20th Division replaced the Sakai Brigade and occupied a range of hills in that area. The China Garrison Army massed the Sakai Brigade at Tunghsien, the Suzuki Brigade in the area north of Peiping, and the Kawabe Group near Fengtai.

On the evening of the 28th, the enemy in the vicinity of Peiping began to retreat southward and, by the 29th, had completely withdrawn from the left bank of the Yungting Ho. An element of the Chinese 38th Division which was south of Tienching, in concert with the Tienching Security Force, attacked the Japanese concession, the China Garrison Army Headquarters, the airfield and other installations in Tienching on the night of 28th, but, at dawn, on the 29th, after being counterattacked by the Japanese reserve force and bombed by its air unit, they retreated to the south bank of the Yungting Ho.

Reinforcement and disposition of the forces
in North China

Soon after the outbreak of the China Incident, being aware of the limited strength of the China Garrison Army and fearing that it might not be possible to localize the incident, the Central Authorities in Tokyo, began the mobilization of three divisions in Japan, to be sent as reinforcements to north China. These divisions were the 5th Division commanded by Lt Gen Seishiro Itagaki, the 6th Division commanded by Lt Gen Hsiao Tani, and the 10th Division commanded by Lt Gen Rensuke Isogai. In addition, the Provisional Air Corps commanded by Lt Gen Yoshitoshi Tokugawa was formed. These units, on arrival in north China, were to be placed under the command of the China Garrison Army commander. The Provisional Air Corps was scheduled to arrive during the latter part of July and the divisions were to arrive successively from about the middle of August until the middle of September.[9]

After the rout of the Chinese 29th Army, the China Garrison Army commander assumed responsibility for maintaining law and order, as well as the maintenance of lines of communication. The newly arrived reinforcements from Japan, together with the 20th Division, were disposed as follows:

The Provisional Air Corps was ordered to conduct reconnaissance

---

9. In order to expedite their arrival in North China, it was decided that their mobilization would be completed upon arrival at their assigned areas.

of the area.[10] The 20th Division was to secure the area in the vicinity of Changhsintien and to protect the troops massing in that area, while the 5th Division was to assemble in and around Hsiyuan and the 6th Division in and around Huangtsun. The 10th Division was ordered to mass south of Tienching and to occupy the area in and around Machang.[11] The Suzuki Brigade was ordered to secure the Pataling area and the Sakai Brigade was returned to the Kwantung Army.

On 6 August, the Nanching Government began reinforcing its units in the Chahar and Hopeh Provinces, and, on 15 August, it issued a general mobilization order throughout China. By the middle of August, the Chinese had two divisions, commanded by Tang Enpo, in Chahar Province and three divisions advancing north through the mountainous region between Hopeh and Shansi Provinces. In addition, it was believed that they had a force of unknown size stationed near Chingyuan.

Early in August a Chinese infantry unit, together with a caval-

---

10. The temporarily organized air unit was returned to the Kwantung Army, when the main strength of the Provisional Air Corps formed in Japan arrived in Tienching via Manchuria on 27 July. Elements of this corps arrived in Chengteh on the same day.

11. The 5th and 6th Divisions arrived in the Tienching area from Japan via Korea about the middle of August. The 10th Division reached Tangku near Tienching about the same time from Japan. Concentration of these troops in the Tienching area was completed on 22 August. Advance elements of the 5th Division proceeded to the Nankou area immediately upon arrival in China in anticipation of operations in that area.

ry unit, occupied Nankou, and the Nationalist Army began to advance steadily into the Chahar Province where the 143d Division of the Chinese 29th Army was stationed. Realizing the necessity of occupying strategic points in the vicinity of Pataling, the China Garrison Army dispatched the Suzuki Brigade, with the Artillery Regiment attached, to attack the enemy in the vicinity of Nankou. However, not only had the Chinese greatly increased their strength but the terrain was rugged and the Suzuki Brigade's attack bogged down. Therefore, in order to make the assault more effective the China Garrison Army commander placed the Suzuki Brigade under the command of the commander of the 5th Division, who had just arrived in the area with advance echelons of his division. The Division commander continued the attack using the Suzuki Brigade and elements of the Division as they arrived in the area. Under unfavorable weather conditions and over rugged terrain the Division fought desperate battles for ten days before finally it was able to break through enemy positions on 23 August, occupy Chuyungkuan, and advance into the plains of Huailai. Here the Division prepared for the next operation and the Suzuki Brigade was returned to the Kwantung Army.[12]

Organization of the North China Area Army

On 31 August 1937, the Order of Battle of the North China Area Army, to include the 1st and 2d Armies, was published (Appendix 1). At the

---

12. In August, there was considerable rain in north China, rivers overflowed their banks and the low plains of Hopeh, especially the area along the Tienching - Pukou railway, became a sea of mud greatly hindering troop movements. The rains also had an adverse effect on subsequent operations.

same time, the commander of the North China Area Army received the following order from the Central Authorities in Japan:

> The commander of the North China Area Army will secure the Peiping - Tienching area and other nearby strategic points and establish law and order in this area.
> In addition, in order to break the enemy's will to fight and thereby hasten the conclusion of hostilities, the North China Area Army commander will destroy the enemy in central Hopeh Province without delay.

Preparations for Combat by North China Area Army

General Terauchi, commander of the North China Area Army, accompanied by his staff, left Tokyo by plane on 1 September, arriving in Tienching on 4 September.[13] There he mapped out the following plan for the coming battle:

Over-all Tactical Plan of the North China Area Army.

   1. Plan

   The Chinese force which has advanced to the line connecting Chingyuan and Tsanghsien and vicinity will be trapped and destroyed. The decisive battle will be waged in the area along the Peiping - Hankou railway and the time for this operations will be early October.

   2. General Plan

   As soon as the 14th Division arrives, the 1st Army will promptly carry out, from the southeast, a large scale encirclement of the opposing enemy and will annihilate him.
   After the 1st Army destroys the enemy's advance units, the North China Area Army's main force will advance to the line

---

13. Because of the bad condition of the airfield at Tienching, caused by weather, General Terauchi travelled with his staff from Tokyo via Seoul to Dairen by air, arriving in Dairen on 2 September. He left Dairen on the night of 3 September by destroyer, arriving in Tangku on the morning of 4 September, and, that same day, travelled from Tangku to Tienching by train.

connecting Ihsien, Paikouhochen, Pahsien and Machang by mid-September and then prepare for an attack on the enemy deployed along the line connecting Chingyuan and Tsanghsien. The boundary between the operational areas of the 1st and 2d Armies will be generally fixed by the river flowing through Hsitien and Tungtien.

The 1st Army will direct its main effort toward the area west of the Peiping - Hankou railway, and surprise and penetrate enemy positions. Its mechanized units will strike swiftly and capture key points along roads and railways behind enemy positions to seal off the enemy's route of retreat. The 1st Army's main body will press the enemy in a generally easterly direction and, coordinating its drive with the westward drive of the 2d Army, will trap and destroy the enemy's main body in the area north of the Chengting - Tsanghsien road.

When the 16th Division arrives, the 2d Army will commence its drive just prior to the movement of the 1st Army. The 2d Army will first strive to advance as far south as possible and then by skilfull maneuver break through the weak points between enemy units and drive a flying wedge to the Chulung Ho, thus severing the escape route of the enemy deployed on the main front. When necessary, the 108th Division may be used in the Tehsien area or the Peiping - Hankou railway area.

The 5th Division will rapidly advance to the vicinity of Yuhsien and Laiyuan, and sever the Peiping - Hankou railway south of Wangtu. Upon the 5th Division advancing to the Laiyuan area, the North China Area Army will open a supply route for the Division leading from the Peiping - Hankou railway area.

The 109th Division is to be used mainly in the Peiping - Hankou railway area, but, when the situation warrants it, an element of the Division may be committed to the Peiping - Suiyuan railway area.

If the enemy should retreat earlier than expected, our forces will make full use of supplies and ammunition thus unexpended and pursue the enemy to the line connecting Hsingtai and Tehsien without pausing, and trap and destroy him in the area north of the line.

The Provisional Air Corps will, at the outset, support the 1st Army in smashing enemy advance units, and the main strength of the air reconnaissance unit will scout the vicinity and rear areas of Chingyuan and Tsanghsien. When the battle reaches the decisive stage, the air units will strive to cut off the enemy's retreat and to prevent the arrival of enemy reinforcements. To this end, air units will, without delay, destroy railway bridges spanning the Huang Ho. Prompt action will be taken to expand and improve airfields in the Peiping - Tienching area.

Line of communication facilities will be strengthened

promptly; the repair of the Peiping - Hankou railway will be speeded up and lateral supply routes by waterways will be opened as the 2d Army advances westward.

On 4 September, the North China Area Army commander issued the following order in preparation for the next offensive:

> The enemy force which has advanced into Central Hopeh Province numbers about 400,000. The enemy in the northern area, namely in and around Chingyuan and Tsanghsien, possess rather strong positions with outer trench defense works some 60 to 70 kilometers in length. In the vicinity of the lines connecting Chohsien - Kuan and Hsiunghsien - Machang, there are several powerful enemy groups. The 1st and 2d Armies will clash with them soon. The enemy's main force, which was in Chahar Province, was dealt a crushing blow by our 5th Division and is now retreating westward. The units of the Kwantung Army have captured strategic points around Wanchuan, and are preparing for the next operation. The boundary between operational areas of the North China Area Army and the Kwantung Army will be the line connecting Chinganpao, Hsiahuayuan and Paoan, plus the part of stream of the Sankan Ho above Paoan. The North China Area Army will be responsible for the area on the boundary.
> The North China Area Army will rush its advance to the Ihsien - Tinghsing - Paikouhochen - Pahsien - Machang line in order to destroy the enemy on the Chingyuan - Tsanghsien line and will then prepare for the next operation.
> The 5th Division will rush to the Yuhsien area close on the heels of the enemy and will then prepare for the operation on the Chingyuan Plain.
> Upon arrival of the 14th Division, the 1st Army will advance to the line connecting Ihsien, Tinghsing, Paikouhochen and Pahsien (including its vicinity) and prepare for an assault against the enemy in and around Chingyuan.
> Pending the arrival of the 2d Army commander, the 10th Division commander will command units assigned or attached to the 2d Army commander and will promptly advance to the Machang area and prepare for an attack against the enemy in and around Tsanghsien.
> The boundary between the operational areas of the 1st and 2d Armies will be the line connecting Langfang and Pahsien; and the area on the boundary will be the 1st Army's area of responsibility.
> The Provisional Air Corps will devote most of its effort to the support of the 1st Army and the 5th Division, and, in addition, will reconnoiter enemy positions in and around the line

connecting Chingyuan and Tsanghsien, as well as the forward and rear areas of the enemy and the movement of enemy forces in the mountainous district west of the Peiping - Hankou railway.
The Provisional Air Corps will also support the 2d Army whenever necessary.
    The rest of the units in North China, which are under the direct command of the North China Area Army, will carry on their previously assigned mission.

On 9 September, when the operational preparations of the 1st Army were well under way, the North China Area Army commander ordered the Provisional Air Corps to support the 1st Army with its main force and the 2d Army with an element. At the same time, the North China Area Army commander delegated to the 1st Army commander the power to deploy the North China Area Army's heavy artillery unit in the area around Lianghsiang to support the 1st Army's operation.

Chahar Operation

Prior to the organization of the North China Area Army the Central Authorities in Tokyo issued an order to the China Garrison Army commander to employ an element of his force to destroy the enemy forces east of Wanchuan. The Central Authorities also ordered the Kwantung Army commander to render assistance to the China Garrison Army from Jehol Province and Inner Mongolia in order to facilitate the Garrison Army's operations. These orders were issued as two hostile divisions of the Kuomintang Army had crossed the border of Chahar Province and captured Nankou and it was felt they were awaiting an opportunity to enter the Peiping - Tienching area.

In accordance with this order, the China Garrison Army commander committed an element of his force to the operation in the middle of August.[14] The Kwantung Army supported the China Garrison Army from Jehol Province and Inner Mongolia by committing an element of its force (three mixed brigades and seven infantry companies) to the operation. Towards the end of August, the China Garrison Army broke through the enemy positions on the border of Chahar Province near Pataling and the Kwantung Army penetrated their lines in the vicinity of Wanchuan on 27 August and continued in pursuit of the retreating enemy. The 5th Division captured Yuhsien mid-September.[15] The 5th Division commander, in accordance with a subsequent order of the North China Area Army, then made preparations to transfer the main body of his division from Yuhsien to the Chingyuan Plain.[16]

However, upon receipt of information that the enemy was building up for an offensive in the border area of Chahar and Shansi Provinces, west of Yuhsien, he decided to destroy these forces prior to the transfer of the division to the Chingyuan Plain. This mission was successfully accomplished within a few days. In addition, a powerful element of the Division destroyed an enemy force near the

---

14. The 11th Independent Infantry Brigade, (Suzuki Brigade) later reinforced by the 5th Division. See page 11.
15. By that time, the 11th Independent Infantry Brigade had returned to the Kwantung Army.
16. The China Garrison Army was integrated into the North China Area Army on 31 August 1937, at which time the commander of the China Garrison Army became the commander of the 1st Army.

Inner Great Wall. In the latter part of September, however, this element was encircled by a superior enemy force and the situation deteriorated to such a degree that it became necessary for the main body of the Division to attack the encircling enemy. Fierce fighting ensued. The Chahar Detachment of the Kwantung Army, driving westward roughly along the Peiping - Suiyuan railway, captured Tatung in mid-September and proceeded to mop up hostile remnants in the area. Upon receipt of information that the 5th Division was fighting desperately against heavy odds, this detachment launched an attack from the north against the enemy forces disposed along the Inner Great Wall and destroyed them late in September. The Detachment then advanced westward in pursuit of the enemy along the Huto Ho, until it reached an area south of Taihsien early in October. After that, the main body of the Chahar Detachment was brought under the command of the 5th Division, and the Division commenced new operations to capture Yangchu.

During this period, an element of the Division, consisting of three infantry battalions and one mountain artillery battalion, commanded by Maj Gen Kunisaki, was ordered by the Division commander to advance to the Chingyuan Plain via Laiyuan and left Yuhsein in mid-September, reaching the Chingyuan Plain early in October.

Also, in mid-October, a powerful element of the Chahar Detachment of the Kwantung Army, on orders from the Kwantung Army, captured Suiyuan and Paotou. (Map 2)

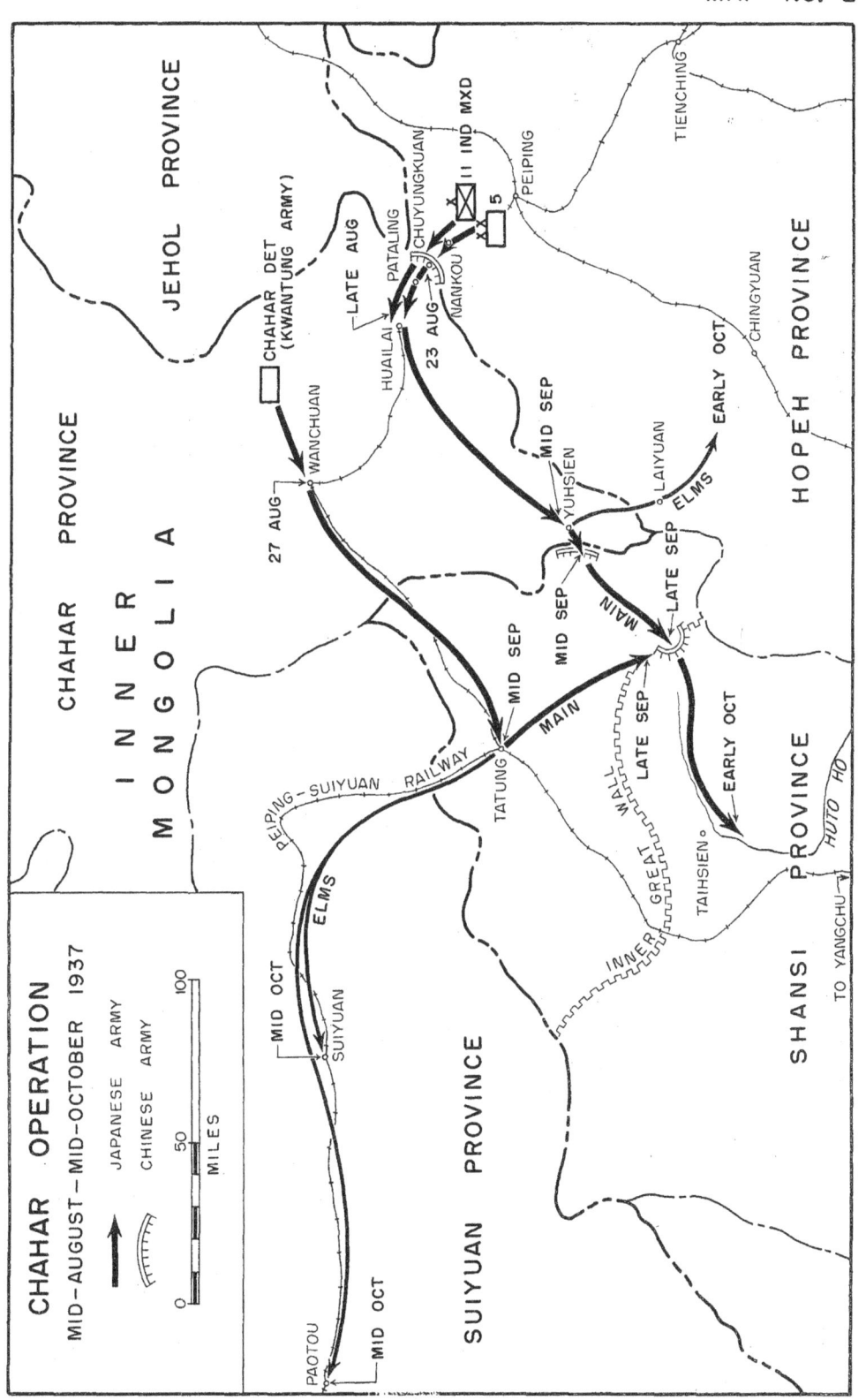

Chohsien - Chingyuan Operation

First Phase (14 - 17 September) (Map 3)

The enemy confronting the 1st Army[17] in early September 1937 consisted of Sun Lien-chung's Army (about $3\frac{1}{2}$ divisions of the 30th Army under the indirect control of the Nationalist Army) disposed west of the Peiping - Hankou railway, and Feng Chan-hai's Army (about one division of the 63d Army of the former Northeastern Army), and Wan Fu-lin's Army (about 3 divisions of the 53d Army of the former Northeastern Army), both disposed east of the railway line. These forces had constructed positions along three lines: (1) a line running from the area north of Fangshan to the bank of the Yungting Ho (2) a line running from the vicinity of Chohsien to east and west of Liuchuanchen, and (3) a line running from the vicinity of Laishui via Kaopeitien to Hsinchiao and east and west of Niutochen. Since early September enemy troops had been advancing steadily overland from existing positions near Chingyuan to the vicinity of Chohsien.

Intending to commence an assault on or about 11 September, the 1st Army ordered its 20th Division, stationed in the Changhsintien district, to be deployed in the vicinity of Lianghsiang to prepare for an attack on Fangshan and the 6th Division, deployed along the Yungting Ho across from Kuan, to prepare to advance. However, the enemy's main strength in and around Chingyuan began advancing overland toward

---

17. Headquarters of the 1st Army was located at Fengtai, southwest of Peiping.

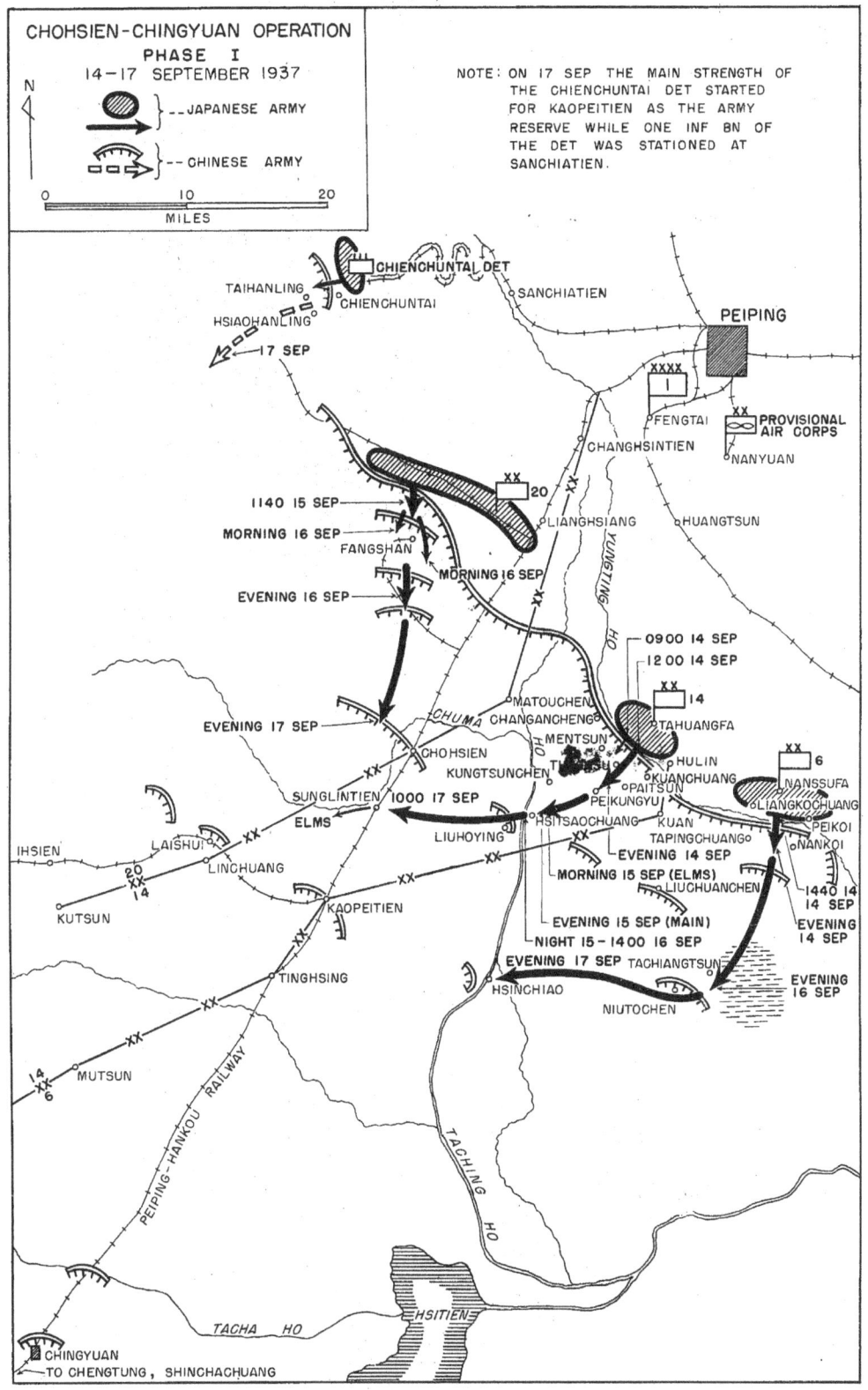

Chohsien and its vicinity, therefore, the 1st Army postponed its offensive for several days in order to deploy the 14th Division, which was due to arrive from Japan,[18] between the 20th and 6th Divisions, and thereby facilitate the trapping and destroying of the enemy in and around Chohsien. The time of the offensive was announced as after sunset of the 14th. However, on the morning of 14 September, the 1st Army commander received the following report from the 14th Division[19] commander:

> On the night of the 13th, the Division received a small-scale enemy attack against its right flank but reconnaissance revealed that the enemy strength in the vicinity of Kuan has diminished considerably.

The 1st Army telephoned the 14th Division for confirmation of the report, and received an answer to the effect that on the night of the 13th, a small enemy unit on the opposite bank near Changancheng had directed fire against the Japanese unit stationed there, but no enemy troops had been seen in the vicinity of Hulin.

The 1st Army commander considered the possibility of the enemy having started to retreat, and ordered the 6th and 20th Divisions to submit a report on their respective fronts. The 20th Division re-

---

18. Advance echelons of the 14th Division landed at Tangku and proceeded to their assigned area west of Peiping on 3 September. However, concentration of the main strength in this area was not completed until 12 September.
19. At that time the 14th Division was preparing to advance in the area along the Yungting Ho near Hulin.

ported no change in the enemy situation, while the 6th Division reported that not only had the enemy shown no sign of withdrawal but, on the contrary, seemed to be increasing his strength.

Subsequently, the Army received a report from the 14th Division to the effect that although the division had sent patrols to the vicinity of Kuanchuang (approximately four kilometers north of Kuan) there were no signs of the enemy in the area. The Division, therefore, had ordered its front units to prepare to advance.

The Army commander, considering the reports of the enemy situation on the 6th and the 20th Division fronts, estimated that the forces opposing these divisions were still in their original positions and that only the troops confronting the 14th Division had been withdrawn wholly or partially or had made a change in disposition. However, he advised each division to take immediate counter-measures to cope with any change in the enemy situation.

At 1000 hours, 14 September, the 1st Army commander sent his Chief of Staff, Maj Gen Hashimoto, together with Colonel Isamu Kinoshita, to the 14th Division headquarters to observe the situation on the 14th Division's front. They arrived by air at the 14th Division headquarters at Tahuangfa at 1140 hours.

By this time, the 14th Division had completed preparations to advance and some elements had already moved forward. The Division commander explained that since there was no enemy confronting the Division, it had begun the river crossing operation in order to secure a foothold on the opposite bank.

Colonel Kinoshita then sent a telegram to Lt Col Takeshi Mori, staff officer in charge of operations of the 1st Army at Fengtai, as follows:

> Enemy troops operating in the Kuangchuang area on the 14th Division front are evidently spread thin. The main force may have retreated.
> The main body of the 14th Division began moving at noon of the 14th and is now advancing toward the line connecting Mentsun, Tunghsu and Paitsun.
> The Chief of Staff has approved this action.

About 1300 hours of the 14th, the Army received a telegram from the 14th Division which stated:

> The Division started moving at 1200 hours. It has crossed the Yungting Ho and is now advancing to the line connecting Mentsun, Tunghsu and Kuangchuang. It will then advance beyond this line. The headquarters will advance to Hulin.

The Army commander, upon receipt of this report, disseminated the information immediately to the 6th and 20th Divisions.

At 1300 hours, the Chief of Staff left the 14th Division headquarters, and arrived at 6th Division headquarters at Nanssufa about 1530 hours to observe the situation in the 6th Division area.

About 1440 hours the 6th Division, in concert with the advance of the 14th Division, had launched an attack against the enemy.

The Chief of Staff, accompanied by the 6th Division commander, proceeded to the Peikoi command post to observe the actual combat situation and, after having affirmed the occupation of the opposite bank by the two flank units, returned to Army headquarters.

Prior to his return, the Chief of Staff sent the following telegram at 1600 hours to report on the situation to the Army commander:

> Although there is no sign of a general retreat by the enemy in view of the advance made by the 6th and 14th Divisions, it is believed appropriate to advance X Day.[20]

However, the telegram had not reached the Army headquarters at 1830 hours, when the Chief of Staff returned to headquarters.

At 1800 hours, the Army commander received from Colonel Kinoshita the following telegram:

> The enemy troops confronting the 6th Division are still in their positions. The Division launched an attack at 1440 hours in concert with the drive of the 14th Division.
> Although there is no sign of a general retreat by the enemy, since the 14th Division has begun its advance, it is believed advisable to advance the 20th Division's attack to X + 1 Day.[21]

Prior to this report, the Army commander had ordered the 20th Division to attack the enemy whenever the enemy showed signs of retreating. However, since the 14th and the 6th Divisions had begun their attack, he issued the following order to the 20th Division:

> The 14th Division crossed the Yungting Ho at noon, has advanced to the sector northwest of Kuan, and is planning to advance to the Chuma Ho line tonight. The enemy on the division's front is retreating to the southwest. The 6th Division began an attack on its front at 1440 hours and is now pursuing the enemy.
> The 20th Division will attack the opposing enemy troops as soon as preparations are completed.

---

20. A 1st Army order on 11 September had set X Day as 14 September with the advance of the 6th Divisions beginning at nightfall of that day. However, with the 14th Division beginning its advance at 1200 and the 6th Division advancing at 1440, the Chief of Staff considered the Army's operational tempo generally should be stepped up.

21. The attack by the 20th Division had been planned for X + 2 Day.

By sunset the 14th Division had advanced almost to Peikungyu while the 6th Division drove to the line connecting Nankoi and Tapingchuang. Both divisions continued to pursue the enemy southward.

The 1st Army's estimate of the enemy situation made on the night of the 14th was as follows:

> It would appear that the hostile 30th Army, which is operating in our 20th Division area has received information that our main force is preparing to attack from the Kuan area, and elements of the 30th Army are now rushing the construction of positions in the area between Chohsien and Liuhoying in order to resist in the northeast area. Also, they are destroying bridges across the Chuma Ho to delay our advance. Moreover, the hostile 53d Army retreating from the banks of the Yungting Ho is attempting to join the 30th Army, when together they will resist from their prepared second and third positions.
> The 20th Division will encounter stubborn resistance from the main body of the 30th Army on the 15th. The 14th Division will also encounter determined resistance at the Chuma Ho line and west, while the 6th Division will meet resistance in the Niutochen area. However, the 6th and 14th Divisions should be able to advance boldly and break through enemy positions on the Chuma Ho and in the areas west of the river, which are not yet fully fortified, and advance to the rear of the hostile 30th Army. No change in present policy relative to the employment of groups is necessary. All that is necessary is to advance.

In view of the situation on the 1st Army front, the North China Area Army commander dispatched Staff Officer Shimoyama to the 1st Army headquarters in Fengtai and Staff Officer Hanaya to the Provisional Air Corps headquarters in Nanyuan to obtain first-hand information on new developments.

Also on the 14th, the 4th Air Brigade headquarters and the 7th Air Battalion which had been incorporated into the Order of Battle of the North China Area Army, were placed under the Provisional Air

Corps.

On the morning of the 15th, the 1st Army commander went to the Lianghsiang command post to inspect the battle front of the 20th Division.

The 20th Division started its attack at 1140 hours, occupied the multi-trench positions north of Fangshan and continued to attack the stubbornly resisting enemy.

At dawn on that day, elements of the 14th Division, continuing their pursuit, had advanced to the left bank of the Chuma Ho and began to prepare to cross the river. Toward evening, the main force of the division advanced to the line connecting Hsitsaochuang and Kungtsunchen on the left bank of the Chuma Ho and prepared for a river crossing operation.

The situation on the 6th Division front was unknown due to a temporary break in the communication system.

The 1st Army commander, on the basis of the over-all situation, decided to pursue the enemy towards the area northwest of Chingyuan without slacking the offensive and, at 1340 hours, issued the following order:

> The majority of the enemy has been put to rout by the heroic efforts of each group.
> The Army will pursue the enemy toward the area northwest of Chingyuan without let up.
> The 20th Division, in accordance with its original mission, will, without delay, pursue the enemy toward the vicinity of Ihsien. After the division has annihilated the enemy operating north of Chohsien, a force, built around three infantry battalions and one field artillery battalion, will be placed under

the direct control of the Army at Chohsien.

The 14th Division will pursue the enemy toward the area southwest of Ihsien.

The 6th Division will pursue the enemy toward the area north of Mancheng.

Operational boundaries will be extended as follows:

The boundary between the 20th and 14th Divisions: A line connecting Chohsien, Linchuang south of Laishui, and Kutsun approximately four kilometers south of Ihsien.

The boundary between the 14th and 6th Divisions: A line connecting Tinghsing, Mutsun (approximately 28 kilometers southwest of Tinghsing) and the bench mark on 415-meter Hill (about 15 kilometers north of Mancheng).

The area on the boundary will be the area of responsibility of the Division on the left. However, the road running from Chohsien through Sunglintien to Laishui, which is within the operational area of the 14th Division, may be used by heavy vehicles of the 20th Division.

Each division will be responsible for protecting railways within its own operational area.

The Army reserve unit (the 50th Infantry Regiment less one infantry battalion) will advance through the sector east of the Peiping - Hankou railway toward the vicinity of Chohsien to sever the retreat route of the enemy confronting the 20th Division. Upon advancing to Chohsien, the reserve unit will return to its original command.

The North China Area Army commander decided to exploit the success of the 1st Army and send it directly against Chingyuan without halting to prepare the line extending east and west from Tinghsing. Based on this plan, the Area Army commander ordered the Provisional Air Corps to support, with its main force, the 1st Army's pursuit of the enemy and the 5th Division's advance to the Chingyuan plain,[22] and, with an element, to support the 2d Army's operation.[23]

---

22. See pages 16 and 17.
23. On 11 September, the 2d Army had occupied Machang and by mid-September was north of Tsanghsien. It occupied Tsanghsien on 24 September.

Also, on the 15th, the 1st Army placed the newly-attached heavy artillery units under the control of the commander of China Garrison Artillery Regiment,[24] and issued the following order:

> Colonel Nobuo Kobayashi, commander of the China Garrison Artillery Regiment will assume command of the 1st Independent Heavy Siege Artillery Battalion, the 2d Independent Heavy Siege Artillery Battalion, and the 1st Independent Heavy Siege Artillery Battery,[25] in addition to the units now under his direct command (less the mountain artillery battalion). The units under Colonel Kobayashi's command will be attached to the 1st Army as the Army Heavy Artillery Unit.
> The Army Heavy Artillery Unit will support the attack of the 20th Division.
> The 20th Division will be responsible for providing quarters and supplies to the aforementioned Unit.

The Area Army commander also announced plans for the disposition of units which were due to arrive in the near future as follows: the 118th Infantry Brigade of the 109th Division was to detrain at Huangtsun and prepare to advance toward the area south of the Yungting Ho via Kuan, while the 6th Heavy Field Artillery Brigade was to enter the command of the 1st Army commander upon arrival at Fengtai.

On 16 September, the 20th Division unleashed its attack in the morning and advanced to the area southwest of Fangshan. It continued

---

24. On 15 September, the China Garrison Artillery Regiment, which was under the direct command of the North China Area Army, was attached to the 1st Army.

25. On 9 September, these heavy artillery units, which were under the direct command of the North China Area Army, were ordered to advance from the vicinity of Peiping to Lianghsiang and to prepare to support the 1st Army, whenever necessary. On 15 September, they were attached to the 1st Army.

its attack into the night in the sector south of Fangshan.

The 14th Division began to cross the Chuma Ho at a point near Hsitsaochuang on the night of the 15th, and, at 1400 hours of the 16th, after the main body of the Division had crossed the river, began to advance toward Sunglintien in pursuit of the enemy.

After crossing the Yungting Ho the 6th Division found its way blocked by a vast marshy area east of Niutochen. Unable for a time to make much headway, the Division finally passed through this area, and, crushing enemy resistance, advanced to the vicinity of Tachiangtsun by evening of the 16th.

On 13 September, the North China Area Army released from its direct control the 3d Battalion of the 59th Infantry Regiment, which had been stationed at Tangshan and which had been guarding the Peiping - Ninghai railway and its neighboring area, and ordered it to return to the 14th Division. On 15 September, the 1st Army ordered the battalion to proceed to Lianghsiang to serve as a reserve unit of the 1st Army. It arrived in Lianghsiang at 1530 on the 18th.

On the 17th, since enemy troops in the Chienchuntai area had withdrawn to the area west of the Tahanling and Hsiaohanling Mountain Ranges, the Army ordered the Chienchuntai Detachment[26] to leave one infantry battalion in the vicinity of Sanchiatien and advance with its remaining units to the vicinity of Kaopeitien and serve as the Army's

---

26. Strength: 23d Infantry Regiment (minus 1 battalion) and 2d Battalion of 45th Infantry Regiment as nucleus, commanded by Colonel Shizuomi Okamoto.

reserve.

The 20th Division, upon completion of a successful night attack southwest of Fangshan, commenced a pursuit action and advanced to the area west of Chohsien at sunset of the 17th. At the same time, the Army ordered the 3d Battalion of the 50th Infantry Regiment, (minus two companies), which was at Lianghsiang as a reserve unit,[27] to advance toward Chohsien via the Peiping - Chingyuan road, in concert with the advance of the 20th Division.

The 1st Army, also ordered the Army Heavy Artillery, which had been deployed in the vicinity of Lianghsiang since the 15th but which it was found unnecessary to use in support of the 20th Division attack, to mass in the vicinity of Changhsintien and prepare to advance and support the attack on Chingyuan, if required.

The 14th Division advanced to the south of Chohsien at about 1000 hours of the 17th, and severed the Peiping - Hankou railway line, while an element of the Division pursued the enemy towards Laishui.

On the morning of the 17th, the 6th Division continued to mop up hostile remnants in the vicinity of Niutochen and, advancing westward, reached the left bank of the Taching Ho near Hsinchiao about sunset.

---

27. After this unit landed at Tanghu on 13 September, it assembled in the Lianghsiang area.

As the attack was generally successful on all fronts, the 1st Army commander decided to send elements as an advance force to Shihpanshan and to the heights on the northern bank of the Tacha Ho, north of Mancheng, to facilitate the forthcoming operation, and issued the following order:

> The Army's attack is developing favorably.
> The 6th and 14th Divisions will promptly send elements to the following points to facilitate the attack against Chingyuan.
> Elements of the 14th Division: If possible to Shihpanshan; otherwise, to the heights north of Shihpanshan.
> Elements of the 6th Division: To the heights on the northern bank of the Tacha Ho, north of Mancheng.

During this period, the main body of the Provisional Air Corps gave the 1st Army direct air cover to facilitate its operations, in addition to bombing Shihchiachuang, Chingyuan, and other places.

Second Phase (18 - 20 September) (Map 4)

The enemy force which had been routed from positions near Chohsien, was composed of the 53d Army (commanded by Wan Fulin and composed of the 116th, 119th and 130th Divisions), the 91st Division of the 63d Army commanded by Feng Chanhai, the 30th Army (commanded by Sun Lienchung and composed of the 27th, 30th and 31st Divisions), the 3d Army (commanded by Tseng Wanchung and composed of elements of the 7th and 12th Divisions) and elements of the 4th Cavalry Division, while retreating from the Chienchuntai area were elements of the 14th Army (commanded by Wei Lihuang and composed of the 10th, 83d and 85th Divisions).

The Japanese 20th Division, in spite of torrential rain, left

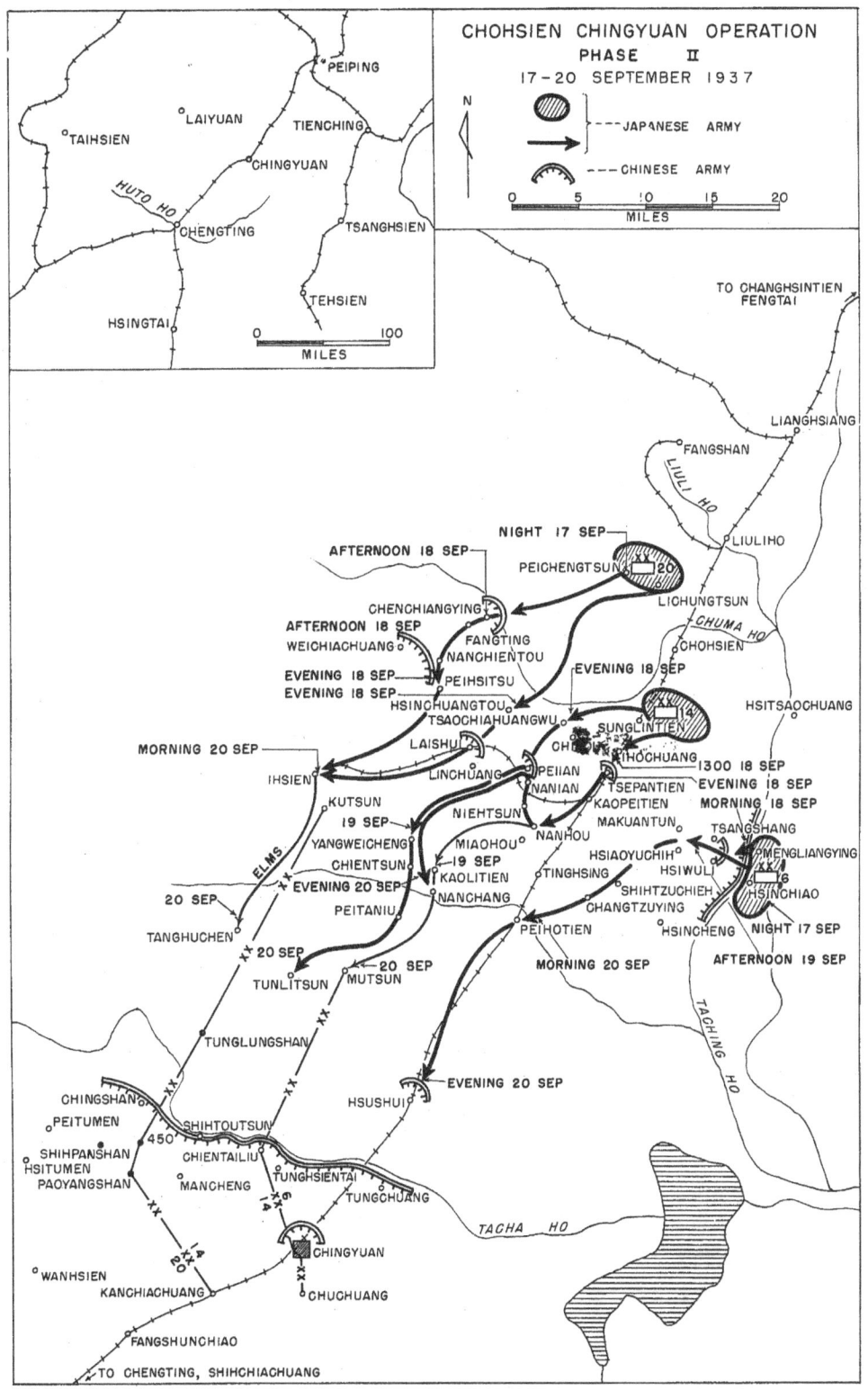

the vicinity of Peichengtsun and Lichungtsun at midnight of the 17th, and, dividing into two columns, continued the pursuit of the enemy through the night. They dislodged powerful enemy forces from the vicinity of Chenchiangying on the upper reaches of the Chuma Ho, and from Fangting and Nanchientou southwest of Chenchiangying on the afternoon of the 18th.

The 14th Division, upon advancing to the area east of Chohsien on the 17th, sent the Tachi Detachment (principally composed of three infantry battalions of the 27th Infantry Brigade and one field artillery battalion) to the Laishui area without delay, in order to seal the escape route of the enemy fleeing to the west of Chohsien and decided to continue pursuing the enemy with the main force of the division. On that day the right column (principally composed of two infantry battalions of the 59th Infantry Regiment and one field artillery battery) left Sunglintien for Yangweicheng via Chikou and Nanian, and the advance guard of the left column (principally composed of two infantry battalions of the 28th Infantry Brigade and two field artillery batteries) left Sunglintien for Chentsun via Kaopeitien, Nanhou and Kaolitien. The rest of the division, forming the main body of the left column, followed the advance guard. On the morning of 18 September, the right column advanced as scheduled and placed itself under the command of the Tachi Detachment commander. The Tachi Detachment, having incorporated the right column into its command, itself became the right column. The vanguard of the left column reached the vicinity of Ihochuang at about 1300 hours on the 18th. Upon discovering that the enemy was occupying a position near Tsepantien, the vanguard unit lost no time in attacking.

On the night of 17 September, the 6th Division assembled troops on the bank of the Taching Ho near Mengliangying and Hsinchiao and prepared to cross the river. On the 18th, the division commander, in order to cross the Taching Ho as rapidly as possible and continue the pursuit of the enemy, and in order to occupy strategic areas north of Mancheng with an element of the division and thus facilitate the battle of Chingyuan, ordered the commander of the 11th Infantry Brigade, who was in command of the left pursuit unit, also to assume command of the right pursuit unit (the main body of the 47th Infantry Regiment), cross the Taching Ho and advance to the area north of Hsincheng. Further, he ordered the cavalry unit (with one infantry battalion attached) to rush to the hilly area north of Mancheng. On the morning of the 18th, the main body of the 47th Infantry Regiment, operating as the right pursuit unit, crossed the Taching Ho near Mengliangying by native boats. The 11th Infantry Brigade commander then ordered the 47th Infantry Regiment, to secure the bank opposite Hsinchiao and thereby provide cover to the main force of the brigade crossing the river near Mengliangying, where the crossing was easier. However, since the enemy had occupied positions extending from the vicinity of Tsangshang to the vicinity of Hsiwuli, the covering force prepared for a night attack against the enemy.

On 18 September, the 1st Army commander directed the battle from the Lianghsiang Command Post and in the wake of the successful advance of the Japanese front line forces, he ordered an element of the 20th Division (approximately three infantry battalions and one field artillery battalion commanded by the 78th Infantry Regiment commander), which had been in the neighborhood of Chohsien to advance to the vicinity of Kaopeitien as the left flank detachment to protect the left flank of the Army. On the afternoon of the 18th, the enemy on the 1st Army's front began a general retreat. Thereupon, the 1st Army commander partially revised his operations plan. He decided to attack the prepared positions in and around Chingyuan, on the momentum of the present drive and pursue the enemy toward the sector west of Chingyuan and then to Shihchiachuang. He then issued the following order at 1800 hours:

> The enemy is retreating in confusion to the south and west.
> The 1st Army will continue to pursue the enemy toward the area west of Chingyuan, and then to Shihchiachuang.
> The 20th Division will rush to Shihpanshan via Ihsien and then advance to the vicinity of the Fangshunchiao and sever the enemy's retreat route. At Ihsien, the 2d and 3d Field AAA Units of the 3d Division will be placed under the direct control of the Army.[28]
> The 14th Division will break through hostile positions near

---

28. On 11 September, these units had been attached to the 20th Division by a 1st Army order.

Mancheng, and advance to the area west of Chingyuan and destroy the enemy. The 3d Battalion of the 59th Infantry Regiment, which is held as the army reserve unit, will return to its original command at Sunglintien.

The 6th Division will advance and attack the enemy from the direction of the Peipin - Hankou railway and thereafter will advance to the vicinity of Chingyuan and annihilate the enemy there. The division will send, without delay, a pursuit unit built around one infantry regiment and one field artillery battalion led by the infantry brigade commander, to pursue the enemy along the Peiping - Hankou railway toward Shihchiachuang. At Tinghsing, the 6th Heavy Field Artillery Brigade (less the 14th Regiment and half of the transport unit) will be attached to the division.

Each division will reorganize as soon as it has advanced to its objective and prepare to pursue the enemy towards Shihchiachuang.

Operational boundaries will be extended as follows:

The boundary between the 20th and 14th Divisions: A line connecting Kutsun, 450-meter Hill, Paoyangshan (approximately 8 kilometers west of Mancheng) and Kanchiachuang.

The boundary between the 14th and 6th Divisions: A line connecting Mutsun, Chentailiu, the western gate of Chingyuan Fortress, the southern gate of the fortress and Chuchuang (about 8 kilometers south of Chingyuan).

Divisions on the left will be responsible for the areas on the boundaries. However, should the 14th Division advance to the vicinity of Mancheng, control of the route connecting Ihsien, Chingshan, Shihtoutsun, Mancheng and Wanhsien will be transferred without delay to the 20th Division.

No troops will be garrisoned within Chingyuan until further notice.

The left flank detachment will pursue the enemy toward Hsushui.

The former Chienchuntai Detachment and the 3d Battalion of the 50th Infantry Regiment will remain at Kaopeitien as the reserve unit of the army.

Units under the command of the 118th Infantry Brigade commander upon arrival at Fengtai will mass at Chohsien.[29] The time will be set by a separate order.

The Army Heavy Artillery Unit will advance toward Tinghsing.

The 1st Army Signal Unit will continue its present assignment.

---

29. These units, which had recently arrived in Tienching and which were commanded by Maj Gen Honkawa, were ordered by the North China Area Army commander at 0900 hours of the 18th to be placed under the command of the 1st Army commander upon their arrival at Fengtai.

At 1200 hours on 18 September, the 1st Army commander received orders from the North China Area Army commander to pursue the enemy toward Chengting, after breaking through enemy positions in the vicinity of Chingyuan. The order also stated that the main force of the 2d Army (16th Division as a nucleus) would advance from Tsanghsien to Chengting and seal off the escape route of the enemy confronting the 1st Army. Further, while an element of the 5th Division was to support the advance of the Tojo Unit of the Kwantung Army, its main force was to advance to the Chingyuan area by way of Laiyuan and the Provisional Air Corp's main force was to cooperate with the 1st and 2d Armies in cutting off the enemy's escape route.

The 1st Army commander then placed one battalion of the 118th Infantry Brigade under the command of the Army Line of Communications Headquarters at Fengtai. Simultaneously, he ordered the main force of the unit to advance to the vicinity of Changhsintien to prepare for the coming operation.

On the 19th, the 1st Army commander, from information obtained through air reconnaissance made by army staff officers and the Provisional Air Corps, estimated the enemy situation as follows:

> The enemy in the Peiping - Hankou railway area has abandoned his intention to resist earnestly in the vicinity of Chingyuan and will probably attempt resistance near Shihchiachuang on the right bank of the Hoto Ho.
> Therefore, though the enemy probably will resist at Chingyuan, it will be only to cover his retreat.

The 1st Army commander dispatched his chief of staff to Liuliho

Command Post to direct the over-all pursuit action. Rail transportation was not satisfactory, especially as the repair of bridges over the Liuli Ho had not been completed. This lack of transportation began to seriously effect supplies to the front line troops. The Army commander, therefore, temporarily suspended the advance of the Army Heavy Artillery Unit, and also the newly attached 6th Heavy Field Artillery Brigade. At the same time, he strove to transport supplies to the front line by employing line of communications motor companies and, the same day, advanced the terminal point of the line of communications to Kaopeitien.

Near sunset of the 18th, the 20th Division advanced to the vicinity of Peihsitsu with the main force of the right pursuit unit, and to Hsinchuangtou northeast of Laishui with the main force of the left pursuit unit. The Division prepared to attack the enemy position extending from a hill west of Weichiachuang to the vicinity of Laishui at dawn of the 19th, but, at dawn, the enemy had begun to retreat and the Division began to advance to the area east of Ihsien, close on the heels of the retreating enemy. Early on the morning of the 20th, the Division captured Ihsien without encountering much opposition. It then assembled its troops near there to prepare for further pursuit action. Later in the day an element of the Division occupied Tanghuchen.

On the evening of the 18th, the vanguard of the 14th Division's left column occupied Tsepantien. Around sunset of the same day, the right column of the 14th Division had advanced to the vicinity of Tsaochiahuangwu and made preparations to attack enemy positions near Peiian and Nanian at dawn of the 19th. At dawn of the 19th, however, the enemy began to retreat and the column advanced toward the area southeast of Ihsien, closely pursuing the retreating enemy. On the 19th, the 14th Division commander decided to continue the pursuit of the enemy south of Ihsien. In accordance with this decision, the right column pursued the enemy south of Ihsien, while the vanguard of the left column advanced towards the vicinity of Peitaniu via Kaopeitien, Nanhou and Kaolitien. The rest of the division, constituting the main body, followed the vanguard of the left column.

Around sunset of the 19th, having advanced to the vicinity of Nanhou, the 14th Division commander discovered that it would be difficult for the main body of the division to pursue the enemy further not only because of the condition of the roads but also because of the obstacle presented by an impassable unnamed river west of Nanhou. The commander assembled his troops northwest of Tinghsing and prepare for further pursuit action and ordered the right column to occupy immediately the hills west of Mutsun in order to facilitate the pursuit by the rest of the division. The vanguard of the left column was directed to construct a bridge near Nanhou and occupy Miaohou and vicinity, in order to protect the massing of the main body of the left column.

However, the construction of the bridge made little progress, so the commander, believing it would be a waste of time to postpone the advance until the bridge was completed, decided to advance the main body of the left column on the 20th by a road which passed through Nanhou, Niehtsun (about two km northwest of Nanhou), Peiian and Yangweicheng.

On the 19th, the right column had advanced to the vicinity of Yangweicheng and the vanguard of the left column to Kaolitien.

Early on the morning of the 20th, the division commander personally led the main body of the left column and reached Nanchang about sunset.

The same day, the right column advanced to the vicinity of Tunlitsun, west of Mutsun and the vanguard of the left column to the vicinity of Mutsun.

At that time the rear motor transport unit of the 14th Division began to fail to keep pace with the frontline forces and supply problems began to crop up. Thus, each front line unit of the division had to depend largely on acquiring supplies from newly occupied areas.

By midnight of the 18th, the greater part of the main force of the 11th Infantry Brigade of the 6th Division completed crossing the Taching Ho and was preparing, together with the river-crossing cover force, to attack the enemy in the vicinity of Tsangshang and Hsiwuli. Around daybreak of the 19th, however, the enemy began to withdraw. The brigade pursued them and, on the afternoon of the same day, advanced to a line connecting Makuantun and Hsiaoyuchih.

On the 19th, the 6th Division commander intending to pursuit enemy troops from the direction of the Peiping - Hankou railway line and annihilate them in the vicinity of Chingyuan, ordered the pursuit unit commanded by the 11th Infantry Brigade commander to advance toward Peihotien along the Shihtzuchieh - Changtzuying - Peihotien road at first and then to pursuit enemy troops toward Chingyuan along the Peiping - Hankou railway. On the 20th, the pursuit unit, in a dawn engagement near Peihotien, destroyed a powerful enemy force retiring from the north, before advancing southward. The unit destroyed another enemy force in the vicinity of Hsushui about sunset of the same day, and occupied the town.

The 1st Army commander, therefore, cancelled the pursuit action of the left flank detachment toward Hsushui and ordered this detachment to proceed to Tanghuchen promptly and return to its original command.

On the 20th, the Army obtained the following intelligence, and immediately transmitted it to the 20th Division:

> Three enemy divisions, the 2d, the 17th and the 25th Division, are in positions near Chingyuan.
> On the 18th, the 25th Division was ordered by the commander of the Chingyuan Defence Force to occupy the area between Tunghsientai, and Tungchuang with one brigade and the mountainous area northwest of this area with another brigade, also to dispose one artillery battalion, on the east side of Mancheng and another at Chingshan. Incidentally, the enemy 25th Division was badly mauled by our 8th Division at Kupeikou during the Manchurian Incident.

According to air reconnaissance the valley opening from Tanghuchen to Chingshan via Tunglungshan is very broad and the roads can be negotiated by heavy vehicles. The reconnaissance also showed that the terrain near Peitumen and Hsitumen approximately eight kilometers west of Shihpanshan, is composed of low hills, and, in general, would permit easy troop movement.

It seems that the sector north of Shihpanshan, which was neglected by the enemy in the beginning, has, since the 18th, been receiving enemy attention as they are now hastily preparing defensive positions in the area.

Your division will advance a part of its strength without delay as close as possible to Shihpanshan and secure a position in its vicinity in order to facilitate our subsequent attack. Your division, no doubt, will take such steps, but nevertheless we should like to remind you of the importance of your mission.

On the same day, an army staff officer was dispatched to the area to effect closer liaison with the 6th Division.

The Third Phase (21 - 24 September)   (Map 5)

On 21 September the enemy continued to retreat in confusion, and the 1st Army relentlessly pursued it to the Tacha Ho line.[30] The 1st Army commander advanced his command post to Chohsien. At the same time, the 2d Army unleashed an assault on enemy positions around Tsanghsien, while the main force of the Provisional Air Corps supporting the 1st and 2d Armies bombed enemy positions in and around Chingyuan and Tsanghsien as well as key points behind the enemy's lines, in order to sever the enemy's retreat route. The North China Area Army commander also ordered the Provisional Air Corps to assign an element of its force to cooperate with the Kwantung Army's air force

---

30. This Japanese force comprised the main strength of the 14th Division, one infantry battalion of the 20th Division and the Cavalry Regiment and one infantry battalion of the 6th Division.

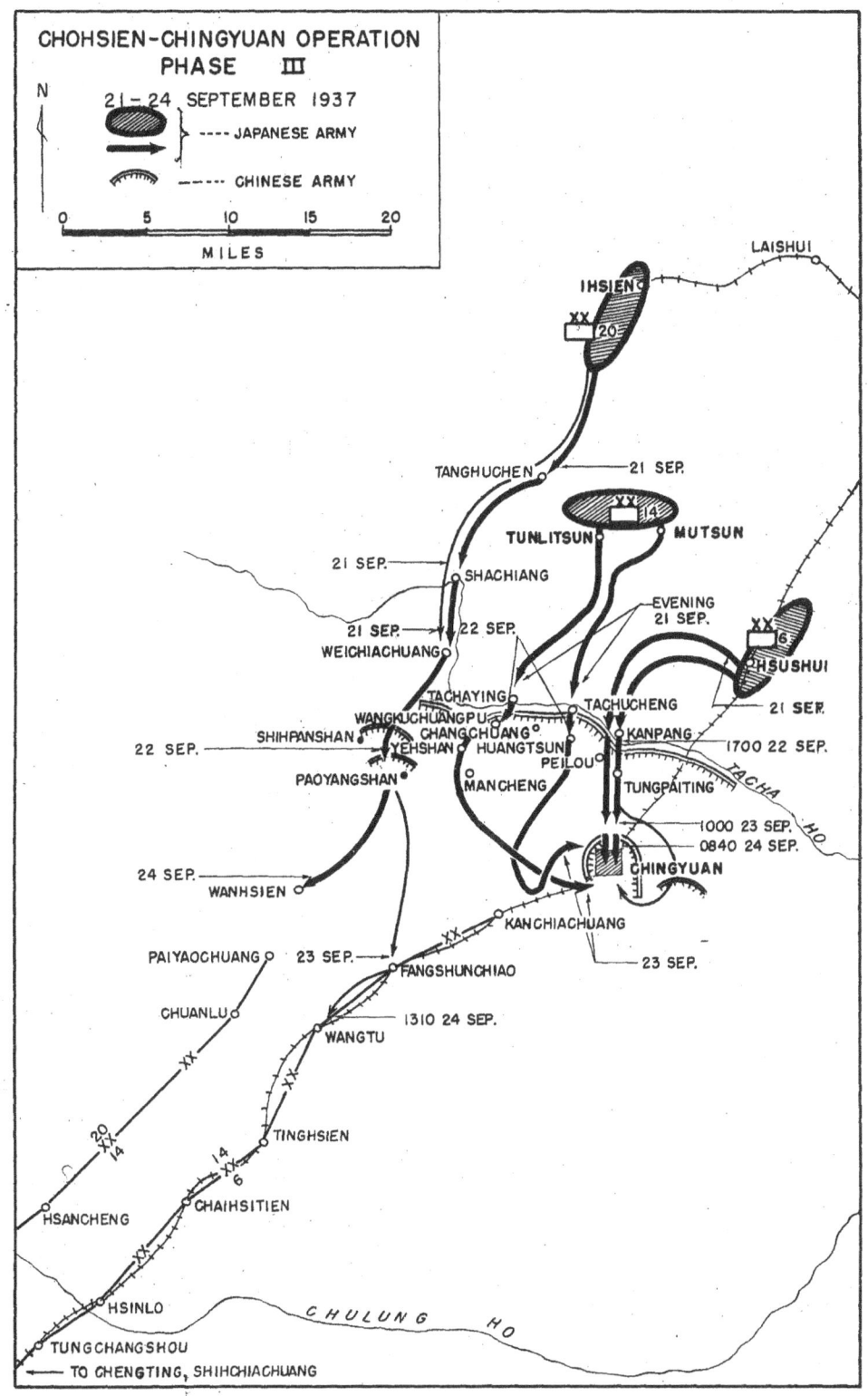

in destroying the enemy air force in Shansi Province.

The vanguard of the 20th Division pursued the enemy in the vicinity of Weichiachuang, and the main force of the Division, the enemy in the area around Tanghuchen and Shachiang. On the 22d, the 20th Division drove southward after breaking through enemy positions in the vicinity of Shihpanshan and, on the 23d, an element of the Division advanced to the vicinity of Fangshunchiao and cut off the enemy's line of retreat.

Meanwhile, the 14th Division launched daring night attacks in the vicinity of Tachaying and Tachucheng on the 21st, advanced to the Yehshan - Changchuang - Huangtsun line on the 22d and, about sunset that day, started a drive toward the sector southwest of Chingyuan to cut off the enemy's line of retreat, arriving in this sector on the 23d.

On the 21st, the main strength of the 6th Division advanced to the area round Hsushui. Later, on the same day, the Division advanced toward Kanfeng, intending to attack enemy positions near Peilou and Tungpaiting, on the 22d. However, because of the delay in artillery preparations, the attack was postponed until daybreak on the 23d, but, hearing of the success of the 14th Division, the time of the commencement of the attack was again stepped up to 1700 hours of the 22d. Around 1000 hours of the 23d, the 6th Division charged into the enemy's outer positions at Chingyuan, having first broken through enemy positions on the banks of the Tacha Ho, south of Kanfang. However, owing to the delayed advance of artillery units, the necessary artillery support did not begin until dusk and the occupation of Chingyuan was correspondingly delayed.

On 21 September, the 108th Division upon arrival at Tienching from Japan, was placed under the direct command of the North China Area Army. It was disposed under the delegated command of the 1st Army to the sector south of Changhsintien along the Peiping - Hankou railway line. Accordingly, the 1st Army commander directed the division to mass between Lianghsiang, Sunglintien and Tinghsing (approximately eight kilometers southwest of Kaopeitien), and on 22 September issued the following order:

> The 108th Division, which is under the direct control of the North China Area Army, will advance to Changhsintien and areas south thereof.
> The units commanded by the 118th Infantry Brigade commander will proceed to Kaopeitien, and assume responsibility for maintaining public peace and order in the area and guarding the railways between Chohsien and Chingyuan, and between Kaopeitien and Ihsien.
> Until the 108th Division troops arrive at Chohsien, an infantry battalion will remain at Chohsien and will be responsible for the maintenance of public peace there.

Since the railway bridge on the Liuli Ho had been repaired, the main strength of the 6th Heavy Artillery Brigade, which had been standing by between Lianghsiang and Toutienchen, was ordered to move to Hsushui on the night of the 22d, and place itself under the command of the 6th Division commander. The heavy artillery which was under the direct control of the Army also was ordered to proceed to Hsushui.

The 1st Army commander had ordered the former Chienchuntai Detachment to move to the vicinity of Kaopeitien, via Fengtai, by train and motor car and to remain as a reserve unit, but, on the 22d, the commander issued another order to the Detachment to move to Hsushui by train and return to its parent unit.

On the 23d, with the fall of Chingyuan imminent, the 1st Army commander decided that a part of the strength should pursue the enemy, and that the main strength should, after regrouping near Chingyuan, proceed immediately toward Shihchiachuang in pursuit of the enemy in that area. He, therefore, issued the following order at 1500:

> Each unit's relentless attack has inflicted heavy losses on the enemy which was entrenched in the fixed positions around Chingyuan and is now fleeing in disorder to the south and southwest.
> The Army will send an element to pursue the enemy to the south and southwest while the main force will be sent to Shihchiachuang in pursuit of the enemy in that area, as soon as the main force completes its grouping in the vicinity of Chingyuan.
> All divisions will consolidate their organization promptly and prepare to advance toward Shihchiachuang in pursuit of the enemy. The time for the advance is set tentatively for the morning of 29 September, but definite orders will be issued later.
> The pursuit unit of the 6th Division hereafter will be placed under the direct control of the 1st Army and shall be called the Army Pursuit Unit. The Army Pursuit Unit will proceed toward Shihchiachuang in pursuit of the enemy by taking the road running parallel to the Peiping - Hankou railway. The pursuit unit organized by the 20th Division, the 3d Battalion of the 50th Infantry Regiment and a part of the motor transport unit, will be placed under the Army Pursuit Unit. At the same time staff officer Major Yanoi will be sent from Army headquarters to the Army Pursuit Unit to act as advisor to the commander of the unit.
> The commander of the 20th Division will send a pursuit unit,

composed basically of an infantry regiment, (minus a battalion) and two field artillery batteries to Fangshunchiao, and place it under the command of the Army Pursuit Unit commander.

The 3d Battalion of the 50th Infantry Regiment will advance to Chingyuan by train and will place itself under the command of the Army Pursuit Unit commander.

The commander of the 6th Division will return a company of the 4th Independent Engineer Regiment to its parent regiment at Chingyuan station.

The operational sector boundary for the pursuit of the enemy toward Shihchiachuang will be decided as follows:

The line connecting Paiyaochuang, Chuanlu, Hsiancheng and Nanwa will be the boundary dividing the operational areas of the 20th and 14th Divisions. The line connecting Kanchiachuang Station, Fangshunchiao Station, Wangtu Station, the northeastern end of Tinghsien, the southwestern end of Tinghsien, Chaihsitien Station, and Tungchangshou will be the boundary dividing the operational areas of the 14th and 6th Divisions. The areas on the boundary line will be the areas of responsibility of the division on the left.

The 5th Independent Machine Gun Battalion, the 1st Independent Light Armoured Car Company and the heavy artillery unit, under the direct control of the 1st Army, and the 6th and 13th Field Gas Platoons will proceed toward Chingyuan and place themselves under the delegated command of the 6th Division commander.

Field AAA units will be stationed as follows to provide air defense:

The 1st Field AAA Unit of the Guards Division will be stationed at Kaopeitien. The 2d Field AAA Unit of the Guards Division and the 1st, 2d and 3d Field AAA Units of the 3d Division will be stationed at Chingyuan under the delegated command of the senior commander.

The 4th Independent Engineer Regiment will continue its road repair work between Chingyuan and Shihchiachuang. A company attached to the 6th Division will be returned to its parent unit at Chingyuan Station.

The 1st Army Signal Unit will be responsible for maintaining liaison between Army headquarters, the division and the Army Pursuit Unit.

The commander will be at the Chohsien Command Post and will enter Chingyuan the day after tomorrow; namely, on the 25th.

At dawn of the 24th, the 6th Division commenced its attack under cover of artillery fire and, at 0840, had occupied part and later occupied the entire city of Chingyuan.

An element of the left pursuit unit of the 20th Division which was in close pursuit of the enemy towards Chengting, captured Wangtu on the 24th at 1310.

On the same day, the 2d Army, which had begun attacking enemy positions around Tsanghsien on 21 September, captured the town. An element of the Provisional Air Corps cooperated with the 2d Army in this operation.

After the fall of Chingyuan and Tsanghsien there was a marked decline in the enemy's fighting power and spirit. The North China Area Army commander, therefore, decided to seize this opportunity, use the main force of the 1st and 2d Armies to pursue the enemy relentlessly, and encircle and destroy him. To this end, at noon on the 24th he ordered the 1st Army to pursue the enemy to Chengting and the main force of the 2d Army to advance to the left bank of the Fuyang Ho and strike the enemy's main force from the rear in a coordinated attack with the 1st Army.

On the 24th, the 1st Army commander ordered the 108th Division[31] to assume positions between Chohsien and Hsushui and to protect the railways north of Chingyuan, while preparing to advance to Shihchiachuang. At the same time, the units commanded by the 118th Infantry Brigade commander were placed under the command of the 108th Division

---

31. The division was attached to the 1st Army by a North China Area Army order on 24 September.

commander.

The Fourth Phase (25 - 27 September) (Map 6)

Immediately after the occupation of Chingyuan on 24 September, the 1st Army commander left the Chohsien Command Post and entered Chingyuan at 1300 hours of the 25th.

On 25 September, the North China Area Army commander ordered the 1st Army commander to send the units commanded by the 118th Infantry Brigade commander to Tienching and place them under the command of the 2d Army.

The 1st Army lost no time in sending its pursuit unit after the enemy retiring towards Shihchiachuang, and assembled its main force in the vicinity of Chingyuan. In preparation for further pursuit, the 1st Army assembled the main force of the 20th Division near Wanhsien, the 14th Division west of Chingyuan, and the 6th Division southeast of Chingyuan.

The pursuit unit of the 1st Army left the vicinity of Chingyuan on the 25th and destroyed enemy forces wherever they were encountered. The unit's main body reached Hsinlo on the 27th. The railway pursuit unit of the 1st Army entered Hsinlo by train on the 26th and began repairing the railway bridge spanning the Sha Ho which had been destroyed by the enemy. The 1st Army commander ordered the pursuit unit to halt in the vicinity of Hsinlo to cover the advance of the main strength of the Army.

After 14 September, Japanese forces were successful in every en-

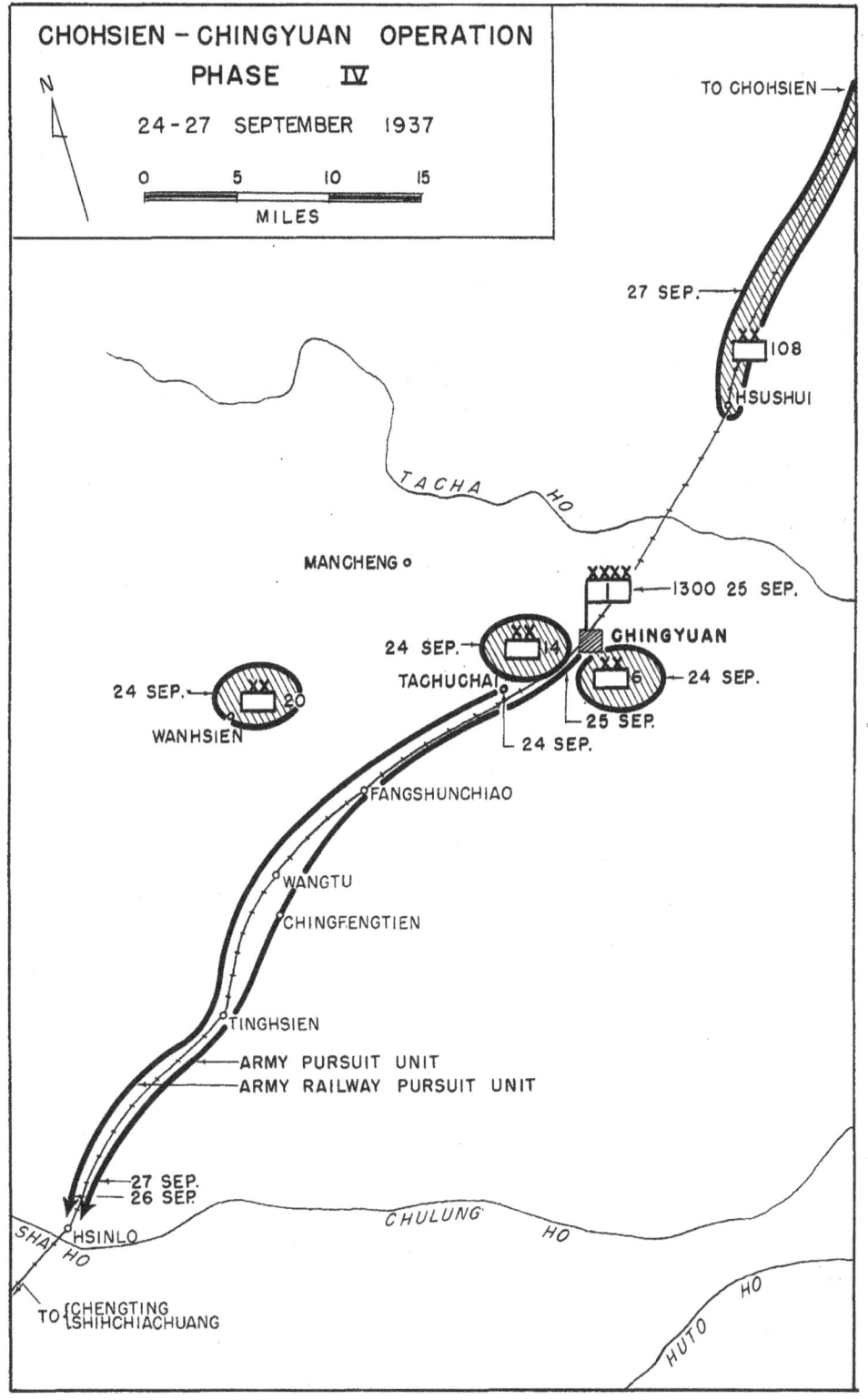

counter with an enemy of superior strength. The 1st Army had quickly occupied Chingyuan, thus denying the enemy the use of his strongly fortified positions near this town and the battle had ended in a rout for the enemy, who had suffered severe losses and was compelled to flee far to the south.

The 1st Army then reorganized its ranks in the vicinity of Chingyuan to prepare for its drive toward Shihchiachuang.

At the same time the 2d Army had advanced to the vicinity of Chiehtichen south of Tsanghsien with the 10th Division, to the northern area of Shahochiao with the 16th Division and to the eastern area of Tacheng with the 109th Division, while the main strength of the 5th Division supported by the Chahar Detachment of the Kwantung Army from the direction of Hunyuan and Yinghsien continued to attack the enemy around the Great Wall west of Lingchiu. (Map 7)

With the enemy retreating toward Shihchiachuang the North China Area Army began to prepare for operations in that area.

Operations in the Vicinity of Shihchiachuang and Fuyang Ho

Preparations for Combat by the 1st Army

From the 24 September, the 1st Army concentrated its main force in the vicinity of Chingyuan.

On 28 September, the 1st Army issued orders from Chingyuan for a drive to Shihchiachuang and vicinity to begin on 1 October. It ordered the Army Pursuit Unit at Hsinlo to protect the advance of the Army,

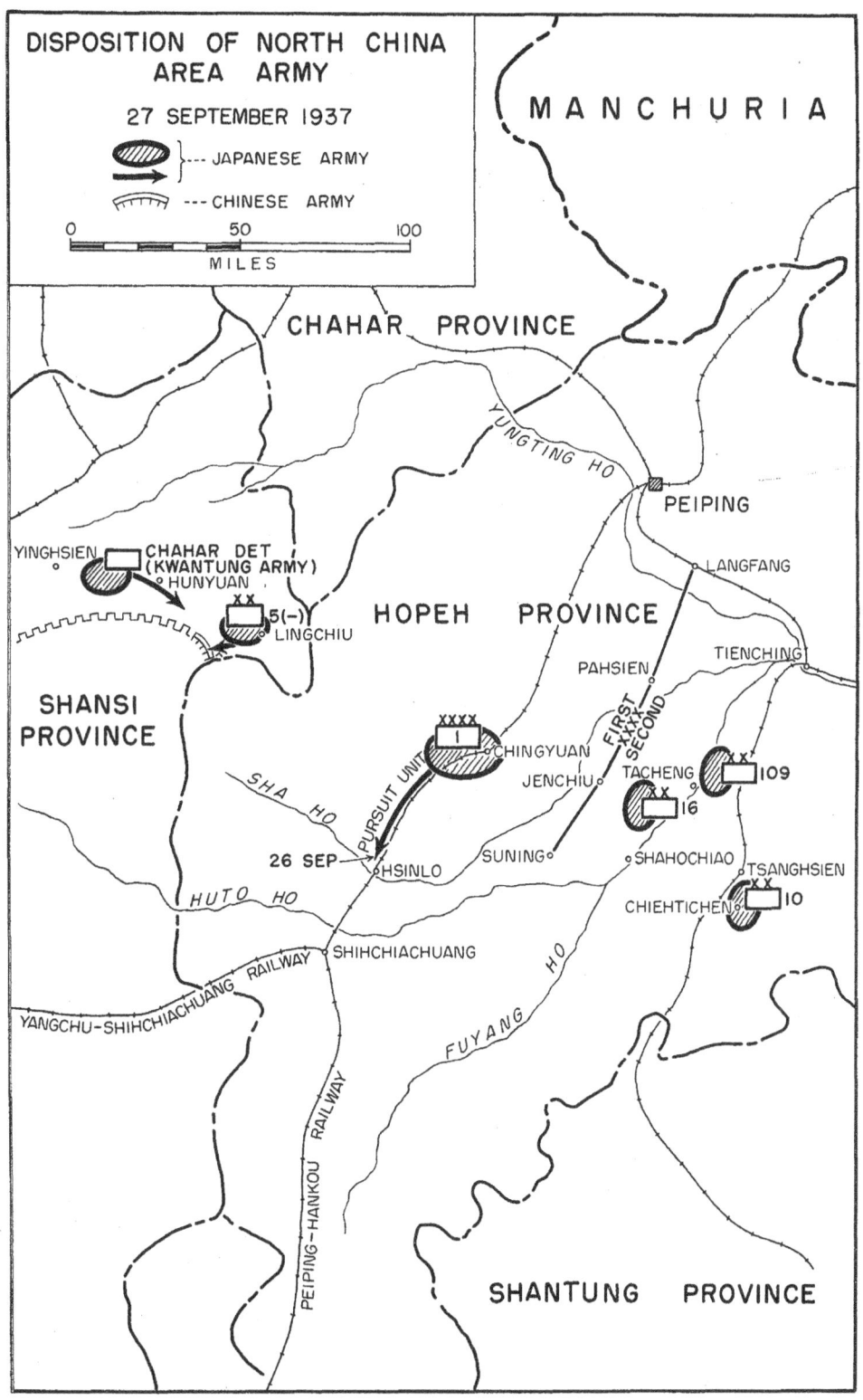

and ordered its divisions to start movement on 1 October and concentrate their forces in the following assigned areas by 9 October, to prepare for the coming drive.

The 20th Division was to advance through the area along the base of the mountains to the west of the Peiping - Hankou railway to the sector northwest of Lingshou. The 14th Division was to proceed through the area generally west of the Peiping - Hankou railway to the sector west of Chengting, and the 6th Division was to proceed through the area generally east of the Peiping - Hankou railway, to the sector northeast of Chengting.

The Army, at the same time, ordered the 108th Division which was placed under its command on 24 September, to proceed along the Chingyuan highway and concentrate in the sector north of Chengting and act as the Army's second line unit.

On 4 October, the Army assembled couriers from all subordinate units at Tinghsien in order to disseminate orders for the attack against the enemy in and around Shihchiachuang.

A summary of the plan of attack was as follows:

> On 9 October the Army will begin its attack on the enemy in the vicinity of Shihchiachuang.
> If the enemy retreats, the Army will pursue him southward without let up and will destroy him in the area north of Hsingtai, together with the enemy located between the Huto Ho and the Fuyang Ho.
> On 9 October, the 20th Division will launch its attack against the enemy along the banks of the Huto Ho and advance to the vicinity of Kaotsien south of Shihchiachuang so as to press the enemy into the southeastern sector and cut the route

of his retreat. During this time, the Division will send a powerful element in the direction of Yangchu on the road running parallel to the Shihchiachuang - Yangchu railway to secure the railway for as long a distance as possible.

On 10 October, the 14th Division will begin an attack on the enemy along the banks of the Huto Ho and advance to the area west of Shihchiachuang. The Division thereafter will quickly advance to the line running from east to west of Hsingtai in pursuit of the enemy along the Peiping - Hankou railway and on the roads parallel to it.

The 6th Division will, upon completion of preparations, capture Chengting, and then attack the enemy along the banks of the Huto Ho and advance to the sector southeast of Shihchiachuang. The Division will then advance its main force, without delay, to the vicinity of Chaohsien and an element to the vicinity of Ningchin and another to Paihsiang and vicinity, to cut the route of retreat of the enemy which is in the sector between Huto Ho and Fuyang Ho.

The plan to cross the Huto Ho will be issued later.

The 108th Division will first take up positions in the sector north of Chengting and, when units of the 6th Division cross the Huto Ho, it will follow up the crossing to exploit the 6th Division's assault and advance to the vicinity of Shulu and destroy the enemy there.

Actual Combat

On 6 October, the 20th, 14th and 6th Divisions of the 1st Army began to advance simultaneously from the line from Chuyang to Tinghsien.

On this day, the North China Area Army issued an order, the gist of which was as follows:

The North China Area Army will destroy in one blow the enemy on the Hopeh Province plain.

The 1st Army will launch an attack at the proper time and destroy the enemy before he has time to retreat. The main effort will be directed against Shihchiachuang and vicinity and, when the enemy line is breached, the enemy will be pursued relentlessly toward Hsingtai and vicinity. Furthermore, the Army will send an element to the strategic area west of Chinghsing to cut the enemy lines of communication to the Shansi Province area. The element will thereafter cooperate with the 5th Division.

At that time, the 5th Division, which had been ordered to capture Yangchu, was attacking Yuanpingchen. The main force of the 2d Army was advancing southwest along the Fuyang Ho, and the advance party of the 16th Division was believed to have reached the vicinity of Fanchiachuang, with the 109th Division in the vicinity of Shenhsien.

On 7 October, the Army commander advanced his command post to Hsinlo.

The 20th Division encountered about two enemy divisions moving northward in the vicinity of Lingshou and Tienyingchen and dealt them a crushing blow.

The 14th and 20th Divisions had advanced to the banks of the Huto Ho and were preparing for further attacks.

On 8 October, the 6th Division deployed siege guns[32] and heavy field artillery pieces, and, receiving support from about 100 artillery pieces in all, stormed Chengting and generally completed mopping up resistance in the city by dawn of the 9th.

Subsequently, an element of the 20th Division succeeded in crossing the river in the vicinity of Tienhsing and pursued the enemy toward Chinghsing. The Division's main force then advanced.

The 14th Division, detecting signs of retreat by the enemy confronting it, advanced its river-crossing schedule and met so little

---

32. 24 cm to 30 cm howitzers, when employed in siege operations (against a fortress) were termed "siege guns." (KOJOHO)

resistance that the spearhead of the vanguard, by the afternoon, had entered Shihchiachuang.

Analyzing the situation, the 1st Army estimated that the enemy on the Huto Ho had begun retreating after suffering heavy losses in the 14th and 20th Division sectors. It, therefore, ordered the divisions under its command to pursue the enemy and advance immediately to designated positions, in order to exploit the success of the battle and destroy the enemy.

Earlier, since the boundary between the 1st Army's area and that of the 2d Army had been extended to the line connecting Suning, Shentse, Chinhsien and Chaohsien, the 1st Army ordered the drive of the 6th and 108th Divisions to halt at that line.

On the 11th, in order to avoid the danger of friendly troops accidentally firing upon each other when the 2d Army troops advanced to the Kaoi area the 1st Army suggested to the Area Army that the boundary line between the 1st and 2d Army be extended further.

On the same day, the 20th Division advanced to the vicinity of Touyutsun, the pursuit unit of the 14th Division to the area north of Yuanshih, and the 6th Division reached Chaohsien.

The 1st Army, therefore, decided to reorganize without delay, after advancing to Hsingtai and Chaohsien and vicinity, and prepare for a further push to the south. It ordered the 20th Division to continue the original mission of its right flank detachment and to quickly reorganize its main force after arriving at the designated position in order to be ready to carry out the operation in the Yangchu area.

The 14th Division was ordered to send an element to pursue the enemy toward Hantan and to reorganize its main force in the vicinity of Hsingtai and prepare for a drive to Anyang.

The 6th Division was ordered to quickly reorganize its troops in the sector between Chaohsien and Luangcheng and be ready for movement to other areas when required.[33]

The 108th Division was ordered to regroup without delay in the vicinity of Meihuachen and to prepare for a drive south through Chaohsien and Paihsiang, and siege guns and a portion of heavy field artillery pieces were ordered to assemble at Chengting and be ready for further action.

On the 12th, the pursuit unit of the 14th Division began attacking a powerful enemy position in the area north of Yuanshih, while the pursuit unit of the 6th Division dealt an annihilating blow to the fleeing enemy south of Chaohsien.

The Army, thereupon, ordered the 6th Division to send its pursuit unit which has reached Paihsiang to Neichiu and to halt the Division's main force at Chaohsien and prepare for further action.

On 12 October, the Area Army ordered the extension of the

---

33. The 6th Division had received an informal Area Army order to move to the Shanghai area.

operational sector boundary between the 1st and 2d Armies to the line connecting Chaohsien, Paihsiang and Nanho and ordered the 6th Division[34] to mass in the vicinity of Shihchiachuang.

On 15 October, the Army headquarters advanced to Shihchiachuang.

The 14th Division continued its pursuit with its mechanized and railway pursuit troops and captured Hantan on the 17th. It reached the Chang Ho line on the 18th.

The 14th Division then endeavored to establish a foothold on the south bank of Chang Ho, and, on about the 27th, built bridges in the vicinity of Fenglochen and near the Peiping - Hankou railway.

About the 27th, the main force of the 14th Division massed between Hsingtai and Hantan and prepared to cope with any emergency which might arise.

The pursuit unit of the 108th Division, which had been pursuing the enemy through Jenhsien, Hokuochen and Tangping captured a strong point for reconnaissance about the 19th in the vicinity of Feihsiang and, on the 23d, inflicted heavy losses on the enemy in the surrounding area, as well as in the vicinity of Chengan on the 24th. Subsequently, the pursuit units began massing in the vicinity of Feihsiang and Chengan.

The main force of the 108th Division was located in the vicinity of Chaohsien as a unit under the direct control of the 1st Army and

---

34. On 12 October, the 6th Division was assigned to the 10th Army and later was transferred to the Shanghai area.

was responsible for maintaining peace and order in Chaohsien and vicinity. (Map 8)

Yangchu Operation

In accordance with the 1st Army order to attack enemy positions in the neighborhood of Shihchiachuang, on 4 October the 20th Division was ordered to attack the enemy on the banks of the Huto Ho. After that, the Division was to send a powerful element toward Yangchu on the road parallel to the Shihchiachuang - Yangchu railway in pursuit of the enemy and to dispose its troops so as to secure as much as possible of the railway.

On 6 October, the North China Area Army ordered the 1st Army to advance an element promptly to strategic points west of Chinghsing and cut off the enemy's line of communication to the Shansi Province area and, at the same time, to act in concert with the 5th Division to capture Yangchu.

The right flank detachment of the 20th Division crossed the Huto Ho and attacked and occupied Chinghsing on 13 October, while its Koito Unit reached Chiukuan, where the drive was slowed down because of a superior enemy force. On the night of the 14th, the 20th Division, dispatched an infantry battalion and a mountain artillery battery from the vicinity of Shihchiachuang to Chinghsing to reinforce the detachment.

On 14 October, the 1st Army ordered the 20th Division commander

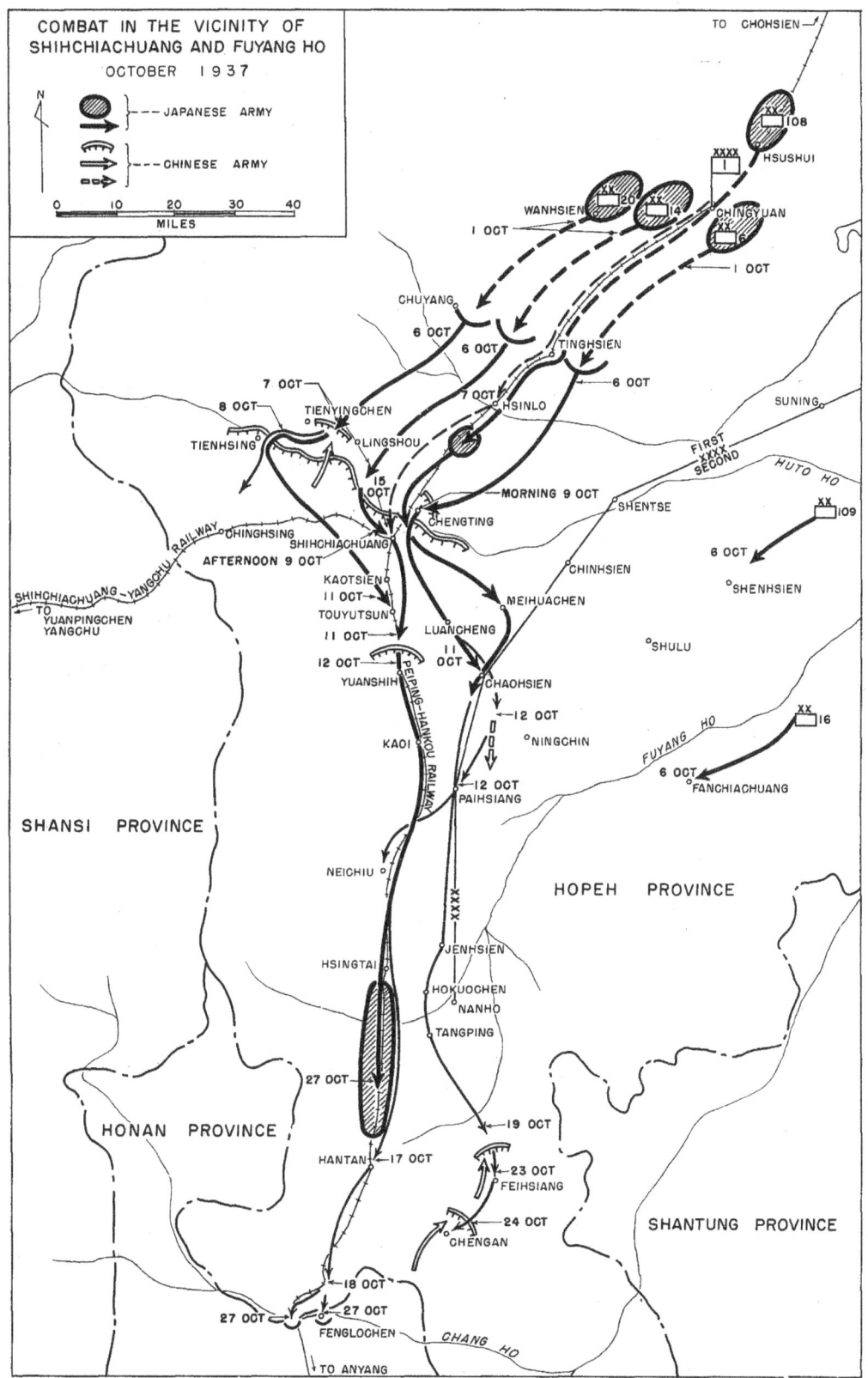

to send three infantry battalions, the main force of the independent mountain artillery regiment and other necessary units as reinforcements to the 5th Division's right flank detachment on the Yangchuan plain to aid the 5th Division's drive on Yangchu. Incidentally, the 5th Division had attacked and occupied enemy positions in and around Hsinkouchen on the 13th.

In accordance with this order, the 20th Division reinforced the right flank detachment with two infantry battalions and an artillery battalion with 10 cm howitzers. These units left Chihchiachuang on the 17th and advanced westward. The area of Chiukuan was known to have been secured by the Koito Unit, but the situation in the Titou area was unknown. Later, a report was received from a staff officer of the 20th Division, who had been dispatched to the right flank detachment, that the detachment had advanced from Chinghsing toward the Hsinkuan area with the main force of the Koito Unit and toward the Niangtzukuan area with about half an infantry battalion by following the railway line. However, although very little resistance had been encountered by the Koito Unit and Chiukuan had been occupied on the 13th, along the railway line there had been heavy fighting with enemy troops entrenched in the hills west of Chinghsing and the Japanese forces had been unable to advance. The commander of the Koito Unit ordered the 3d Battalion to advance to Titou. The battalion, however, was encircled by a superior enemy force in the neighborhood of Titou on the 14th and suffered heavy casualties. It succeeded in breaking through the enemy encirclement and returned to Chiukuan. During this period, the main force of the Koito Unit had attacked the enemy north of Hsinkuan and advanced from the hills west of Chiukuan to Kantaoi and the hills southeast thereof, but remnants of the enemy were still manning positions dug in on hills flanking both sides of the Chiukuan - Chinghsing road.

On 17 October the Area Army issued the following order:

> The 1st Army will rush a powerful element to the Shinchiachuang - Yanchu railway area. The element will break through enemy positions there and advance to Yutzu and vicinity to facilitate the 5th Division's drive on Yangchu.

On the 18th, the right flank detachment of the 20th Division massed six infantry battalions, a mountain artillery regiment, an artillery battalion with howitzers of 10 cm caliber, a trench mortar battalion, a light armored company and an engineer company between Chinghsing and Chiukuan and, on the 19th, ordered the Koito Unit to continue the attack on Hsinkuan. Two infantry battalions, a mountain artillery battery, an artillery battalion with howitzers of 10 cm caliber and a trench mortar company, were dispatched to attack first the enemy on hills west of Chinghsing and then to attack enemy troops in the area of Niangtzukuan.

On the 19th, the right flank detachment attacked the enemy west of Chinghsing and advanced roughly to the line running north-south of Chuangtou.

The 5th Division continued to attack the enemy in the neighborhood of Hsinkouchen, and the enemy began to erect fortifications along a line east and west of Hsinhsien and in the vicinity of Yangchu. In view of the shifting of enemy troops from the vicinity of Wutai to the Niangtzukuan area, the Army ordered the 20th Division to occupy the Yangchuan Plain.

In order to occupy the Yangchuan Plain, the 20th Division decided first to attack the enemy at the Great Wall near Niangtzukuan. On the 20th, therefore, it ordered the right column (formed around 6 infantry battalions, 2 field artillery battalions, 2 artillery companies with 15 cm guns, a mountain artillery battalion and 2 trench mortar companies) to attack the enemy in the Chinghsing - Hsinkuan - Shihmenkou road area and in areas north of the road. The left column (formed around 4 infantry battalions, a mountain artillery battalion and a trench mortar company) was ordered to destroy the enemy in the area along the Weishanchen - Tseyuchen - Shihmenkou road and then advance to the rear of the enemy confronting the right column, to facilitate the attack of that column. The remaining units were ordered to mass in the neighborhood of Chinghsing.

On the 21st, the Area Army ordered the 1st Army to employ a unit built around the 20th Division with an infantry brigade (minus a regiment), a mountain artillery battalion and an engineer company from the 109th Division[35] in a co-ordinated action with the 5th Division, to

---

35. These units of the 109th Division were attached to the 1st Army on 21 October 1937.

occupy the Yangchu Plain. At that time, the 5th Division was still fiercely attacking enemy positions in Hsinkouchen. The Area Army order also directed the 5th Division to begin the drive on Yangchu, after it had occupied enemy positions at Hsinkouchen, recouped its strength and made thorough preparations.

In accordance with the Area Army order, the 1st Army ordered the newly attached units of the 109th Division, which were named the Hsiyang Detachment, to attack Hsiyang from the direction of the Tsanhuang - Chiulungkuan - Hsiyang road. At that time, however, the 109th Division was massed in the vicinity of Tangshan and during the operations near the Fuyang Ho had lost a considerable number of horses. Consequently, although the organization of the Detachment was accelerated not only by drawing horses from within the Division, but also by obtaining a considerable number of horses from 1st Army Headquarters in order to prepare for the mountain operations, the early departure of the detachment was not possible.

The right column of the 20th Division advanced from the vicinity of Shihchiachuang on the 21st and successively occupied the hills southwest of Chuangtou. Also, after a pitched battle on the 24th, it occupied the 1066 meter hill southeast Hotaoyuan. On the same day, the advance force of the left column of the 20th Division surprised the enemy in the neighborhood of Chitoutsun and then advanced to Mashantsun.

The right column occupied Niangtzukuan on the 26th. On the same day the left column destroyed about two divisions of the enemy in the vicinity of Sungkoutsun and then, advancing north, occupied the 1387 meter hill and Paimuching and pushed to the rear of the enemy in the Niangtzukuan area.

On the night of the 26th, the 20th Division commander designated the right column as the right pursuit unit and directed it to pursue the enemy to the Yangchuan Plain. At the same time, the left column was designated the left pursuit unit and ordered to pursue the enemy relentlessly to Pingting via Paimuching, and the main body of the Division was ordered to advance from Hsinkuan to Pingting.

The Army, in order to exploit the fall of Niangtzukuan and to occupy the Yangchu Plain on the momentum of its drive, ordered the 20th Division to continue its attack on the enemy and advance first to the area south of Yutzu and then to the Yangchu Plain. It also ordered the Hsiyang Detachment to place itself under the command of the 20th Division commander at Hsiyang. At the same time, the Army withdrew an artillery regiment with 15 cm howitzers, an artillery battalion with 10 cm cannons, two trench mortar companies and an engineer company from the area along the Peiping - Hankou railway to employ these units in the Shansi Operation.

The Koito Unit which had been in the Chiukuan area advanced to the attack during the morning and pursued the enemy toward Paimuching, after effecting a break-through in the vicinity of Hsinkuan.

An element of the right pursuit unit destroyed the enemy on the hills northwest of Chuchengchen and the main force of the pursuit unit destroyed the enemy on the hills west of Shangpanshihtsun.

The left pursuit unit advanced to the vicinity of Hsiaochiaopao by evening and continued its attack into the night in the area south of Shihmenkou, finally destroying the enemy.

In accordance with the Area Army order, the 109th Division (minus the 118th Infantry Brigade and a cavalry battalion) was placed under the command of the 1st Army on the 26th, so that it might be employed promptly in the campaign to occupy the Yangchu Plain from the mountains west of the Peiping - Hankou railway line.

On the 28th, the Army ordered the newly attached 109th Division upon completion of its preparations to advance to Hsiyang along the Tsanhuang - Chiulungkuan - Hsiyang road, but since the Division had previously transferred its healthy horses to the Hsiyang Detachment, it was short of the ncecessary pack horses for operations in the mountainous area and was unable to depart from the vicinity of Tangshan until 1 November. Much time was spent and much trouble was experienced by the Division in organizing its pack horse unit, for horses had to be drawn from the Division's Transport Unit or captured Chinese horses obtained from the 1st Army and from other sources.

In accordance with the Army order to advance to the area south of Yutzu, the 20th Division resolved to pursue the enemy to the Yangchu Plain after occupying the Yangchuan Plain and replenishing its supplies. It directed an element of the right pursuit unit to pursue the enemy toward Hsinhsingchen and an element of the left pursuit unit to pursue the enemy toward Mataoling. The remaining main force was ordered to mass near Yangchuan and Pingting.

On the 29th, the left pursuit unit of the Division, with the support of the divisional artillery's main force, began attacking an enemy force of about a division and a half, which was occupying positions near Hsiputsun, and captured Pingting.

In the Hsinkouchen area, there was no change in the situation as late as 2 November, but, on 3 November, the enemy in this area began a general retreat with the 5th Division in pursuit.

On 2 November, the 20th Division ordered the right pursuit unit to pursue the enemy relentlessly toward the vicinity of Mingchienchen and, on 3 November, ordered the left pursuit unit to depart from the neighborhood of Pingting and pursue the enemy toward the vicinity of Yutzu along the Mataoling - Sungtachen - Shiahu - Yutzu road, while the Division's main force was to leave Pingting on 4 November and advance toward Changchingchen in the wake of the right pursuit unit.

On 3 November, however, as the situation on the 5th Division's front had improved, the 20th Division attached the main force of the field artillery regiment to the right pursuit unit and ordered it to make an all-out pursuit of the enemy.

Occupation of Yangchu

On the night of 3 November, the Area Army ordered the 1st Army to occupy Yangchu and Yangchu Plain and, at the same time, placed the 5th Division under the 1st Army's tactical command. To achieve its objective the 1st Army issued the following orders:

> The 5th Division will attack Yangchu, while an element of the Division will advance toward Fenyang in pursuit of the enemy.
> The 20th Division will advance an element to occupy the area northwest of Yutzu to keep watch on enemy positions southeast of Yangchu. The main force of the 20th Division will, after advancing to Yutzu, continue pursuit of the enemy toward Chiehhsiu
> The 20th Division will advance the Hsiyang Detachment to Yutzu.
> The 109th Division will depart from Yuanshih on 4 November and begin to advance toward Yutzu via Hsiyang.

Marked progress was made in the bold pursuit action of the 5th Division and its pursuit unit advanced to Yangchutu by the afternoon of 5 November. Between Mingchienchen and Wulitsun, the right pursuit unit of the 20th Division dealt a crushing blow to approximately two enemy divisions, which were advancing northward from the direction of Yutzu toward prepared enemy positions southeast of Yangchu, before advancing toward Hsiaotienchen.

On 6 November, the 5th Division advanced to the gates of Yangchu and prepared to attack. At the same time, the Division urged the enemy within the city to surrender.

In the vicinity of Hsiaotienchen, the right pursuit unit of the 20th Division attacked the enemy on the west bank of the Fen Ho, and subjected a retreating enemy force of not less than 10,000 to artillery fire, inflicting heavy losses.

In the Peiping - Hankou railway area, several divisions of Sung Cheyuan's Army had advanced to Taming and areas to the north and had assumed offensive positions. Therefore, the 1st Army decided to exploit its success on the Yangchu Plain and destroy the enemy in the Taming area.

To this end, the Army ordered the 20th Division to advance an element in pursuit of the enemy to Pingyao and to concentrate its main force in the area north of Taiku and prepare to advance to Shihchiachuang.

The capture of Yangchu already was certain, therefore, due to the situation in the area along the Peiping - Hankou railway, the 104th Brigade, the 15 cm howitzer unit, the special mountain artillery battalion, and the mortar battalion, which were massed near Chinghsing, were ordered to suspend their westward drive and change their course of advance toward the Peiping - Hankou railway area to assume new missions.

On 8 November, the 5th Division launched a general attack on Yangchu. It occupied the walls of the city at a little past 0900 hours and then proceeded to conduct mopping-up operations within the city. An element of the Division advanced to Chingyuan on 9 November. On 12 November, the Army, in accordance with the Area Army order, changed the direction of advance of the 5th Division to Shihchiachuang.

The left pursuit unit of the 20th Division continued in pursuit

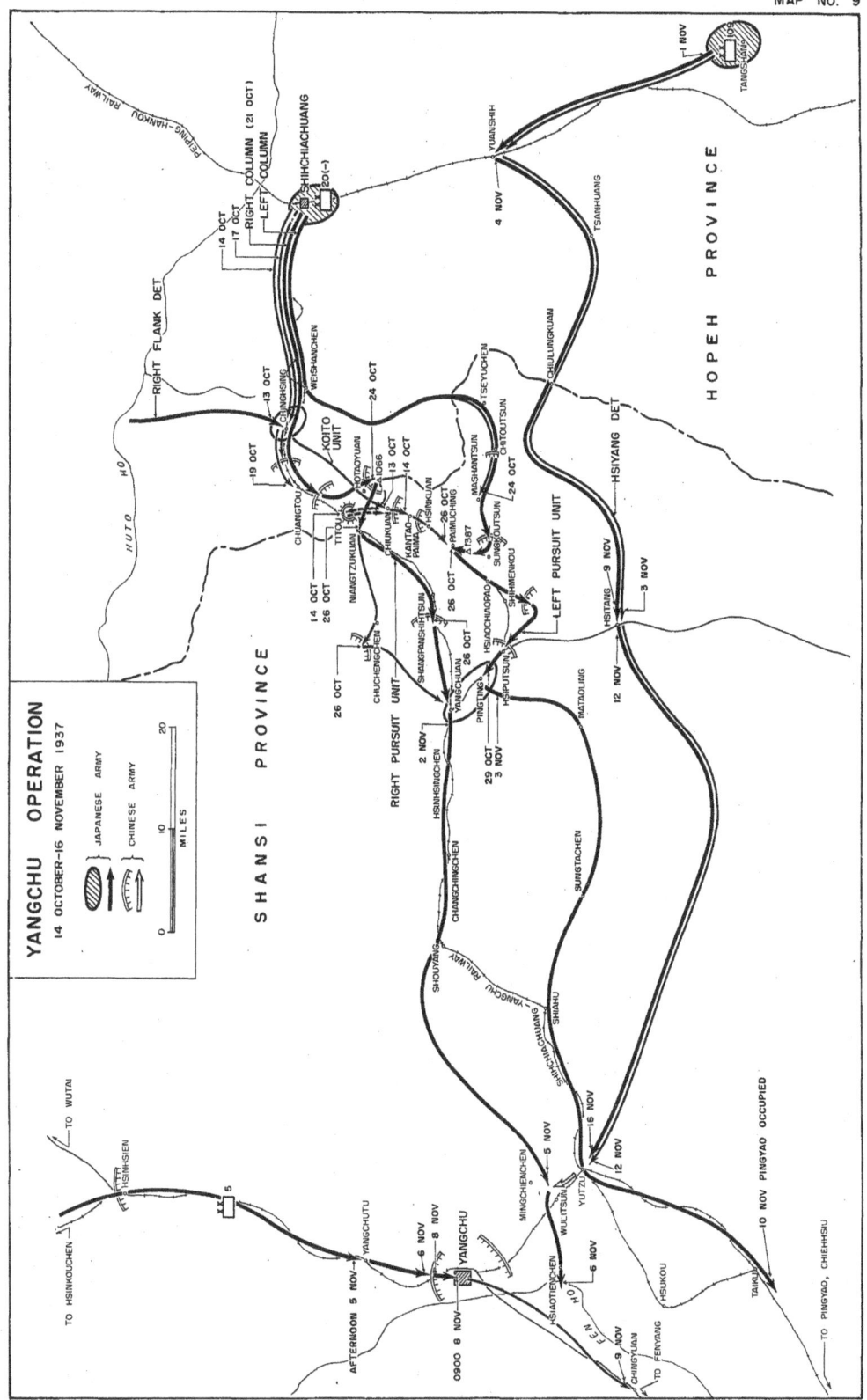

of the enemy and occupied Pingyao on 10 November. The Hsiyang Detachment advanced to Hsiyang on 3 November and to Yutzu on 12 November.[36]

The 109th Division arrived at Hsiyang on 9 November and, on the 12th, leaving behind a garrison unit built around one infantry battalion, the Division advanced westward and reached Yutzu on 16 November. (Map 9).

---

36. The original Japanese manuscript states that the Hsiyang Detachment advanced to Hsiyang on 12 November. Actually, it advanced to Hsiyang on the 3d and to Yutzu on the 12th.

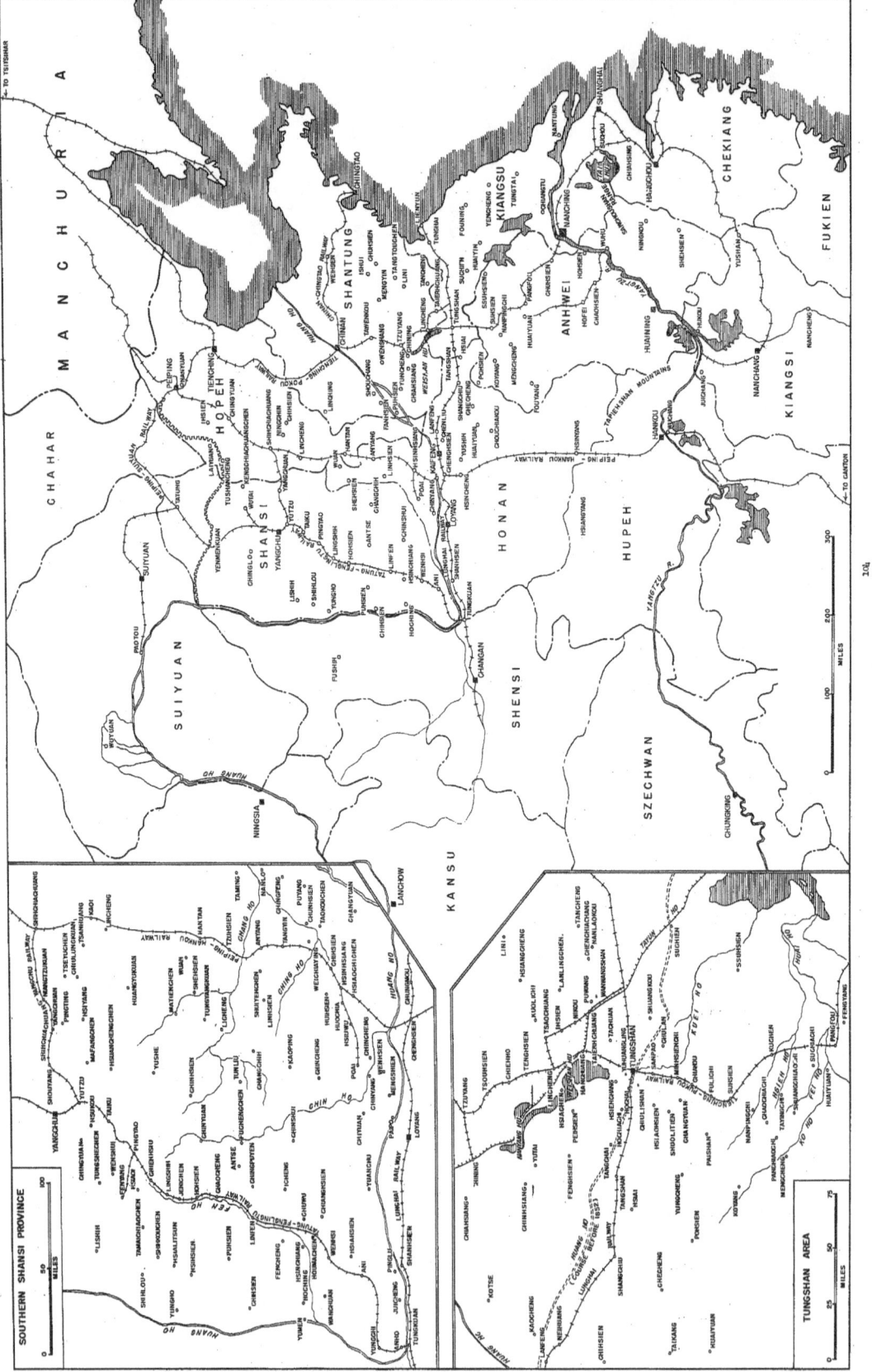

CHAPTER II

Hopeh, Tungshan and Wuchang - Hankou Operations

General Situation Prior to the Hopeh Operation[37]

Japanese Situation

On 18 December 1937, Imperial General Headquarters[38] ordered the North China Area Army commander to undertake operations in areas along the Chinan - Chingtao railway and along the left bank of the Huang Ho above Chinan. At the same time, Imperial General Headquarters stated that orders would be issued later in regard to operations around Chingtao and in southern Shansi Province. On 8 January 1938, it directed the North China Area Army to commence operations in these latter areas whenever the situation appeared favorable.

Accordingly, in mid-December the North China Area Army commander ordered the 1st Army to secure and hold its presently occupied areas and, at the same time, to prepare to advance south to the banks of the Huang Ho. Further, he ordered the 2d Army to occupy Chinan as quickly as possible.

---

37. Although this is known as the Hopeh Operation, actually it covers the North China Area Army's operations from mid-December 1937 to the end of March 1938 north of the Huang Ho and from mid-December 1937 to mid-January 1938 in the Shantung Province.
38. To deal with the situation in China, Imperial General Headquarters was established in the Imperial Palace in Tokyo on 17 November 1937.

The 1st Army commander, therefore, immediately assigned the defense of the Yangchu Plain area to the 20th and 109th Divisions (less the Honkawa Brigade) and that of the west Hopeh Province to the 14th and 108th Divisions.[39]

On 10 January, the North China Area Army commander ordered the 1st Army to conduct operations in the area along the left bank of the Huang Ho, along the Peiping - Hankou railway front and in southern Shansi Province, the 2d Army to occupy Chingtao, and the Provisional Air Corps commander to support the 1st Army with its main strength while supporting the 2d Army with an element. The Provisional Air Corps was also ordered to destroy hostile air strength in the area along the Lunghai railway.

In the early part of January 1938, with the organization of the Mongolia Garrison Group,[40] the operational boundary between the Group and the 1st Army was established as the Inner Great Wall, west of

---

39. From late October, 1937, the main strength of the 14th Division had been stationed between Hsingtai and Hantan, while an element had been stationed at Taming. Also, from late October, the main strength of the 108th Division had been stationed around Chaohsien with elements near Feihsiang and Chengan.

40. The Order of Battle of the Mongolia Garrison Group was established on 4 January 1938 and Lt Gen Shigeru Hasunuma was appointed commander. The Group was built around the 26th Division as a nucleus. (The 11th Independent Infantry Brigade, which had participated in the early part of the China Incident was later expanded into the 26th Division.) The Group was placed under the direct command of Imperial General Headquarters and was assigned the mission of securing important points in Inner Mongolia and southern Chahar Province. Its headquarters was at Wanchuan. On 4 July 1938, the Order of Battle of the Mongolia Garrison Army was issued and the Group became the Army. On 7 July, the Army was assigned to the North China Area Army.

Tushancheng and the Great Wall, bordering the Suiyuan and Shensi Provinces. On 15 January, therefore, the 1st Army commander attached three second reserve infantry battalions[41] and some cavalry and artillery companies[42] to the 109th Division and assigned it to garrison duty in the area south of the Inner Great Wall, mainly to guard the railway connecting Yenmenkuan and Yangchu and line of communications installations, in addition to its existing duties.[43]

Also on 15 January, the North China Area Army commander reassigned the Honkawa Brigade,[44] which had previously been attached to the 2d Army, to the 109th Division. He also attached the 16th Division,[45] which had been returned from Central China, to the 1st

---

41. The term of service of the Japanese soldier was two years active service, five years and four months reserve service after completion of active service and ten years second reserve service after completion of reserve service. The soldier could be called up for active service whenever necessary during his reserve or second reserve service.

42. The North China Area Army had attached these units to the 1st Army, which had, prior to this date, used them as guard units in the logistical zone.

43. The 109th Division was already charged with the defense of the Yanchu area, and had been ordered to secure Chingyuan and Hsukou as strong points vital to the future offensive from this area.

44. This Brigade, composed mainly of three infantry battalions and one cavalry battalion, was commanded by Maj Gen Shozo Honkawa. (Note: The Japanese manuscript says one mountain artillery battalion. This is an error.) It had been attached to the 2d Army on 25 September 1937 but was returned to the 109th Division on 15 January 1938.

45. Originally, the 16th Division was assigned to the 2d Army. It was transferred to the Shanghai Expeditionary Army in late October 1937. On 15 January 1938, it was returned to the North China Area Army which, in turn, attached it to the 1st Army.

Army. These groups began arriving in the 1st Army's operational area in the latter part of January.

Following the invasion of Chinan late in December, the 2d Army, about the middle of January, occupied the areas along the Chinan - Chingtao railway, as well as the area between Chining and Mengyin.

In order to occupy Chingtao, the North China Area Army transferred the 5th Division from the 1st Army to the 2d Army, but before the division reached its objective, Japanese Navy troops occupied Chingtao on 10 January.

The 2d Army then began to consolidate in the occupied areas.

In the Central China area, the Shanghai Expeditionary Army,[46] after occupying Chuhsien late in December, advanced an element to the area along the Tienching - Pukou railway line. In early February this force advanced to Pangfou.

---

46. The Shanghai Expeditionary Army was dispatched from Japan on 15 August 1937, landing in Shanghai late in August. Its mission was to support the small Japanese Navy unit already fighting in that area. On 7 November, the Central China Area Army was organized and the Shanghai Expeditionary Army was assigned to the Area Army, continuing its operations under the control of the Area Army. The enemy around Shanghai began to retreat on 12 November. On 1 December, Imperial General Headquarters ordered the Central China Area Army to attack Nanching and the Shanghai Expeditionary Army together with the 10th Army engaged in this operation. Nanching was captured on 13 December. On 20 December, an element of the Shanghai Expeditionary Army occupied Chuhsien. (Monograph 179, Central China Area Operations, Vol. 1). In late January 1938, an element of the 13th Division of the Shanghai Expeditionary Army began to attack the enemy south of Pangfou and, by the beginning of February, had occupied Pangfou. (Monograph 70, China Area Operations Record, Vol. 1.)

In general, the Army was responsible for air operations in the North China area, while the Navy was responsible for those in the Central and South China areas.

The Japanese Army's air strength in China from January to April 1938 consisted of 24 air squadrons, of which 14 (5 reconnaissance squadrons, 3 fighter squadrons, 3 light bomber squadrons and 3 heavy bomber squadrons) in addition, to one reconnaissance squadron organized locally for long-range reconnaissance, were stationed in north China, and 10 in central China. The Air Force in north China first used Yangchu, Shihchiachuang, Chinan, and then Anyang as base airfields, and, as the operations progressed, it used Linfen, Ani, Hsinhsiang and Lincheng as first-line airfields.

Enemy Situation

Chiang Kaishek established war sectors in accordance with the expanding battle areas. He appointed a commander to each sector who was responsible for the defense of that sector.[47]

The main strength of the enemy in the Shansi Province area (the Second War Sector), commanded by Yen Hsishan, had retired to the southern part of the province after the loss of Yangchu, while the majority of the hostile force, commanded by Cheng Chien, in the area along the Peiping - Hankou railway (the First War Sector) fled to the right bank

---

47. Although the exact boundaries of these sectors are unknown, approximate areas are shown on Map 10.

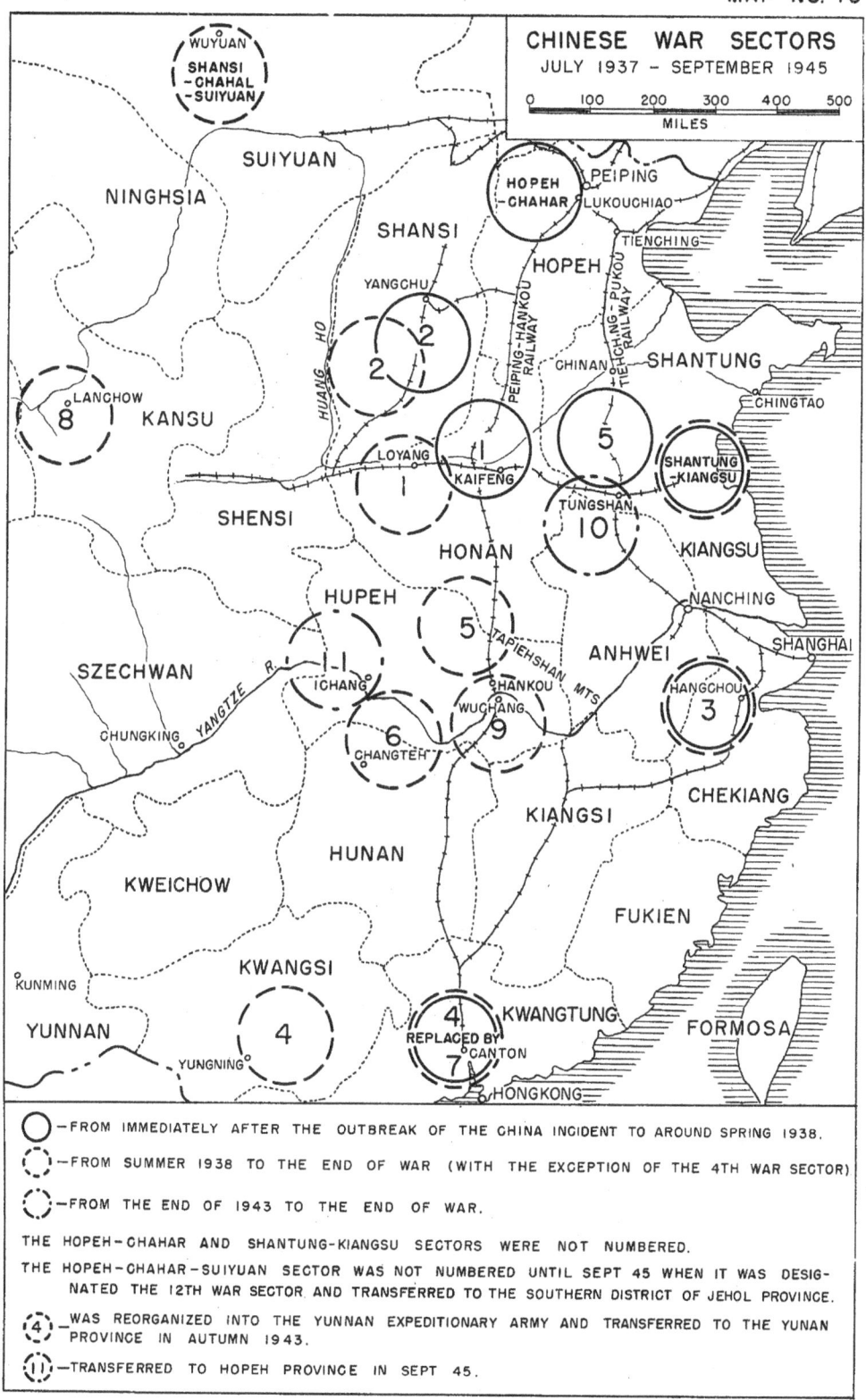

of the Huang Ho. However, a powerful element of the enemy was still in the Hsinhsiang Plain. The enemy in these areas constructed strong positions and endeavored to check the Japanese advance by destroying roads between enemy positions and the Japanese Army. Hostile strength in late January was estimated at about twenty-seven divisions in the Second War Sector and thirty-six divisions in the First War Sector.

It was estimated that the enemy in the area along the Tienching - Pukou railway (the Fifth War Sector) was planning an attack against the Japanese 2d Army. In addition, Chinese communist forces in the mountainous area near Wutai, Yushe and Chinglo in Shansi Province were conducting guerrilla raids against the flanks and rear of the Japanese Army.

The number of enemy planes at the beginning of 1938 was estimated to be between 350 and 450, approximately half of which were of Soviet manufacture, with a monthly importation of planes from Russia between 70 and 80 planes. Although the enemy air force remained quiescent for a time after the fall of Nanching, it attempted raids against the Japanese occupied areas after the beginning of the year, and began using Lanchow, Changan, Hsiangyang, Hankou, Nanchang and Nancheng as third-line airfields (base airfields), Shanhsien, Hsinyang, and Yushan as second-line airfields (used as departure points by bomber units and as standby fields by the fighter units), and Loyang, Chouchiakou, Hofei, and Shehsien as first-line airfields. In addition, it used many advance fields in front of the first-line airfields.

Operational Plan of the 1st Army

The 1st Army commander, upon receiving informal instructions in December 1937 relative to operations in the area north of Huang Ho, had formulated an operational plan on 25 December, in general, as follows:

> The 14th Division will commence action on 11 February and occupy the Hsinhsiang Plain. The 20th Division will commence action on 23 February and occupy the plains of Linfen and Yungchi. The operation will be completed on or about 10 March. When the operation is completed, four divisions[48] will be assigned to consolidate occupied areas.

The general course of action of each group was specified, but, in January 1938, as the 16th Division had been attached to the 1st Army and the Honkawa Brigade had been returned to the 109th Division, some changes were made in the plan, and, on 26 January 1938, the 1st Army commander issued an order relative to the mopping up operations north of the Huang Ho. The gist of this order was follows:

Chart: Table of Troop Distribution of 1st Army.

> The 14th Division will advance steadily southward, leaving the vicinity of Anyang on 11 February and occupying the Hsinhsiang Plain. A powerful element of the Division will further pursue the enemy along the Chinyang - Chincheng - Chinshui - Icheng - Chuwu road and will advance into the Chuwu Plain. The unit to advance by way of the Taming - Puyang road will advance to the Chang Ho and south thereof before 11 February.
> The 108th Division will follow the 14th Division, and advance southward. It will leave the Wuan - Shuiyehchen line on 13 February, and occupy the Changchih Plain before sending a powerful element in pursuit of the enemy by way of the Tunliu - Fuchengchen - Linfen road into the Linfen Plain. In addition, the Division will assign an element, composed principally of three infantry

---

48. These were the 14th, 20th, 108th and 109th Divisions.

Table of Troop Distribution of 1st Army

Chart No 1

Force	Units Lacking	Attached Units					
		Inf & cav	HMG units	Mecz units	Arty and Trench mtr units	Engr units and supplies	Air def Unit
14th Div		2 inf bns.	1 HMG bn.	1 L armd car co, 1 Tank bn.	1 fld arty btry, 1 mt arty btry, one 15cm how brig (less 1 bn), one 10cm gun bn, 1 bln co.	2 brig mtl cos 30 collapsible boats	1 AAA Unit
108th Div	2 inf bns, 1 arty btry		1 HMG bn.		1 mt arty btry, one 15cm how bn, 1 L mtr bn.		"
16th Div*	1 inf bn.						"
20th Div**				1 L armd car co	1 mt arty regt, one 15cm how regt (less 1 btry), one 10cm gun bn, 1 L mtr bn.	1 ind engr regt, 1 brig mtl co, 30 collapsible boats	"
109th Div		2 2d res inf bns, 1 2d res cav co	1 HMG bn.		one 15cm how co, 1 2d res fld arty btry.		"
Shihchia-chuang Garrison Force		1 inf bn belonging to the 16th Div					
Force under direct control of the Army						1 sig unit	1 AAA Unit
Remarks	The main body of the Provisional Air Corps, 2 squadrons each of recon planes and fighters, 3 squadrons each of light and heavy bombers will participate in this battle. * One inf bn will be deployed at Linching, one at Taming and one at Anyang. Two inf bns, one arty bn and one engr regt at Tzuhsien. ** Two 15cm how btries will be transferred to the 109th Div after the breakthrough of enemy positions near Lingshih has been effected.						

battalions, to garrison Yangchuan and Hsiyang.

The 20th Division will leave the vicinity of Chiehhsiu on 23 February, and will occupy the plains of Linfen and Yungchi. An element after skirting around enemy positions near Lingshih will, before the 23d, advance south beyond the line extending to the east and west of Chiehhsiu.

The 109th Division will destroy the enemy in and around Lishih and drive enemy remnants west across the Huang Ho.

The 16th Division will mass its strength between Kaoi and Hantan, and, at the same time, will assign an element to garrison Taming, Linching and Anyang. After 11 February, the Division will hold a force composed principally of two infantry battalions, one artillery battalion and one engineer regiment in Tzuhsien so that it will be available for the 1st Army when required.

As of 11 February, operational boundaries will be established as follows: (Map 11)

Boundary between the 14th and the 16th Divisions:

Line connecting Linhsien, Tangyin, Taokouchen, Changyuan and Lanfeng. The area on the boundary will be the area of responsibility of the 16th Division.

Boundary between the 14th and the 108th Divisions:

Line connecting Linhsien and Kaoping. The area on the boundary will be the area of responsibility of the 108th Division.

Boundary between the 108th and the 16th Divisions:

Line connecting Chiulungkuan, Huangyukuan, Matienchen, Shehsien and Linhsien. The area on the boundary will be the area of responsibility of the 108th Division.

Boundary between the 20th and the 109th Divisions:

Line connecting Chinyuan, Hohsien, Hsihsien and Yungho. The area on the boundary, except Chinyuan, will be the area of responsibility of the 20th Division; Chinyuan will be the responsibility of the 109th Division.

Boundary between the 109th and the 108th Divisions:

Line connecting Kengchiachuangchen, Shouyang, Mafangchen, Hsuanchengchen and Chinyuan. The area on the boundary will be the responsibility of the 109th Division.

Boundary between the 108th Division and the area defended by Line of Communications Command:

Line connecting Niangtzukuan and Chiulungkuan. The area on the boundary will be the responsibility of the 108th Division.

Boundary between the area defended by the Line of Communications Command and the operational area of the 16th Division:

Line connecting Chiulungkuan, Tsanhuang, Kaoi, Ningchin and Chihsien. The area on the boundary, except Kaoi, will be the area defended by the Line of Communications Command; Kaoi will be the responsibility of the 16th Division.

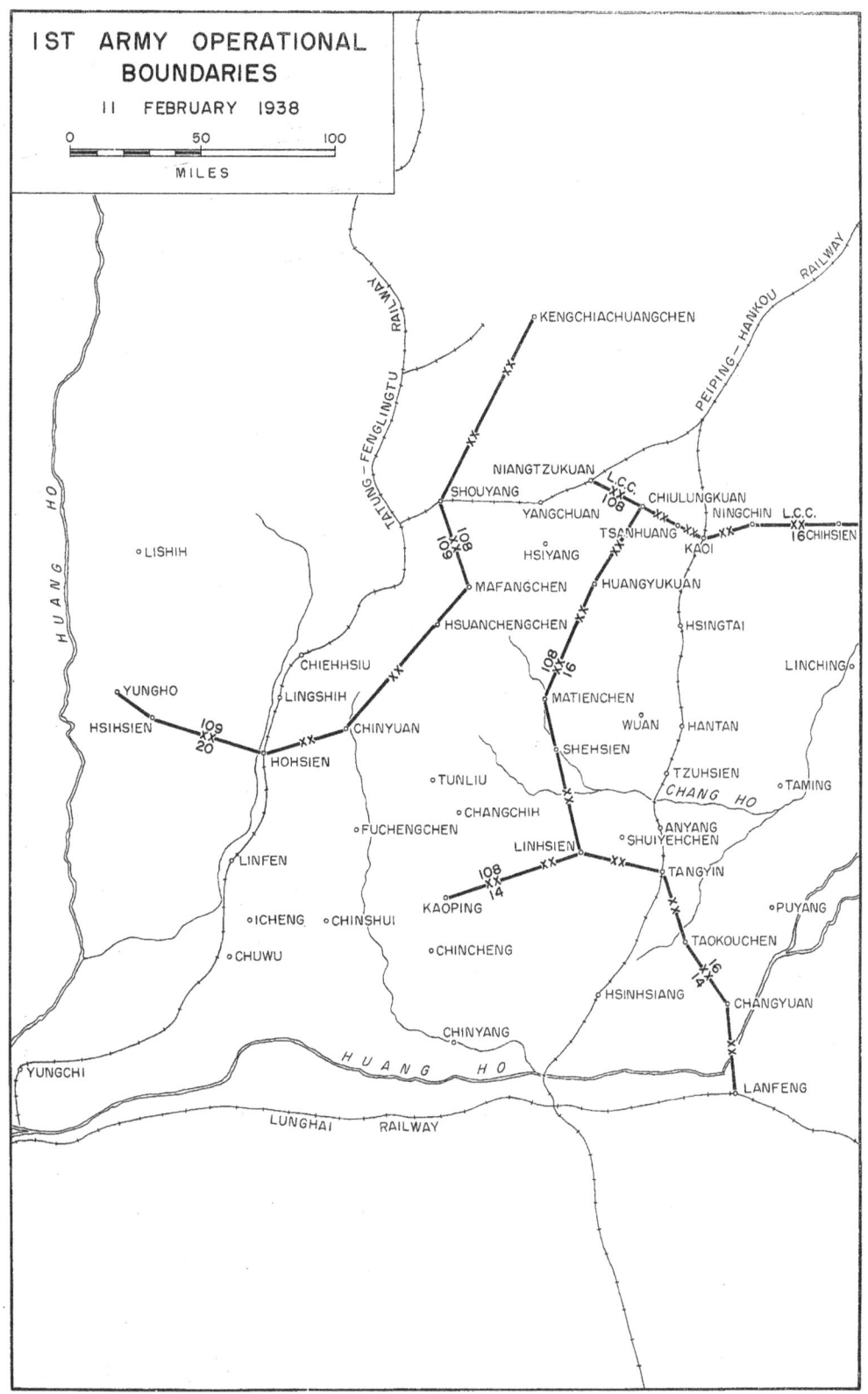

Honan Province Operation North of the Huang Ho
Operation of the 14th Division

The Tachi Detachment (composed mainly of five infantry battalions, one field artillery battalion, one heavy field artillery battalion and one mountain artillery battery and commanded by Maj Gen Yoso Tachi) of the 14th Division left Taming on 7 February and, after destroying the enemy in and around Nanlo, Chingfeng and Puyang, occupied Changyuan on the 13th. The Detachment then advanced to the vicinity of Hsiaochichen on the 17th.

The 14th Division, massed its main strength at Anyang. On 11 February, it launched an assault with its right flank detachment, (composed principally of two infantry battalions and one mountain artillery battalion and commanded by Colonel Toyama), its right wing unit (composed principally of four infantry battalions and one light armored car company and commanded by Maj Gen Sakai) and its left wing unit (composed principally of two infantry battalions and one field artillery battalion and commanded by Colonel Ishiguro). It met with only slight opposition and successively occupied multiple enemy positions extending west and east of Weichiaying. On 13 February, it advanced to a line on the right bank of the Ching Ho and prepared to attack enemy positions in the area northwest of Chihsien.

On the afternoon of the 15th, the Division, with the right wing unit (organized around the former right flank detachment and one infantry battalion transferred from the former right wing unit and with

Maj Gen Sakai remaining as the right wing unit commander); the central unit (organized around two infantry battalions of the former left wing unit and commanded by Col Ishiguro), and the left wing unit (organized around three infantry battalions of the former right wing unit and commanded by Colonel Morita)[49] began an attack directed mainly against the plateau area west of the Peiping - Hankou railway. Huihsien was occupied on the 16th and Hsinhsiang on the 17th. Also on the 17th, the main body of the division left the area north of Hsinhsiang and, dividing into two columns on the 18th, pursued the enemy toward Chinyang. At the same time, the left pursuit unit (consisting of the former Tachi Detachment plus the former left wing unit) captured Hsiuwu. On the 20th, this unit captured Chincheng and, on the 21st, Menghsien. One infantry battalion and one artillery battalion of the unit remained at Menghsien while its main body was massed near Chinyang. The main body of the Division with the right pursuit unit (composed principally of four infantry battalions, one field artillery battalion, one mountain artillery battalion and one heavy field artillery battalion and commanded by Maj Gen Sakai) after skirting north of Hsiuwu and mopping up the remnants of the enemy in its path of advance, occupied Poai on the 20th, Chinyang on the 21st and Chiyuan on the 22d. Thus, the subjugation of the Peiping - Hankou railway area north of the Huang Ho generally was completed.

---

49. The light armored car company of the former right wing unit and the field artillery battalion of the former left wing unit were held in reserve.

In order to consolidate the occupied areas, the main body of the Division was massed at Chinyang until the 25th, when the main force moved to Poai, leaving an element at Chinyang. At the same time, in accordance with a 1st Army order, an element was sent to Shansi Province in pursuit of the retreating enemy, with orders to accomplish its mission in the following manner:

The Ishiguro Detachment (composed principally of two infantry battalions, one field artillery battalion and one heavy field artillery battalion and commanded by Colonel Ishiguro) was ordered to leave Chinyang on the 24th and to pursue the enemy into the Chuwu Plain by advancing along the Chinyang - Chincheng - Chinshui - Icheng - Chuwu road.

The Sakai Detachment (composed principally of three infantry battalions, one field artillery battalion, one mountain artillery battalion and one heavy field artillery battalion and commanded by Maj Gen Sakai) was ordered to leave Chiyuan on the 25th and pursue the enemy into the Chianghsien Plain by advancing along the Yuanchu - Chianghsien road.

The Ishiguro Detachment left Chinyang on the 24th, attacked the enemy entrenched in the rugged mountainous area and, on the 27th reached the Chin Ho line, west of Chincheng. The Sakai Detachment left Chiyuan on the 25th and, on the same day, advanced to the area east of Yuanchu. However, because of the extremely bad condition of the roads between Chiyuan and Yuanchu, one field artillery battalion and one heavy field artillery battalion of the Sakai Detachment were compelled to return to Chiyuan.

Movement of the 16th Division

After 11 February, the 16th Division secured its operational area in accordance with the 1st Army order.

On the 16th, the 1st Army commander ordered the 16th Division to secure Kaoi, Anyang, Puyang and Linching and to keep watch on the Huang Ho line, also to send an element to Taokouchen to destroy the enemy in that area and to secure the Hsinhsiang - Chihsien railway and other line of communication facilities. He also stated that the unit massed at Tzuhsien was available to the Division.[50]

Accordingly, the Ohno Detachment, (built around one infantry battalion and two field artillery batteries and commanded by Colonel Nobuaki Ohno) was sent to Hsinhsiang. It left Anyang on the 20th and, after mopping up the enemy forces in Chunhsien and Taokouchen, arrived at Hsinhsiang on the 26th. It then secured the left rear of the Army by garrisoning in the vicinity of Hsinhsiang. (Map 12)

Southern Shansi Province Operation

Operation of the 108th Division

On 13 February, an advance detachment of the 108th Division,

---

50. In accordance with a 1st Army order of 26 January 1938, the 16th Division commander, by 11 February, had assembled a force composed of two infantry battalions, one artillery battalion and one engineer regiment at Tzuhsien for use by the 1st Army, as desired.

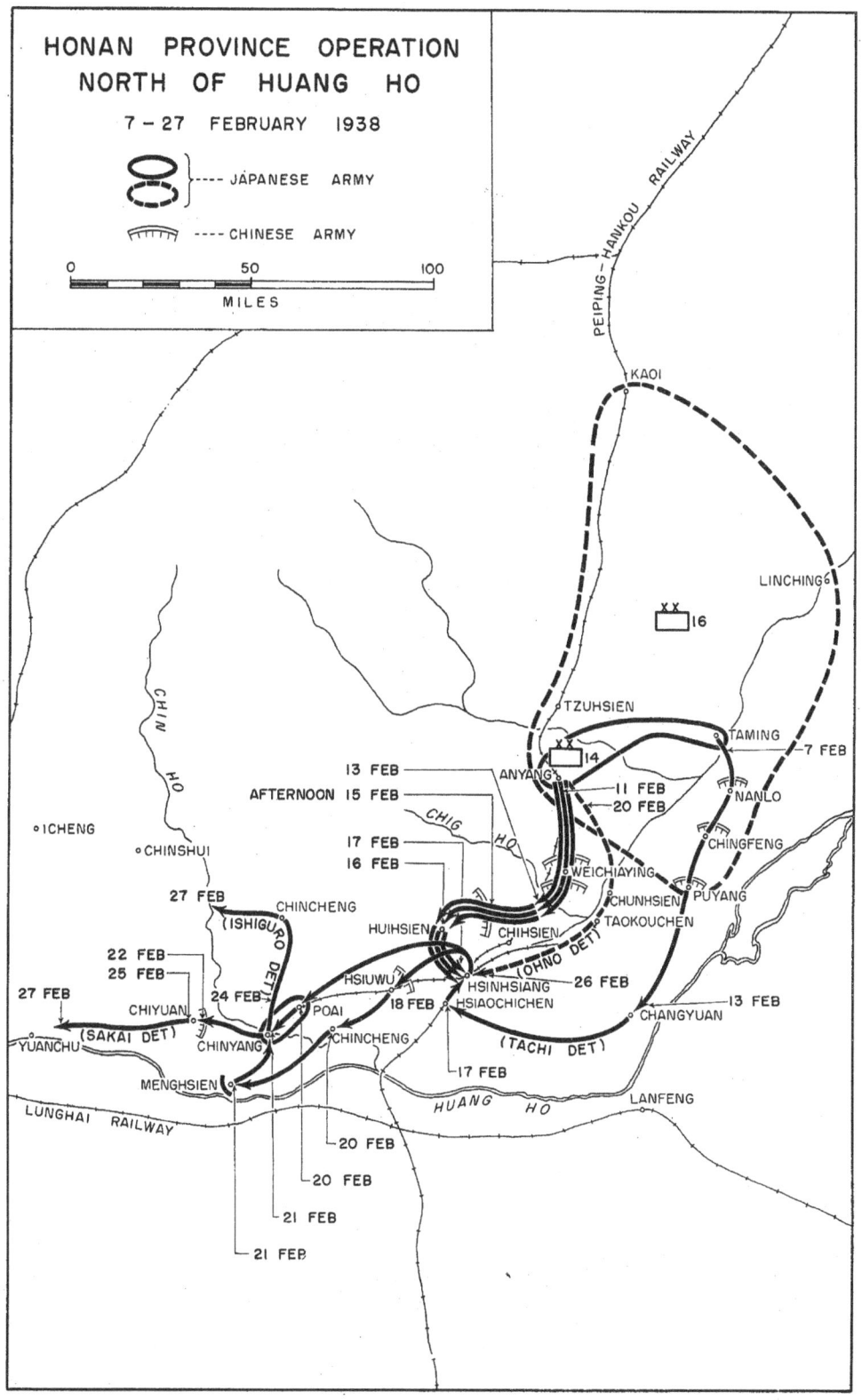

(commanded by Maj Gen Shiro Tomabechi and consisting mainly of three infantry battalions, one field artillery battalion, two mountain artillery batteries and two heavy field artillery batteries) together with a unit of the right flank detachment, (commanded by Colonel Shizutaka Kudo and consisting mainly of five infantry companies and one mountain artillery battery) left the vicinity of Wuan, encircled and attacked the enemy positions in the mountain fastness of Tungyangkuan and put the enemy to flight. Immediately shifting to the pursuit, they captured Licheng on the evening of the 17th and Changchih at dawn of the 20th, thereby attaining the objective of the first phase of the operation.

The 108th Division, thereafter, ordered its main force to defend the vicinity of Changchih and to maintain peace and order in that district, while on the 25th the Linfen Detachment (commanded by Major General Tomabechi and consisting mainly of three infantry battalions, three mountain artillery batteries, one heavy field artillery battery and one mortar battalion, and reinforced by one infantry battalion and one field artillery battalion) was ordered to pursue the enemy in the direction of Linfen via Fuchengchen.

The Linfen Detachment left Changchih on the afternoon of the 21st, marched through steep and rugged mountain ranges in pursuit of the enemy and by the 26th had advanced to Chingpuyen on the outskirts of the Linfen Plain.

Operation of the 20th Division

On 11 February, the 20th Division launched an action from the vicinity of Taiku and Yutzu, advanced on the 13th to Pingyao, and, on the 16th, to the vicinity of Chiehhsiu and east of Hsiaoi. It then began to prepare for an attack on enemy positions around Lingshih.

On the 16th, the Division's right flank detachment, (commanded by Maj Gen Yoshito Takagi and consisting mainly of three infantry battalions, one field artillery battery and two mountain artillery batteries) captured enemy positions in the vicinity of Hsiaoi and, on the 17th, proceeded westward through Tamaichiaochen. After defeating an enemy force which counterattacked with several times the Japanese strength in the vicinity of Shihkouchen on the 21st, and again in the vicinity of Hsialitsun on the 24th, this detachment entered Hsihsien on the 26th. It immediately began to advance toward Linfen, leaving behind one infantry battalion and one mountain artillery battery at Puhsien.

On the 21st and 22d, the main force of the Division moved from the line connecting Hsiaoi and Chiehhsiu and, on the 23d, began attacking the enemy entrenched along a line running east and west through Jenichen. The Division carried out an encircling attack by the right wing unit, (commanded by Colonel Tsuneichi Kobayashi and consisting mainly of three infantry battalions, four field artillery batteries and two mountain artillery batteries) from the area west of the Fen Ho, the center unit, (commanded by Major Goro Yamane and consisting mainly of about one infantry battalion) toward Lingshih and the left wing unit, (commanded by Maj Gen Yoshio Kozuki and consisting mainly of three infantry battalions, one field artillery battery and two mountain artillery batteries) from the area east of the Fen Ho. However, a large enemy force commanded by Yen Hsishan and with an estimated strength of about seven or eight divisions[51] counterattacked along the entire front on the 23d, and, on the 24th, a fierce chaotic battle began which lasted for two days. The Japanese troops fought well, and, assisted by a maneuver by the right flank detachment from the area east of Linfen, the Division finally succeeded in putting the enemy to flight on the 26th. It then advanced to the vicinity of Hohsien and continued pursuing the retreating enemy toward Linfen.

Operation of the 109th Division

On 12 February, the 109th Division launched an action from the vicinity of Yangchu and Chingyuan. On the 16th, its advance detachment, (commanded by Maj Gen Nagahide Tanifuji, and consisting mainly of four infantry battalions and one mountain artillery battalion,)

---

51. At that time, the strength of a Chinese division was estimated at 10,000, whereas the main strength of the 20th Division was approximately 16,000. Yen Hsishan held a further four or five divisions in reserve in this area but apparently having received information that the Linfen Detachment was advancing from the east and the 14th Division was assembling around Chinyang, he decided to hold these divisions to protect southern Shansi Province.

captured Wenshui. The Sasaki Detachment, (consisting mainly of one and a half infantry battalions and two mountain artillery batteries) captured Tungshechen. On the 17th, the advance detachment occupied Fenyang. The Division then began to prepare for an operation in the direction of Lishih.

On the 21st and 22d, the Division advanced westward from the vicinity of Tungshechen and Fenyang in three columns - the Sasaki Detachment, the Tanifuji Detachment (consisting mainly of three infantry battalions and one mountain artillery battalion under the command of Maj Gen Tanifuji) and the Honkawa Detachment (consisting mainly of two infantry battalions and one mountain artillery battalion under the command of Maj Gen Honkawa) - and captured Lishih on the evening of the 24th. By the 27th, part of the Division had advanced to the banks of the Huang Ho.

The main force of the Division then returned to the Yangchu Plain and began mopping up enemy remnants which were creating disturbances at the rear of the Division.

Pursuit Operation in Southern Shansi Province

On the night of the 24th, the 1st Army, taking advantage of the fact that the enemy's main force in the Shansi Province was engaged along the 20th Division front, decided to encircle and destroy the enemy in the plains of southern Shansi Province. It, therefore, issued the following order:

>The commander of the 20th Division will continue his present mission.

> The commander of the 108th Division will rush the Linfen Detachment to Linfen.
> The commander of the 14th Division will order the Ishiguro Detachment to advance to the Huang Ho ferry in the vicinity of Yumen, via Chuwu as speedily as possible, and simultaneously rush the Sakai Detachment to southern Shansi. An element of this detachment will advance to the Shanhsien ferry and the main force will advance to the Tungkuan ferry. All detachments are charged with the mission of cutting off the retreat route of the enemy's main force.

The 20th Division, continuing its pursuit of the enemy, reached Chaocheng on the 27th and the Linfen Detachment of the 108th Division captured Linfen on the same day. Also on the 27th, the Ishiguro and Sakai Detachments of the 14th Division advanced to the Chin Ho line and Yuanchu respectively.

In order to control the pursuit by the various groups in the southern Shansi Plain, the 1st Army commander issued further orders on the night of the 27th:

> The commander of the 108th Division, after the Linfen Detachment attains its mission, will leave behind one infantry battalion and one artillery battery at Linfen to participate in the mopping-up operation under the command of the 20th Division commander, as well as to guard the rear of the 20th Division. The main force of the detachment will return to Changchih.
> The commander of the 14th Division will place the Ishiguro and Sakai Detachments under the command of the 20th Division commander upon their arrival in the vicinity of Chinshui and Yuanchu, respectively.

Simultaneously with the issuance of this order, the 1st Army commander extended the operational boundaries between the various groups as follows:

> Between the 20th and 108th Divisions: The line connecting Chinyuan, Fuchengchen and Chinshui. Jurisdiction over the area

on the line will be the responsibility of the 20th Division, except Chinyuan, which will be under the jurisdiction of the 108th Division.

    Between the 108th and 14th Divisions: The line connecting Kaoping and Chinshui. Jurisdiction over the area on the line will be the responsibility of the 108th Division, except Chinshui, which will be under the control of the 20th Division.

    Between the 20th and 14th Divisions: The line connecting Chinshui and Yuanchu. Jurisdiction over the area on the line will be the responsibility of the 20th Division.

On the 28th, the 20th Division arrived in the vicinity of Linfen. It halted there for supplies and, on 4 March, left the line connecting Fencheng and Chuwu.

The commander of the Division then issued the following order:

    The pursuit unit, commanded by Maj Gen Kozuki and consisting mainly of four infantry battalions, one light armored car company, two mountain artillery batteries, one 10cm gun battalion and 35 motor cars, will pursue the enemy toward Yungchi and the Tungkuan ferry.
    The Hoching Detachment, commanded by Maj Gen Takagi and consisting mainly of three infantry battalions, one field artillery battery and two mountain artillery batteries, together with a cavalry unit, will advance toward the Yumen ferry in the vicinity of Hoching.
    The Sakai Detachment[52] will send its main force toward the Shanhsien ferry and an element toward the Juicheng ferry.
    The Ishiguro Detachment will pursue the enemy toward Hoching after advancing to Chuwu.

A raiding party of the pursuit unit, commanded by Colonel Kyo Kanaoka, and consisting of half a motorized infantry battalion and one 10cm gun battalion, captured Yungchi on the 6th and the Tungkuan ferry on the 7th, while the main force of the pursuit unit advanced

---

52. This Detachment had advanced to Wenhsi on 3 March, but had been compelled to leave infantry regimental guns and an antitank unit together with one infantry battalion at Yuanchu, because of the extremely bad condition of the roads between Yuanchu and Wenhsi.

to Yungchi on the 8th.

The cavalry unit, together with an element of the Hoching Detachment, captured the Yumen ferry on the night of 6 March, while the main force of the Hoching Detachment, on the 6th and 7th, defeated about 10,000 enemy troops in positions in the mountainous region north of Hoching.

On the 8th, the Sakai Detachment captured Juicheng and Pinglu. Thus, all main ferry points along the Huang Ho in the southern Shansi Province were controlled by the Japanese Army.

The Ishiguro Detachment, after defeating the enemy on the right bank of the Chin Ho on 28 February, captured Chinshui on 2 March and arrived at Chuwu on the 6th. It then began regrouping there.

Leaving an element behind at Linfen, the main force of the Linfen Detachment left Linfen on the 3d, and upon arrival at Changchih returned to its parent organization, the 108th Division.

The 20th and 14th Divisions, after occupying the north bank of the Huang Ho, shelled the Lunghai railway on the opposite side of the river from the vicinity of Anho, Juicheng, Pinglu, Paipo and Wenhsien. (Map 13)

Air Operations During the Hopeh Operation

Based on orders, received from the North China Area commander on 10 January, the Provisional Air Corps commander directed the Nakahira Unit (composed of two reconnaissance squadrons) to continue to render support to the 2d Army; the Yamase Unit (commanded by Col Masao Yamase

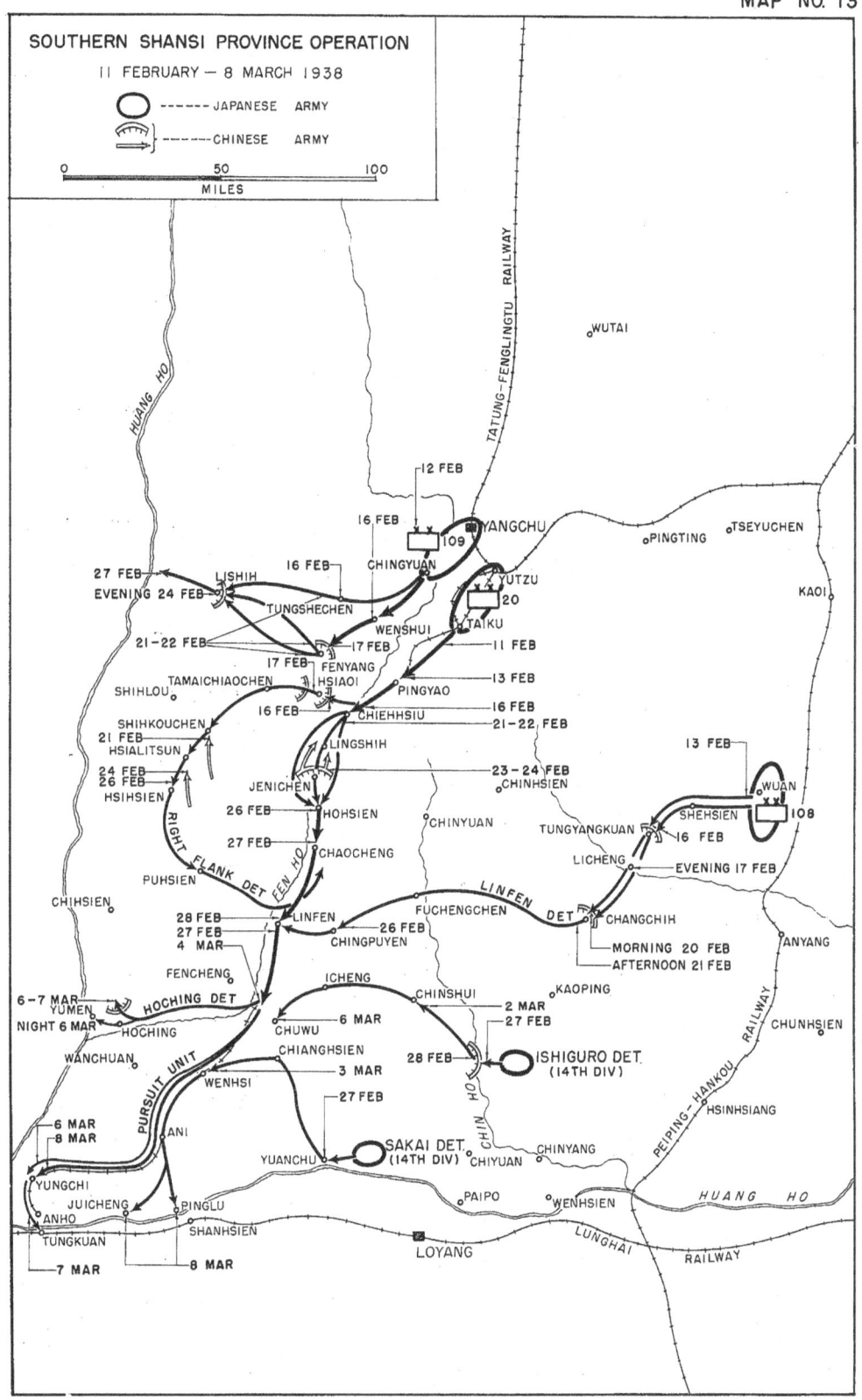

and composed of three and a half squadrons including half a reconnaissance squadron, one fighter squadron, and two light bomber squadrons) to support, from the Yangchu airfield, divisions of the 1st Army in the Shansi Province areas; the Giga Air Brigade (commanded by Maj Gen Tetsuji Giga and composed of seven and a half squadrons including one and a half reconnaissance, two fighter, one light bomber, and three heavy bomber squadrons) to support, from Anyang and Hantan airfields, the 1st Army in the Peiping - Hankou railway area, and, at the same time, to destroy enemy air strength along the Lunghai railway.

Prior to the Hopeh Operation the Provisional Air Corps had been engaged chiefly in terrain reconnaissance and in reconnoitering the enemy situation for the 1st Army, but with the commencement of the Hopeh Operation, the Giga Air Brigade bombed strategic enemy rear targets, especially railway bridges across the Huang Ho, trains and convoys, in order to cut off enemy communications to the rear. At the same time, it supported the 14th Division and later the 108th Division. Subsequently, when the enemy was put to rout, the Brigade bombed enemy troops retreating from Linfen, and then bombed the enemy along the Tatung - Yungchi railway. The Yamase Unit supported the 20th and 109th Divisions.

Operation to Annihilate Enemy Air Strength

Although the enemy air force had not been active prior to the middle of January 1938, it became quite aggressive from that time onward and a report was received to the effect that it was planning to attack Peiping on the lunar New Year's Day. Therefore, late in January, the Provisional Air Corps seized the initiative and attacked Loyang, Linfen, Tungshan and Shangchiu airfields. Especially noteworthy were the exploits of the Giga Air Brigade which engaged and destroyed enemy planes (12 planes shot down) at Loyang airfield on 30 January, causing the enemy to abandon its plan to attack Peiping. Although enemy planes became active again in this area from the middle of February, the Provisional Air Corps did not deliberately engage the enemy air force because the Corps was then busily engaged in supporting the Hopeh Operation. But by early March, when the Hopeh Operation began to draw to a close, the Provisional Air Corps was able to concentrate on destroying enemy air strength. It organized combined fighter - bomber attack units under its direct command (the 1st Air Unit commanded by Col Yamase and composed mainly of one fighter and two light bomber squadrons, and the 2d Air Unit commanded by Col Ryuichi Torita and composed mainly of two fighter and two heavy bomber squadrons) and attacked and inflicted severe damage on the Hsiangyang and Changan airfields on 8 March. The Provisional Air Corps at this time received a report that the enemy air unit was planning to abandon Changan airfield and, considering a strike before the enemy withdrew a necessity, it attacked Changan airfield on the 11th and again on the 14th with considerable success (5 enemy planes were destroyed on the 11th). As soon as the 4th Air Brigade Headquarters (commanded by

Maj Gen Tomo Fujita and attached to the Provisional Air Corps on 18 February) arrived at Anyang in mid-March, the Corps commander placed the attack units, which were under the direct command of the Corps, under the Fujita Air Brigade and ordered the Air Brigade to operate mainly from airfields in and around Anyang and destroy enemy air units wherever they could be found and, at the same time, to support the ground operation of friendly forces.

Situation after the Campaign

Although the main strength of the enemy had retreated to the south of the Huang Ho, a powerful element had retreated to the mountainous area of the Shansi Province. There it joined forces with the communist troops already entrenched in that area and proceeded to harass the Japanese troops. The 1st Army commander, therefore, decided that this force must be destroyed and, on 10 March, ordered the 20th Division to secure the southern Shansi Plains; the 14th Division, the Hsinhsiang Plain; the 16th Division, the area between Kaoi, Anyang, Puyang and Linching; the 109th Division, the Yangchu Plain and the vicinity of Lishih, and the 108th Division, the Changchih Plain and the vicinity of Yangchuan and Hsiyang. The order further stated that these divisions would complete mopping-up operations by the end of April. This was accomplished in the following manner:

Wanchuan and vicinity - remnants of the enemy in this area were put to flight by the 20th Division about mid-March.

Chihsien - the enemy entrenched here was mopped up by the 20th Division during the latter part of March.

Shihlou, Yungho and vicinity - the enemy entrenched in the mountainous districts was mopped up by the 20th and 109th Division during the early part of April.

Taiku, Chinhsien and vicinity - remnants of the enemy in these area were mopped up by the 109th Division from 14 to 24 March.

Area north of Changchih - from 8 to 16 April, the 108th Division assisted by the 16th and 109th Divisions mopped up and completely uprooted the enemy in this area.

Antse, Chinyuan and vicinity - these areas were mopped up by the 20th Division from 2 to 26 April.

Area east of Chunhsien - the 16th Division conducted mopping up operations in this area from the latter part of March to the early part of April.

Tseyuchen and vicinity - mopping up operations, directed mainly against communist troops, were conducted by the Army Line of Communications force, the 108th Division and the Pingting Garrison from 27 to 29 March.

Although the enemy suffered heavy losses during these operations, the desired result was not achieved. Communist troops, particularly in the vicinity of Wutai and the area north of Changchih, were not completely wiped out and powerful forces continued to roam the countryside harassing the Japanese rear. It was evident that the need existed for more aggressive campaigns and mopping-up operations in order to establish peace and order in the area. This was especially true as, with the withdrawal of various 1st Army units during the latter part of April for the Tungshan Operation, enemy guerrilla activity within the Army's jurisdictional area increased markedly.

Tungshan Operation

General Situation Prior to and During the Battle in the vicinity of Taierhchuang

After the Shantung Operation in January 1938, the enemy began harassing the Japanese forces in the occupied area with guerrilla warfare. These guerrillas were especially active in the 10th Division[53] and 13th Division areas.[54]

The 13th Division began operations along the banks of the Huai Ho during the latter part of January and, by the early part of February, had overwhelmed and destroyed the guerrillas in that area. However, the enemy forces in the 10th Division's area of responsibility gradually increased in strength and from the early part of February became increasingly aggressive. About the middle of February

---

53.. The 10th Division was commanded by Lt Gen Rensuke Isogai, and was responsible for the security of Chinan, Tzuyang and vicinity.
54. The 13th Division was commanded by Lt Gen Rippei Ogisu and was garrisoned in the vicinity of Chuhsien and along the left bank of the Yangtzu River. This Division was under the command of the Central China Area Army.

they attacked the Japanese troops in the area west of Tzuyang with a large well-equipped force, compelling the Japanese troops to withdraw.

Mopping up Operations in the 2d Army Sector

Lt Gen Nishio, commander of the 2d Army, which was composed principally of the 10th and 5th Divisions, was responsible for security in the area along the right bank of the Huang Ho and areas along the Tienching - Pukou and Chingtao - Chinan railways in the Shantung Province. He considered a drive to the Lunghai railway necessary and, in December 1937, presented his views to the North China Area Army commander. The Area Army commander was in complete accord with the 2d Army commander's recommendations, but when the plan was submitted to Imperial General Headquarters in Tokyo, it was disapproved.

Although from early February, the 2d Army continued to mop up enemy remnants in its occupied area, powerful enemy units immediately in front of the Army still constituted a direct threat. The 2d Army commander, therefore, decided to attack and smash this enemy force once and for all. He ordered the 10th Division to drive back the enemy in the vicinity of Wenshang and Chining to the west of the Tayun Ho and the 5th Division (commanded by Lt Gen Seishiro Itagaki and garrisoned along the eastern section of the Chingtao - Chinan railway) to advance an element toward Lini in order to facilitate the 10th Division's operation.

On the morning of 20 February, the 10th Division commander began the operation with the Nagase Detachment, commanded by Maj Gen Takehira Nagase and composed mainly of four and a half infantry battalions and two field artillery battalions. This detachment defeated the enemy in the vicinity of Chining, and pursued it west beyond the Tayun Ho, finally occupying Chiahsiang on the 25th.

The 5th Division's Katano Detachment left Weihsien by motor vehicle on the 21st, broke through Chuhsien and Ishui, occupied Tangtouchen on 5 March, and then prepared to attack the enemy in the vicinity of Lini.[55]

The 2d Army's Attack in the Vicinity of Tayun Ho

About this time there were approximately eleven enemy divisions active on the 2d Army front. These divisions were composed of three divisions of the Kuomintang Army, three divisions of the Shantung Army, four divisions of the Szechwan Army and one division of irregulars. Reports were received to the effect that about five of these divisions in the Tienching - Pukou railway area would conduct an offensive against the 10th Division around the middle of March.

In order to foil the enemy's plan to counterattack, the 2d Army

---

55. This detachment was originally commanded by Colonel Teiken Katano, and was composed mainly of one and a half infantry battalions and one mountain artillery battery. However, because the situation was deteriorating in the vicinity of Lini, the 5th Division commander decided to place the detachment under the command of the Brigade commander, Maj Gen Jun Sakamoto, and to increase its strength to two infantry battalions, one field artillery battalion and one mountain artillery battery. Therefore, on 23 February, the General together with the reinforcements, left Weihsien to join the Detachment. The Detachment then became known as the Sakamoto Detachment.

commander decided to attack first. On 13 March, he ordered the 10th Division to attack the enemy in the Tienching - Pukou railway area north of the Tayun Ho and the 5th Division to take Lini immediately and then to continue to advance toward the Ihsien area with an element in order to facilitate the 10th Division's operations. To maintain peace and order in the area, he further ordered the 10th Division, after it had destroyed the enemy north of Tayun Ho, to secure Ihsien and areas to the south.[56]

The 10th Division commander assigned the Seya Detachment, commanded by Maj Gen Hajime Seya and built around four and a half infantry battalions (after the 15th, six battalions), approximately three field artillery battalions, one heavy field artillery battalion and one heavy field artillery battery, to carry out this mission.

On 14 March, the detachment left the area south of Tsouhsien. It broke through enemy positions in and around Chiehho and occupied Lincheng on the 17th and Tenghsien on the 18th. Its right pursuit unit, composed principally of one infantry battalion and one field artillery battery, occupied Hanchuang on the 19th. At the same time, its left pursuit unit, composed principally of one infantry battalion

---

56. Prior to this order, on 11 March, the North China Area Army commander, in order to give the 2d Army greater striking force, attached to it for one month a force from the 114th Division composed principally of three infantry battalions. This force was employed to secure the rear area of the 2d Army.

and one field artillery battery, occupied Ihsien. Then, in accordance with the Division's order that, "The Detachment will secure the Tayun Ho line in the vicinity of Hanchuang and Taierhchuang, garrison Lincheng and Ihsien with an element, and then rush to the Lini area as large a force as possible to support the 5th Division's operations," the Detachment commander, on the 23d, dispatched an element (the former left pursuit unit) to Taierhchuang, and massed the main force of his Detachment in the vicinity of Ihsien and Lincheng. He ordered the Lini Detachment composed principally of one infantry battalion, one light armored car company, one field artillery battery and one mountain artillery battery, to proceed from Lincheng to Lini.

On 25 March, the Lini Detachment was encircled by a superior enemy force in the neighborhood of Kuolichi. The Seya Detachment commander had planned to send his main strength against Taierhchuang, but was now compelled to use this force to destroy the enemy in the vicinity of Kuolichi. The unit dispatched to Taierhchuang succeeded in occupying one corner of the village of Taierhchuang on the 27th, but was unable to make any further progress because of the enemy's superior strength and strongly fortified positions. The enemy used 15cm howitzers for the first time in this battle. After repulsing the enemy in the hills north of Kuolichi with the Detachment's main strength on the 28th, the commander directed the entire strength of the Detachment in an assault against Taierhchuang on the 30th. It succeeded in reaching the Tayun Ho line near Taierhchuang, but by 5 April had not succeeded in occupying the village of Taierhchuang.

Air Support of the 2d Army in the Vicinity of Tayun Ho

In the middle of March, when the 2d Army was about to begin its drive toward the Tayun Ho line the North China Area Army commander ordered the Provisional Air Corps commander to increase its air strength in the 2d Army area. The Corps commander, therefore, prepared the Tawenkou airfield and assigned four heavy bombers to the Nakahira Unit, and, as the enemy ground forces in the 2d Army area increased sharply, the commander sent a light bomber squadron and part of a fighter unit to this area in the latter part of March in order to render greater support to the 2d Army's operations.

Sakamoto Detachment's Battle near Taierhchuang

The 5th Division's Sakamoto Detachment (which was being gradually reinforced until by 17 March it was composed of approximately six infantry battalions, two field artillery battalions and one mountain artillery battery) attacked Lini on 14 March, but was unable to take the town. As the situation in the Seya Detachment area was critical, the Sakamoto Detachment commander decided to withdraw from the vicinity of Lini on the 29th, in order to go to the assistance of the Seya Detachment. On the 30th, the Sakamoto Detachment began to move toward Taierhchuang, and, overcoming enemy resistance on the way, arrived to the east of Taierhchuang at Puwang on 2 April.[57] It was surrounded

---

57. As the Detachment commander had left one element southwest of Lini and another at Hsiancheng in order to guard the Detachment's rear, the strength of the Detachment was reduced to approximately four infantry battalions and two artillery battalions.

by a superior enemy force in the neighborhood of Puwang and fierce fighting ensued. The battle raged until 5 April when the commander of the Detachment decided to withdraw. However, the position on the Seya Detachment front made him reverse this decision and he did not withdraw his force until 7 April.

Communications between the 5th Division headquarters at Chingtao and the 10th Division headquarters at Tzuyang and the Sakamoto and Seya Detachments were slow and often difficult. On 4 April, judging that the Seya Detachment would already have occupied Taierhchuang and that the Sakamoto Detachment's mission of supporting the Seya Detachment would be fulfilled, the 5th Division commander ordered the Sakamoto Detachment to change its course of advance and occupy Lini. Also, the Sakamoto Detachment commander judging that the Seya Detachment already would have occupied Taierhchuang notified the Seya Detachment on 5 April that he was planning to conduct a wheeling maneuver to attack the enemy in the vicinity of Lini. This report greatly shocked the Seya Detachment commander and, as a consequence, the Seya Detachment withdrew from the battlefield near Taierhchuang on 6 April. On the 6th, the Sakamoto Detachment commander learned that Taierhchuang had not been taken and informed the Seya Detachment commander that he would postpone the wheeling maneuver. However this information did not reach the Seya Detachment commander in time to prevent his withdrawal from the battlefield.

The Sakamoto Detachment withdrew from around Puwang on the evening of the 7th. Although on the 7th, the 2d Army commander planned to have the two detachments continue their attacks, his orders did not reach them through the 5th and 10th Divisions in time, as both detachments were already on the move. On the 8th, the 2d Army commander ordered the 10th Division commander to coordinate the action of the two detachments and to destroy the enemy's resistance by establishing bases for an offensive roughly on a line in the vicinity of Ihsien.

The main force of the Seya Detachment massed near Ihsien on the evening of the 8th, and that of the Sakamoto Detachment near Kuolichi on the 9th. Also on the 9th, an element of the Seya Detachment occupied Hanchuang. The two detachments, under the direction of the 10th Division, then prepared for further operations along a line extending from the south of Ihsien to the northeast of Kuolichi. (Map 14)

Co-operation of the Provisional Air Corps at Taierhchuang

At the beginning of April, at the height of the battle near Taierhchuang, the commander of the North China Area Army ordered the commander of the Provisional Air Corps to reinforce that part of his strength cooperating with the 2d Army by diminishing the strength operating with the ground forces west of the Peiping - Hankou railway.

The Corps commander, therefore, ordered the Terakura Air Brigade (consisting of three reconnaissance squadrons, one fighter squadron and one light bomber squadron, commanded by Maj Gen Shozo Terakura,

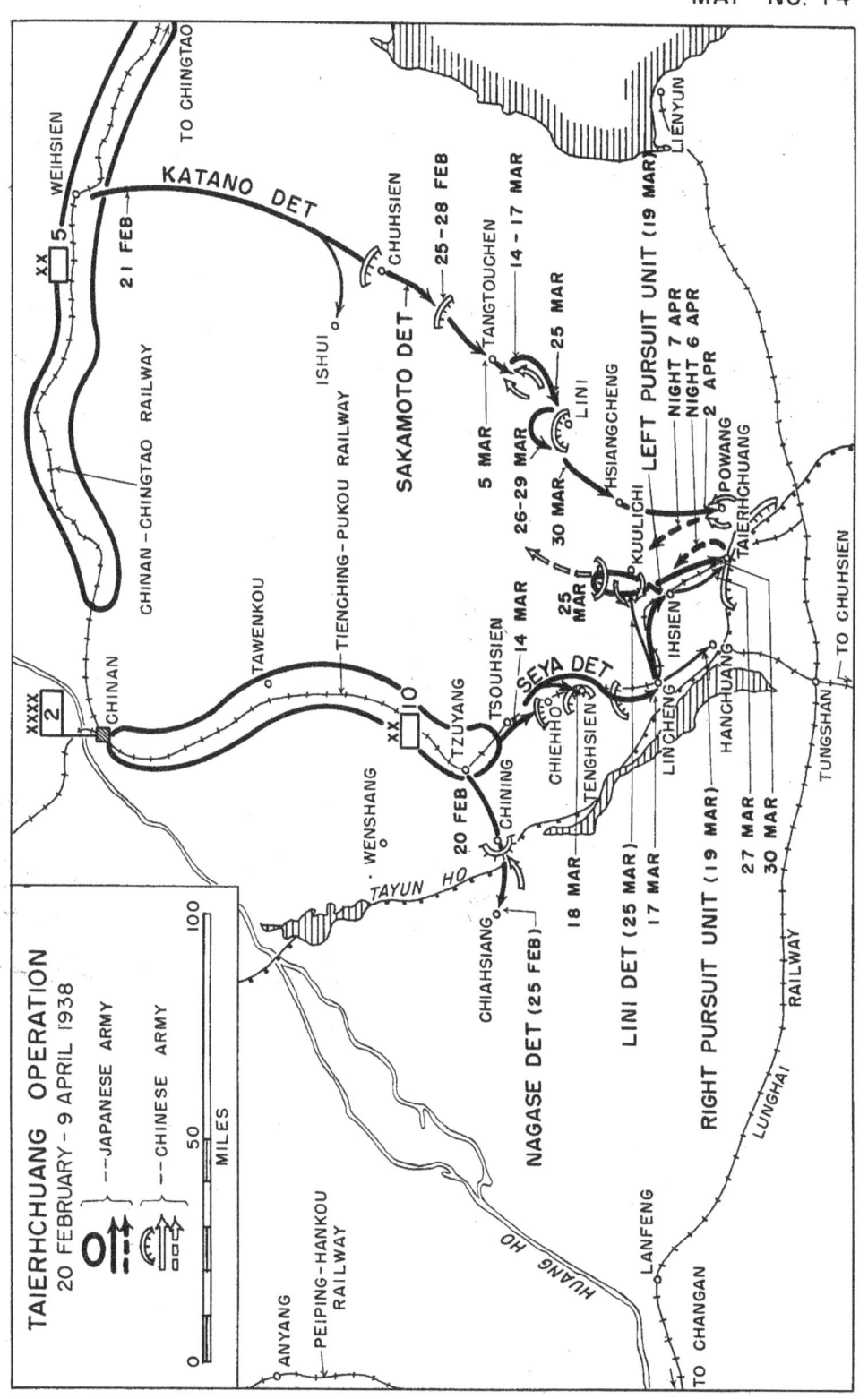

who had succeeded Maj Gen Giga on 9 March) to remain in the Tienching - Pukou railway area and to support the 2d Army and also to cooperate with the Fujita Air Brigade in destroying enemy air strength advancing toward the Lunghai railway district east of and including Lanfeng. At the same time, the Corps commander ordered the Fujita Air Brigade (consisting of two reconnaissance squadrons, four fighter squadrons and two heavy bomber squadrons) to destroy the enemy air strength in the Peiping - Hankou railway area as well as to support the 1st Army (mainly the 14th Division) and, when necessary, to support the 2d Army.

The Terakura Air Brigade,[58] with its main body in the Tienching - Pukou railway zone (the main strength of this body was disposed at Tsuyang) and the Fujita Air Brigade, with its main body in the Peiping - Hankou railway zone (the main strength of this body was disposed at Anyang) and an element (one fighter squadron) in Shansi Province, supported the Seya and Sakamoto Detachments and later cooperated with the adjustment of these fronts and the 2d Army's counter-offensive after 18 April. At the same time, the Fujita Brigade attacked the enemy air force near Changan destroying a number of enemy planes.[59]

---

58. The 10th Air Regiment, dispatched from the Kwantung Army, reached Nanyuan on 15 April, and the commander of the Provisional Air Corps assigned it to the Terakura Air Brigade. At the end of June, this Regiment was returned to the Kwantung Army.

59. Although the exact number of planes destroyed at Changan is unknown, the total number destroyed from 4 April to 5 July was 34 planes shot down, and 4 destroyed on the ground Planes destroyed at Changan were included in this report.

Tactical Command by Imperial General Headquarters

Judging that the Japanese forces were absorbed in the stabilization and pacification of the occupied areas and that they had exhausted their fighting strength and were unable to continue the offensive and believing that they (the Chinese) had won a signal victory in the battle near Taierhchuang, the morale of the enemy increased tremendously and they began to talk boastfully about destroying the Japanese forces. An extensive propaganda campaign was conducted in China and abroad which crystallized the anti-Japanese sentiments of the Chinese people and prompted positive action in the form of an "aid-to-Chiang" policy by powers friendly to the Chiang Kaishek regime.

Accordingly, Imperial General Headquarters decided on a new offensive campaign to deal a crushing blow to the Chinese forces concentrated in the Taierhchuang area, because such a blow would not only eradicate incessant nuisance actions on the front of the 2d Army but would also be highly effective as a morale factor.

Therefore, Imperial General Headquarters summoned to Tokyo the officers in charge of operations of the North China Area Army and the Central China Expeditionary Army,[60] and issued orders on 7 April

---

60. The Order of Battle of the Central China Expeditionary Army was published on 14 February 1938. At that time, the headquarters of the Central China Area Army, the Shanghai Expeditionary Army and the 10th Army were deactivated and the headquarters personnel returned to Japan. All forces under these headquarters were placed under the command of the Central China Expeditionary Army.

stating:

> Imperial General Headquarters plans to destroy the enemy forces in the vicinity of Tungshan.
> The North China Area Army will destroy the enemy near Tungshan with a powerful element and occupy that sector north of the Lunghai railway which is east of Lanfeng.
> The Central China Expeditionary Army will cooperate with the North China Area Army in the action near Tungshan by detailing an element to occupy the Tienching - Pukou railway south of but excluding Tungshan, as well as the area in the vicinity of Hofei.

Furthermore, the following directive was issued concerning the close liaison to be observed between the North China Area Army commander and the Central China Expeditionary Army commander during the campaign in the vicinity of Tungshan. This directive was named the "Essentials for the Tactical Guidance of the Operation in the Vicinity of Tungshan" and was to be used as a reference in carrying out liaison. Imperial General Headquarters, at the same time, ordered the lifting of restrictions in the employment of the 114th Division by the North China Area commander.[61]

Essentials for the Tactical Guidance of the Operation in the Vicinity of Tungshan

Operational Plan.

> A powerful element of the North China Area Army and an element of the Central China Expeditionary Army will defeat the enemy near Tungshan and will occupy the Tienching - Pukou

---

61. In mid-February 1938 when the 114th Division was transferred from Central China to the North China Area Army command, Imperial General Headquarters limited the employment of the 114th Division by the North China Area Army commander to the Peiping - Tienching sector.

railway area as well as the area in the vicinity of Hofei.[62]
The operation is scheduled to be launched late in April.

Essentials.

    1. The North China Area Army, with about four divisions, will assume the offensive against the Lunghai railway and will destroy the enemy in that area.

        To attain this objective, it will advance its main force from the north to destroy the enemy in the vicinity of Tungshan, while an element of about one division will be dispatched from the vicinity northeast of Kaifeng towards the enemy's route of retreat in the vicinity of Shangchiu.

    2. The Central China Expeditionary Army will use about two divisions (an element will be assigned to the rear guard) and move from the south to cooperate with the operation of the North China Area Army.
        For this purpose, the attack will be launched from the sector along the Tienching - Pukou railway and special effort will be directed to intercepting the enemy's route of retreat.

    3. The North China Area Army will seize the Tienching - Pukou railway north of Tungshan (to include Tungshan) and, after defeating the enemy, will occupy that sector north of the Lunghai railway, which is east of Kaifeng.

    4. The Central China Expeditionary Army, after repelling the hostile forces, will occupy the Tienching - Pukou railway south of Tungshan (but to exclude Tungshan) as well as the area in the vicinity of Hofei.

    5. After the termination of the above operation, the North China Area Army will dispose about three divisions in the area south of the Huang Ho while the Central China Expeditionary Army will dispose about two divisions along the Tienching - Pukou railway south of Tungshan (excluding Tungshan) as well as in the area in the vicinity of Hofei.

In order to carry out liaison between Imperial General Headquarters and the operational area during the Tungshan Operation, Imperial General

---

    62. The occupation of the Hofei area was planned in view of the prospective operation against the enemy in the Wuchang - Hankou area.

Headquarters dispatched Maj Gen Gun Hashimoto and staff to the operational area for the period from mid-April to the end of May. This group was known as the Imperial General Headquarters Liaison Team.

Prior to the Tungshan Operation, the North China Area Army had completed the organization of the China Garrison Group and four independent mixed brigades. Imperial General Headquarters then assigned the China Garrison Group and three independent mixed brigades to the North China Area Army and one independent mixed brigade to the Mongolia Garrison Group.[63] The North China Area Army, in turn, attached two independent mixed brigades to the 1st Army and one independent mixed brigade to the 2d Army.

In view of the increased enemy fighting strength, the Imperial General Headquarters ordered the Kwantung Army on 10 May to dispatch two mixed brigades (each mainly composed of six infantry battalions and two field artillery battalions) to north China. Upon arrival they were attached to the North China Area Army.

In addition, the Imperial General Headquarters assigned the 10th Air Regiment from the Kwantung Army to the North China Area Army on 14 April.

On 15 May the Imperial General Headquarters specified that the

---

63. The basic manuscript states in error that the North China Area Army attached one independent mixed brigade to the Mongolia Garrison Group. At this time, the Mongolia Garrison Group was under the direct command of Imperial General Headquarters. It was not until 7 July 1938, after it had been re-designated the Mongolia Garrison Army, that it was assigned to the North China Area Army.

operational boundary between the North China Area Army and the Central China Expeditionary Army would be the Lunghai railway west of Tungshan and the Kuei Ho. However, on 30 May it was changed to the line connecting Founing, Ssuhsien, Nanpingchi, Mengcheng, and Fouyang.

Operational Command of the North China Area Army

On 10 April the North China Area Army commander decided on the over-all plan for the operational command of the Tungshan Operation:

Operational Plan.

> A great enemy force will be drawn into the Tungshan area and in the area east of the Tienching - Pukou railway. First, the route of retreat of this force will be cut by an enveloping movement west and southwest of Tungshan and later it will be destroyed and Tungshan will be occupied.

Essentials of Command.

The First Phase.

> The 2d Army will be reinforced promptly with the 16th Division, the 2d Tank Battalion and one heavy field artillery battalion.[64] The 2d Army will contain the enemy primarily in the vicinity of the Hanchuang - Ihsien - Lini line. At the same time, it will prepare for future attacks.
> An agreement will be made with the Central China Expeditionary Army to divert the enemy to the sector southeast of

---

64. The 114th Division had already been attached to the 2d Army on 8 April. In addition, the main units attached to the 2d Army by the North China Area Army during the engagement were as follows: (1) On 5 May, two infantry battalions were dispatched to Chinan from the China Garrison Group and placed under the direct command of the North China Area Army commander. Subsequently, reinforced by an infantry battalion and a mountain artillery battery, this unit was organized into the Hirayama Detachment on the 9th and attached to the 2d Army on the 10th. Later, the Army attached the Detachment to the 16th Division. (2) In accordance with Imperial General Headquarters orders of 10 May, two mixed brigades attached to the North China Area Army from the Kwantung Army were attached to the 2d Army on 11 May.

Tungshan by an element occupying the area northwest of Huaiyin.

The Second Phase.

With the completion of preparations by the 2d Army, offensive action in the form of a surprise attack will be launched in late April. A powerful group will advance southward from the western side of Weishan Hu to cut off the enemy's route of retreat in the sectors west and southwest of Tungshan. In co-operation with an element of the Central China Expeditionary Army, it will subsequently envelop Tungshan, completely occupy the town and annihilate the enemy. (Depending on the situation, the action from the west side of Weishan Hu may be suspended and the direct route to Tungshan taken when the enemy will be defeated in the area north of the prepared positions of Tungshan.)

About a division of the 1st Army, after crossing the Huang Ho between Lanfeng and Fanhsien shall defend the Lunghai railway east of Lanfeng and shall cooperate with the 2d Army. (If possible, the crossing should be carried out simultaneously with the attack of the main force of the 2d Army). A force formed around four infantry battalions, a field artillery battalion, and a 10cm howitzer battalion of the above division shall be transported to the Chining area by rail and assigned the task of covering the crossing of the river by the division's main force.

In order to contain the enemy west of Lanfeng, a show of strength will be made on the north bank of the Huang Ho, but no effort will be made to establish a foothold on the south bank of the river.[65]

The operational boundary of the 1st and 2d Armies shall be along the line connecting Shouchang, Yuncheng and Shangchiu, while the area on the boundary shall be the responsibility of the 1st Army.

The main force of the Provisional Air Corps shall co-operate with the 2d Army.

The Third Phase.

Simultaneous with the capture of Tungshan, the 2d Army shall occupy the area east of Lanfeng near the Lunghai railway and prepare for future action.

---

65. This restriction was placed on the element on the north bank of the Huang Ho as the 1st Army had no reserve units to reinforce it and it was felt that it did not have sufficient strength to actually engage the enemy.

The Central China Expeditionary Army shall secure the area along the Tienching - Pukou railway south of Tungshan (excluding Tungshan).

According to the situation, the 1st Army may, by employing a part of the troops south of the Huang Ho, seize both Kaifeng and Chenghsien, but a separate order will be issued relative to such action.

The Provisional Air Corps' main strength shall attack key points at the enemy's rear and destroy his air force, while an element shall cooperate directly with each Army group.

Operational Command of the Central China Expeditionary Army

The Central China Expeditionary Army, which previously had drafted a plan for the operational command of the Tungshan Operation and which had been making preparations accordingly, worked out the following battle plan on 24 April:

Operational Plan.

In co-operation with the North China Area Army, the Central China Expeditionary Army shall contact and destroy the enemy west of Tungshan.

The time for the decisive battle is fixed tentatively for mid-May.

Essentials of Command.

The offensive by the Army is expected to commence about 5 May, but, depending on the situation, it may be launched about the end of April. The Army, disposing the 9th and 13th Divisions side by side, shall destroy the enemy to the front and advance rapidly to a line connecting Chaochiachi and Mengcheng.

At this juncture, the left division (13th Division) shall assume responsibility for the main attack and, after advancing to a line linking Chiachiachi and Mengcheng, the Army shall proceed to the Shangchiu - Pohsien area, the Tungshan - Yungcheng area, or to the Tungshan area, depending upon the enemy situation in the Tungshan area.

In any event, a part of the Army shall be employed to seize the vicinity of Suhsien.

Independently of this plan, the Army on 21 April ordered the 101st

Division to advance as many as possible of the troops stationed in the area north of the Yangtzu River (those employed in the occupation and garrisoning of Tungtai and Nantung) toward Founing in order to facilitate the Army's future operations.

Also, on 23 April, the Army ordered the 6th Division to employ a force built around four infantry battalions, to defeat the enemy near Hohsien and then conduct operations in the area along the Hohsien - Chaohsien - Hofei road in order to contain the enemy in the Hofei area and thus facilitate the operations of the Army.

Air Operational Areas

For the battle of Tungshan no boundary was stipulated between the operational areas of the Provisional Air Corps of the North China Area Army and the 3d Air Brigade of the Central China Expeditionary Army, but the reconnaissance areas were separated by the line connecting Tungshan, Shangchiu, Chouchiakou and Hsiyang.

Navy air units, according to an Army-Navy agreement, engaged in attacking the area along the Lunghai railway east of the line connecting Tancheng and Suchien, as well as the area south of a line connecting Pohsien and Chouchiakou, and airfields at Loyang, Chouchiakou, Hofei, Shehsien, Changan, Hsinyang and Tungshan. They were also used to reinforce units in the area along the Tienching - Pukou railway, when necessary. They were especially active in attacking the rear of the enemy.

Operation by the North China Area Army (Map 15)

2d Army Operation to Contain the Main Force of the Enemy

On 12 April, the North China Area Army commander ordered the 2d Army to put into operation the first phase of the plan for the Tungshan Operation.[66]

After the battle at Taierhchuang, the 2d Army, employing the 10th Division (with the Sakamoto Detachment attached), occupied the area northeast of the line connecting Hanchuang, Ihsien and Kuolichi, and repelled repeated enemy attacks.

With the reinforcement of troops, the Army assumed the offensive on the 18th and advanced to the line connecting Nikou, Wanwangshan and Chenchiachang by the 26th, while an element seized Lini on the 19th and Tancheng on the 24th, before proceeding to the area north of Nanlaokou.

After 26 April, although the Army carried out vigorous attacks, little progress was made. Therefore, the Kusaba Detachment, (commanded by Maj Gen Tatsumi Kusaba, and composed mainly of three infantry battalions and a field artillery battalion, and stationed near Tsaochuang) of the 16th Division was attached to the 10th Division on 27 April, while the Katagiri Detachment (commanded by Col Katagiri and composed mainly of two infantry battalions and a field artillery battalion, and stationed

---

66. See page 100.

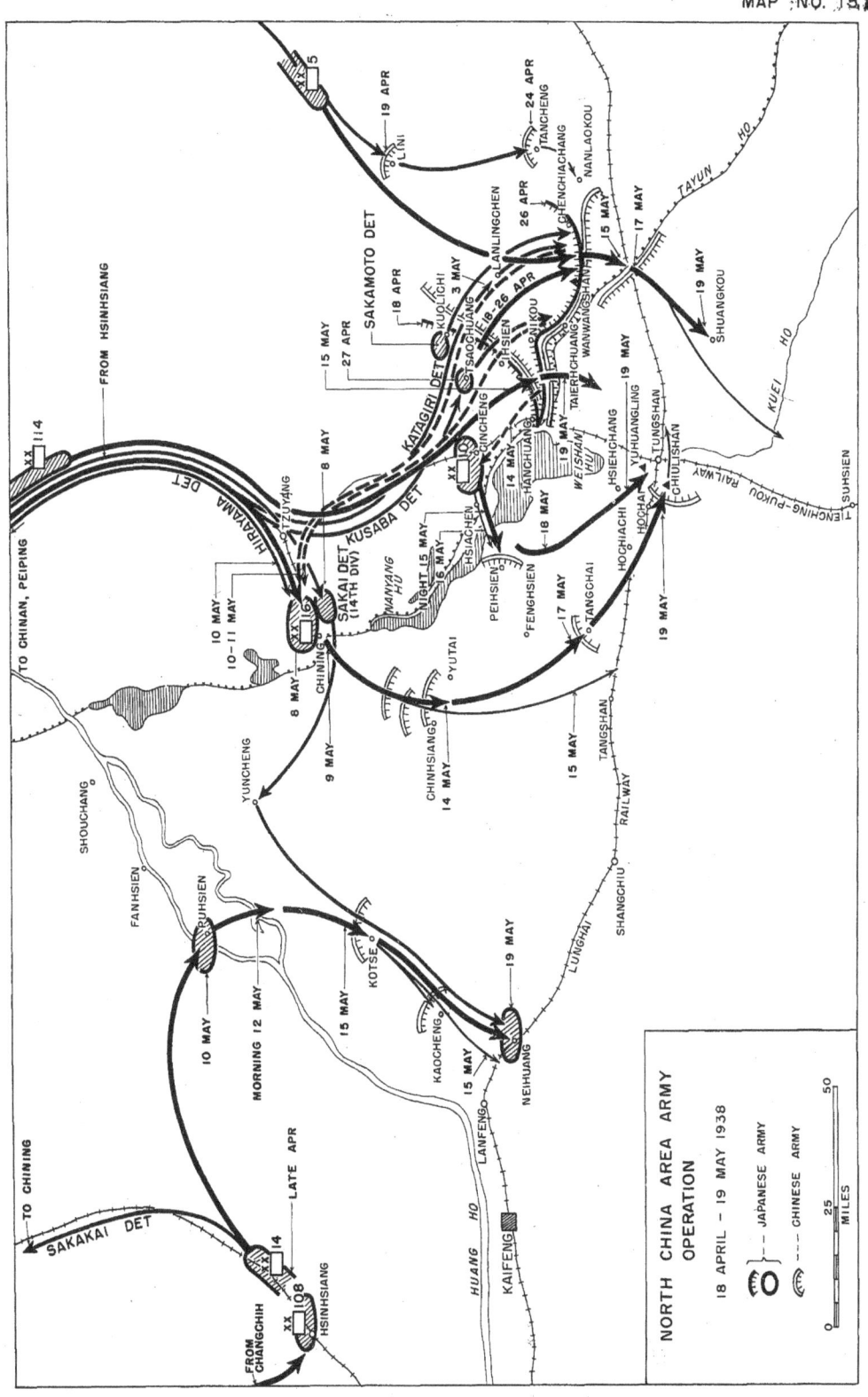

in the vicinity of Lanlingchen) of the 16th Division was attached to the 5th Division on 3 May, and the offensive was continued but still without obtaining the desired results.[67] The Army continued making preparations for the Tungshan Operation, while securing, until mid-May, the important line near the occupied areas and, at the same time, containing a superior enemy force of an estimated strength of over 40 divisions.

Disposition of the North China Area Army for the Battle of Tungshan

The North China Area Army commander decided on 23 April to destroy the enemy in the Tungshan area and occupy the area east of Lanfeng and north of the Lunghai railway line. He, therefore, disposed the 2d Army so that it might, upon concentration of its troops, launch an offensive against the confronting enemy, force him into a major decisive battle west of Tungshan and finally capture Tungshan. He also disposed the 1st Army so that powerful elements[68] could cut the Lunghai railway line between Lanfeng and Shangchiu, after crossing the Huang Ho

---

67. The 114th Division and the 5th Independent Mixed Brigade, both attached to the 2d Army, were mainly employed in defending the rear of the Army.

    In accordance with a 2d Army order of 6 May, the Sakamoto Detachment was detached from the 10th Division and returned to its parent unit as the 10th and 5th Divisions were both employed on the same battle line. Also, in accordance with an Army order, the Kusaba Detachment was returned to its parent unit on 9 May and the Katagiri Detachment on the 10th in order that they might participate in the second phase of the Tungshan Operation. Both units overtook the main force of the division in from 10 to 12 days.

68. The 1st Army employed the 14th Division for this operation.

under cover of an element to be sent by train to the vicinity of Chining, from where it could attack the enemy from the rear.

At the same time, the Area Army commander placed two infantry battalions of the China Garrison Group under the command of the 2d Army commander.[69]

Outline of the Operational Progress of the 2d Army

His Imperial Majesty appointed Lt Gen Prince Naruhiko Higashikuni as commander of the 2d Army on 3 April. At the end of April, the 2d Army began its operational preparations to capture Tungshan by destroying the enemy in the vicinity thereof. It planned to advance its main force from the area southwest of Nanyang Hu and Weishan Hu to the west of Tungshan and an element from the area east of Weishan Hu to the east of Tungshan.

The main force of the 16th Division completed the concentration of its troops in the vicinity of Chining on 8 May and, by order of the 2d Army, left there the following day. It advanced to a line connecting Chinhsiang and Yutai on the 14th, after breaking through a series of enemy positions. Its raiding force cut the Lunghai railway line east of Tangshan on the 15th

On the 14th, the 2d Army commander saw signs of preparation for

---

69. These two infantry battalions, which belonged to the 4th Independent Mixed Brigade, were originally attached to the 1st Army but were later temporarily attached to the China Garrison Group. On 23 April, they were attached to the 2d Army. These two infantry battalions are not those referred to in note 64.

action among the enemy troops in the Tungshan area and ordered the front line forces of the 10th Division west of Taierhchuang to turn over their defense mission to the 114th Division and then to advance quickly to the vicinity of Hochiachi and Hochai by crossing Weishan Hu near Hsiachen. He also ordered those units of the 10th Division (composed mainly of three infantry battalions and one artillery battalion) east of Taierhchuang be left behind and placed under the command of the 5th Division commander.

The gradual replacement of the 10th Division by about half the strength of the 114th Division began on the 14th. As the transfer made progress, the troops of the 10th Division, relieved from their defense duties, were assembled in the vicinity of Lincheng. At midnight, on the 15th, they began to cross the lake and some had successfully landed on the opposite shore before dawn the following morning.

On the 16th, the 2d Army commander believing that although the enemy had withdrawn, its greatest strength was still somewhere east of Tungshan, decided to advance the Army's main force to the area west of Tungshan as quickly as possible. He, therefore, ordered the 16th and 10th Divisions to rush their forces immediately to the line connecting Hsiehchang and Yuhuangling. The 16th Division captured Tangchai on the 17th and Chiulishan on the 19th, while elements advanced to the area east of Tungshan. The 10th Division launched an attack against the enemy in the vicinity of Peihsien on the 16th, but failed to capture the town. Elements of the Division made a second attack on the 17th, and a third on the 18th, when the enemy began to withdraw to the southeast, pursued by the Japanese force. On the 19th, the main force of the Division advanced to the west of Yuhuangling. On the same day, the elements joined the main force of the division.

On the 15th, in the area east of Weishan Hu elements of the 114th Division replaced the 10th Division. By order of the 2d Army, the 114th Division pursued the enemy toward Tungshan on the 18th, and crossed the Tayun Ho west of Taierhchuang the following day.

The 5th Division, after absorbing elements of the 10th Division east of Taierhchuang, reached the Tayun Ho on the 15th and carried out a forced river crossing on the 17th. Its raiding force (composed of one infantry battalion, one field artillery battery, and one light armored car company) drove towards Suhsien, while the rest of the Division advanced to the vicinity of Shuangkou on the 19th.

Outline of the Operational Progress
of the 1st Army

On 15 April, in accordance with a North China Area Army order, the 1st Army commander ordered the 14th Division which was then on garrison duty near Hsinhsiang and commanded by Lt Gen Kenji Doihara, to make preparations to advance to the vicinity of Lanfeng, by crossing the Huang Ho somewhere between Lanfeng and Fanhsien. As a result, the 14th Division was relieved from its garrison duty by the 108th Division and other units towards the end of April and completed the concentration of its troops in the vicinity of Puhsien on 10 May. Meanwhile, the Division commander, by order of the 1st Army, ordered the Sakai Detachment (commanded by Maj Gen Takashi Sakai and composed principally of four infantry battalions, one field artillery battalion and one heavy field artillery battalion) to advance to Chining by train and to provide cover from the right bank of the Huang Ho for the river crossing by the main force of the Division. The Detachment assembled its troops at Chining on 8 May. The 1st Army commander received an order from the North China Area Army commander on 10 May to the effect that the Sakai Detachment was to be placed under the command of the 2d Army after capturing Yuncheng and that the main force of the 14th Division would cross the river without waiting for fire cover from the Sakai Detachment. Therefore, on the same day, he ordered the 14th Division to cross the Huang Ho at an appropriate time after finishing its preparations, so that it would cut the Lunghai railway line between Lanfeng and Shangchiu and also secure a strategic point near Lanfeng. The 14th Division crossed the river before daybreak on the 12th and captured Kotse on the 15th. Also, on the 15th elements advanced in pursuit of the enemy and closed in upon Kaocheng, while the cavalry unit cut the Lunghai railway line. By order of the Area Army, the Sakai Detachment was brought back under the command of the Division the same day. The Division then concentrated its troops in the vicinity of Neihuang on the 19th.

Cooperation of the Provisional Air Corps

Toward the end of April the commander of the North China Area Army, in preparation for the Tungshan Operation, ordered the Provisional Air Corps to cooperate with the ground operations, especially those of the 2d Army, along the Lunghai railway and also to cooperate closely with the 3d Air Brigade of the Central China Expeditionary Army and the Naval Air Unit.

Accordingly, the Corps commander cooperated chiefly with the 2d Army and with the 14th Division of the 1st Army[70] without making any radical changes in the disposition of the Corps strength.

About the middle of May, as soon as the enemy near Tungshan began to retreat, the Provisional Air Corps, according to a North China Area Army order, bombed, with its main strength, the enemy in flight and also enemy trains running westward on the Lunghai railway, inflicting much damage.

Operation by the Central China Expeditionary Army (Map 16)

The 6th Division's Sakai Detachment (commanded by Maj Gen Tokutaro Sakai and composed principally of four infantry battalions and two field artillery battalions), which had been directed to proceed toward Hofei, crossed the Yangtzu River on 23 April, captured

---

70. The 14th Division was attached to the 2d Army during the Tungshan Campaign from 2 June to 13 June.

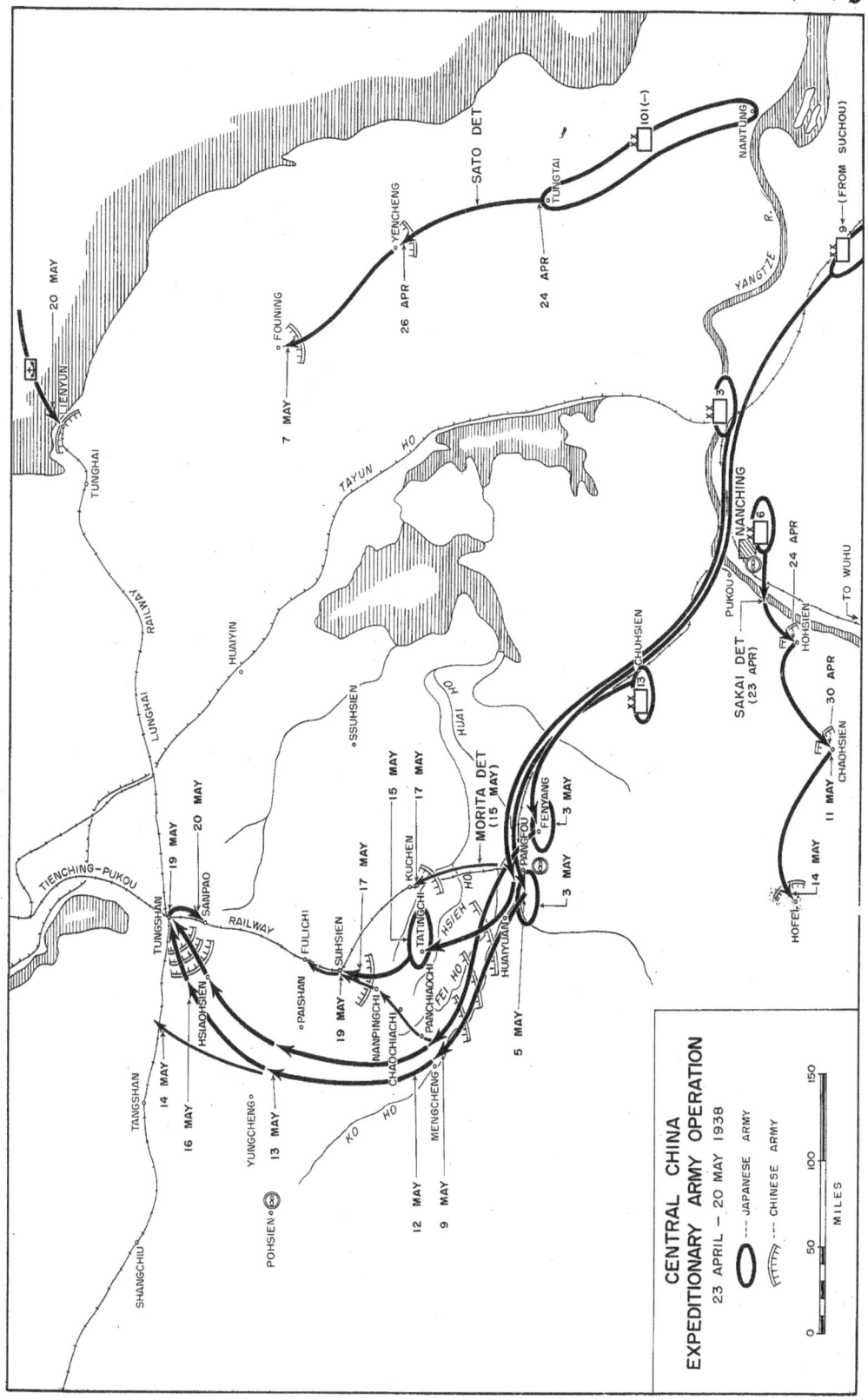

Hohsien on the 24th and Chaohsien on the 30th. It halted there to make operational preparations for its action in the Hofei area but, on receipt of information that the enemy near Hofei had moved northward, it left Chaohsien on 11 May and occupied Hofei on the 14th, where it remained during the operation in order to guard the left flank of the Army and to prepare for the Huaining Operation.[71]

The 101st Division's[72] Sato Detachment (commanded by Maj Gen Shozaburo Sato and formed around five infantry battalions and one field artillery battalion) which had been directed to proceed toward Founing, left Tungtai on 24 April and, breaking through enemy positions near Yencheng on the 26th, captured Founing on 7 May, thereby threatening the rear of the enemy confronting the 2d Army.[73]

---

71. Early in June this Detachment joined the main force of the 6th Division and proceeded toward Huaining.
72. The basic Japanese manuscript gives this Division as the 6th Division. This is an error.
73. About the middle of May, the Central China Expeditionary Army commander began working on a plan to attack and capture Tunghai in order to build a supply base for those forces operating north of the Huai Ho. For this purpose, he made preparations for the Sato Detachment to capture Tunghai by a northward drive from Founing, while another striking force formed around one infantry battalion of the 101st Division, was to capture Lienyun in cooperation with the Navy. However, the plan was called off when a naval force captured the port single-handed on 20 May. The Sato Detachment stayed in the vicinity of Founing until the 101st Division started a westward drive to participate in the Wuchang - Hankou Operation and then, by order of the Army, the Detachment withdrew from the vicinity of Founing toward the end of June. Two infantry battalions and one field artillery battalion (less one battery) commanded by Maj Gen Sato, assembled in the vicinity of Nanching while the remaining three infantry battalions and one field artillery battery were left south of Tungtai to garrison that area.

On 13 April, the commander of the Central China Expeditionary Army ordered the 9th Division then guarding the vicinity of Suchou to mass in the vicinity of Fenyang, and the 13th Division to assemble in the sector between Pangfou and Huaiyuan.

On 3 May, these divisions completed massing in their assigned areas.

On 5 May, the Army advanced northward and broke through enemy positions entrenched in depth in the sector on the left bank of the Fei Ho and on both banks of the Ko Ho, and, advancing to the line connecting Panchiaochi and Mengcheng on the 9th, prepared for the next drive.

At that time a powerful element of the enemy force was attempting to check the northward advance of the Central China Expeditionary Army, while continuing with its main force the attack against Japanese troops in the area northeast of Tungshan. The main enemy line of communications seemed to be the Lunghai railway and the roads connecting Tungshan, Yungcheng and Pohsien. The Expeditionary Army estimated that a superior enemy force was occupying positions on the northern bank of the Hsieh Ho and in the vicinity of Kuchen, and that in the sector between Suhsien and Tungshan enemy troops were steadily increasing from the north. Considering this situation, the Army commander planned to use an element (the right flank detachment of the 9th Division, composed principally of three infantry battalions and one mountain artillery battalion) to provide security for the Army's right flank against enemy attacks from the direction of Suhsien, and to advance the main force to the line connecting Paishan and Yungcheng, to cut the enemy's retreat route. On 12 May, the Army commander ordered the Army's main body to leave the line connecting Panchiaochi and Mengcheng, while ordering the advance of the 3d Division, which was concentrating in the vicinity of Pangfou and Huaiyuan, to the vicinity of Tayingchi.

On the 12th, the Army commander estimated, on the basis of various reports, that the enemy's main force had begun to retreat and, deciding to seize the enemy in the area west of Tungshan, ordered the Army's main force to advance to Hsiaohsien and areas north thereof and also to sever the Lunghai railway line.

The Army's main force occupied the line connecting Paishan and Yungcheng on the 13th, while a raiding party severed the Lunghai railway on the 14th. On the 16th, the main force advanced to Hsiaohsien and areas northwest thereof and, on the 19th, occupied Tungshan after breaking through strong enemy positions prepared several lines in depth. It advanced to Sanpao on the 20th.

The 3d Division brushed aside enemy resistance and completed massing the greater part of its force at Tayingchi on the 15th. The Army commander then ordered the commander of the 3d Division to assume command of the 9th Division's right flank detachment which was in the vicinity of Nanpingchi and to capture Suhsien. The 3d Division while overcoming stubborn enemy resistance in the vicinity of Nanpingchi on the 17th, occupied Suhsien on the 19th, at the same time, sending an element on to Fulichi.

Earlier, on the 15th, the Morita Detachment (composed principally of two infantry companies and two railway companies) was ordered to advance north along the Tienching - Pukou railway and capture Kuchen. The detachment advanced northward, defeating the enemy in its path of advance and occupied Kuchen on the 19th.[74]

Cooperation of the 3d Air Brigade

In the middle of April, the Central China Expeditionary Army made the following agreement with the Navy Air Unit in regard to the Tungshan Operation.

> Bombing and reconnoitering in cooperation with the Army advancing to the east of the 13th Division's line of advance shall be chiefly the responsibility of the Army air units.
> The air base of the Navy Air Unit shall be Nanching, but, when necessary, naval aircraft may land at Pangfou.
> Air battles against enemy planes shall be fought chiefly by the Navy Air Unit.
> In order to cooperate with ground operations, preparations shall be made by the Navy Air Unit to attack the enemy on the left flank of the 3d, 6th and 13th Divisions, to bomb important enemy rear points, troops and positions, and also to cooperate with the forces east of the Tienching - Pukou railway by carrying out bombing operations, when necessary.

For the Tungshan Operation, in accordance with the Expeditionary

---

74. The Morita Detachment, which was commanded by Lt Col Morita, railway battalion commander, was under the direct command of the Central China Expeditionary Army. The detachment was inactivated the day it occupied Kuchen and its two infantry companies were returned to the 3d Division which was then occupying Suhsien. The two railway companies under the command of Lt Col Morita were charged with the responsibility of maintaining rail transportation between Suhsien and Pukou.

Army's plan for the employment of air units, the 3d Air Brigade commander concentrated his main strength in the Pangfou - Nanching sector on 17 April and used this force to cooperate with the unit fighting along the Tienching - Pukou railway. Elements were stationed at Hangchou and Wuhu to reconnoiter the enemy situation on the southern front and to cooperate with ground units in the area. At the same time, preparations were carried out to destroy enemy planes operating in the area of the action radius of the Air Brigade.

While these preparations were being made, the Air Brigade did not carry out any bombing raids but reconnoitered the enemy situation and terrain continuously. On 5 May when the ground forces began advancing from the banks of Huai Ho, the Air Brigade cooperated with the 9th and 13th Divisions in capturing Mengcheng and multiple enemy positions northwest of Huaiyuan. After the 12th, the Air Brigade supported the 3d Division's attack against strong enemy positions near Nanpingchi and also supported the attack of the main body of the Army against enemy positions west of Tungshan. From the middle of May, when the enemy began to retreat, the Brigade bombed the enemy in flight, inflicting much damage.

During this operation the Brigade reported shooting down five enemy planes over Pangfou and Wuhu on 30 April, destroying five more on the Pohsien airfield on 11 May and shooting down one enemy plane, which came to raid Mengcheng, on 20 May.

Pursuit by the North China Area Army
(Map 17)

In view of the fact that the enemy was falling back toward the southwest after abandoning Tungshan, the North China Area Army commander decided on 17 May to mop up hostile remnants in the vicinity of Tungshan and then to capture various key points along the Lunghai railway line, east of Lanfeng, but not including Langfeng. He, therefore, ordered the 2d Army to annihilate hostile remnants still operating east of the Kuei Ho. He also ordered that an element of the 2d Army be dispatched immediately to the Yungcheng area to engage the retiring enemy and that another powerful element capture Shangchiu.

Further, he ordered the 1st Army to instruct its 14th Division to cooperate with the 2d Army in capturing Shangchiu.

In accordance with the above orders, the 2d Army commander, in turn, on the 18th, ordered the 13th Mixed Brigade to advance towards Yungcheng. The same day, he ordered the 3d Mixed Brigade to attack and capture Shangchiu. Earlier, the 13th Mixed Brigade had left Tsitsihar in Manchuria and arrived at Tzuyang on the 15th and, by the 18th, was located in the vicinity of Fenghsien. Also, the 3d Mixed Brigade had reached Tzuyang on the 16th, from Tsitsihar, and, on the 18th, had arrived at Yutai.

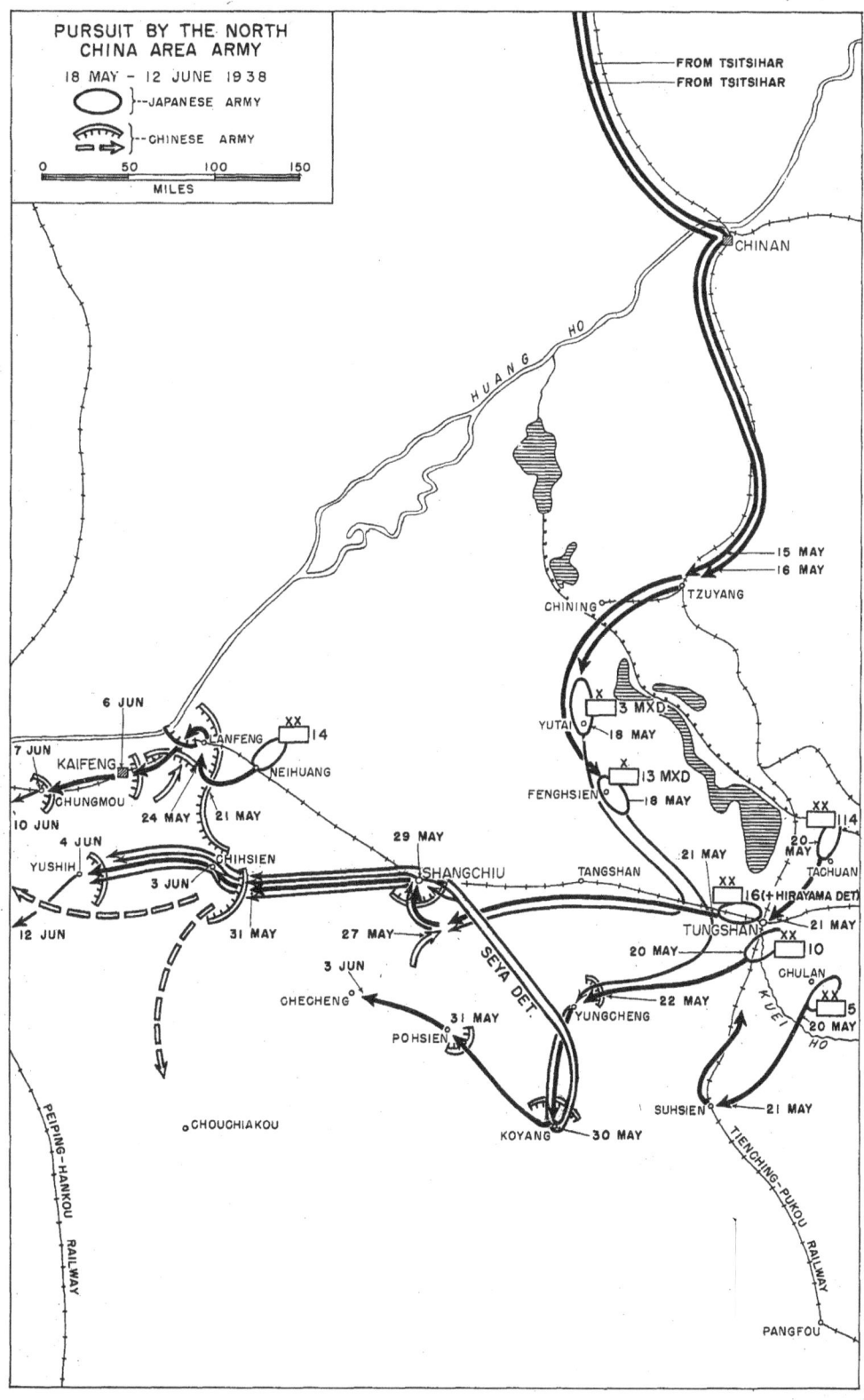

The 2d Army commander, on the 19th, determined to pursue and destroy the retreating enemy and to capture strategic points along the Lunghai railway line, ordered the 114th and the 5th Divisions to pursue the enemy along the Tienching - Pukou railway line between Tungshan and Suhsien, the 16th Division to capture Shangchiu and the 10th Division to rush towards Yungcheng in search of retiring hostile troops and to destroy them as they were found. The 3d Mixed Brigade, then participating in the attack against Shangchiu, had been newly attached to the 16th Division while the 13th Mixed Brigade had been attached to the 10th Division.

The 114th and 5th Divisions advanced to the line of hills south of Tachuan and Chulan on the 20th and then to Tungshan and Suhsien the following day. Later, they engaged in mopping up operations against hostile remnants along the Tienching - Pukou railway line.[75]

The 16th Division began its pursuit from the vicinity of Tungshan on the 21st, and elements attacked hostile positions near Shangchiu on the 27th. Meanwhile, the main force of the Division destroyed some 2,000 enemy troops in an engagement south of Shangchiu. It captured Shangchiu on the 29th and then advanced to the west destroying the retreating enemy.

The 10th Division left the vicinity of Tungshan on the 20th, and advanced to the vicinity of Yungcheng on the 22d, mopping up hostile

---

75. The 114th Division was subsequently assigned garrison duty in the vicinity of Tungshan.

remnants. It captured Koyang and Pohsien on the 30th and 31st respectively.

The 14th Division broke through the enemy's positions extending from Lanfeng to Chihsien, south of Lanfeng, on the 21st and captured Lanfeng on the 24th. However, the enemy in the area received reinforcements until its strength was estimated to be more than ten divisions. The 14th Division was unable to withstand the attacks of this powerful enemy and retreated to the northwest where it continued to hold its crossing point on the Huang Ho.

On the 28th, the 2d Army commander, in accordance with an Area Army order, in order to destroy the enemy in Lanfeng, directed the 16th Division to advance to the sector midway between Lanfeng and Kaifeng. Simultaneously, he ordered the 13th Mixed Brigade to overtake the 16th Division by motor vehicles after seizing Koyang, and enter the command of the 16th Division. Further, he ordered the Seya Detachment, formed around approximately three infantry battalions of the 10th Division, to immediately enter the command of the 16th Division.

The 16th Division continued its pursuit, and, on the 31st, advanced to the sector southeast of Chihsien, when the main force of the opposing enemy retreated to the west of the Peiping - Hankou railway, while an element fled to Chouchiakou.

On 2 June, the 14th Division was attached to the 2d Army. On the same day, the Army commander, in accordance with an Area Army order, directed the main force of the 2d Army to pursue the enemy towards the Chungmou - Yushih line and the main force of the 10th Division to advance to the vicinity of Checheng. The main strength of the Army occupied Chihsien and Checheng on the 3d, Yushih on the 4th, Kaifeng on the 6th, and Chungmou on the 7th, while elements cut the Peiping - Hankou railway south of Chenghsien on the 10th and southeast of Hsincheng on the 12th.

On 8 June, the Army commander decided to concentrate the main force of the units which had been pursuing the enemy at a point near the line to which they had advanced, and disposed the troops accordingly. However, on the 12th, the enemy destroyed the banks of the Huang Ho northeast of Chenghsien, and diverted the river towards the southeast. Accordingly, the Army concentrated its forces in the sector east of the Kaifeng - Chihsien - Yungcheng line.[76]

On and after 23 May, the 5th Division, which had been pursuing the enemy along the Tienching - Pukou railway, engaged in mopping up the remnants of the enemy east of that sector of the Tienching - Pukou line, which is south of Tungshan and north of Suhsien. After

---

76. The 3d and 13th Mixed Brigades dispatched from the Kwantung Army were returned to their original command on 11 June.
   The 14th Division, in compliance with a North China Area Army order, gradually returned to the command of the 1st Army between 14 and 24 June.
   The Hirayama Detachment was ordered to return to its original command on 29 June.

2 June, having successfully completed the mopping-up operation, the 5th Division assembled in the sector south of Tungshan.

The Provisional Air Corps cooperated with the 14th Division in capturing Lanfeng, and later, when the Division was encircled by a superior enemy force, aided the Division by transporting provisions by air, as well as bombing the enemy force. In the middle of June, when the 14th and 16th Divisions were separated from the other units by the diversion of the Huang Ho, the Provisional Air Corps facilitated the withdrawal of these divisions from the inundated area by reconnoitering the situation in the area, bombing counterattacking enemy forces and transporting provisions by air.

Operations to annihilate enemy strength before, during and after the Tungshan Operation were executed on 4 April, 10 April, 20 May and 5 July against the Changan and Hsinyang airfields and in the areas around Shangchiu and east of Lanfeng. In these operations, a total of 34 enemy air planes were destroyed, (four planes on the ground) and several hangars were bombed and destroyed.

Pursuit by the Central China Expeditionary Army (Map 18)

The Central China Expeditionary Army commander, received information on 18 May that the enemy was falling back southwestward from the Tungshan - Suhsien area. This made him resolve to pursue, overtake and destroy the enemy, and, for this purpose, he took the following steps:

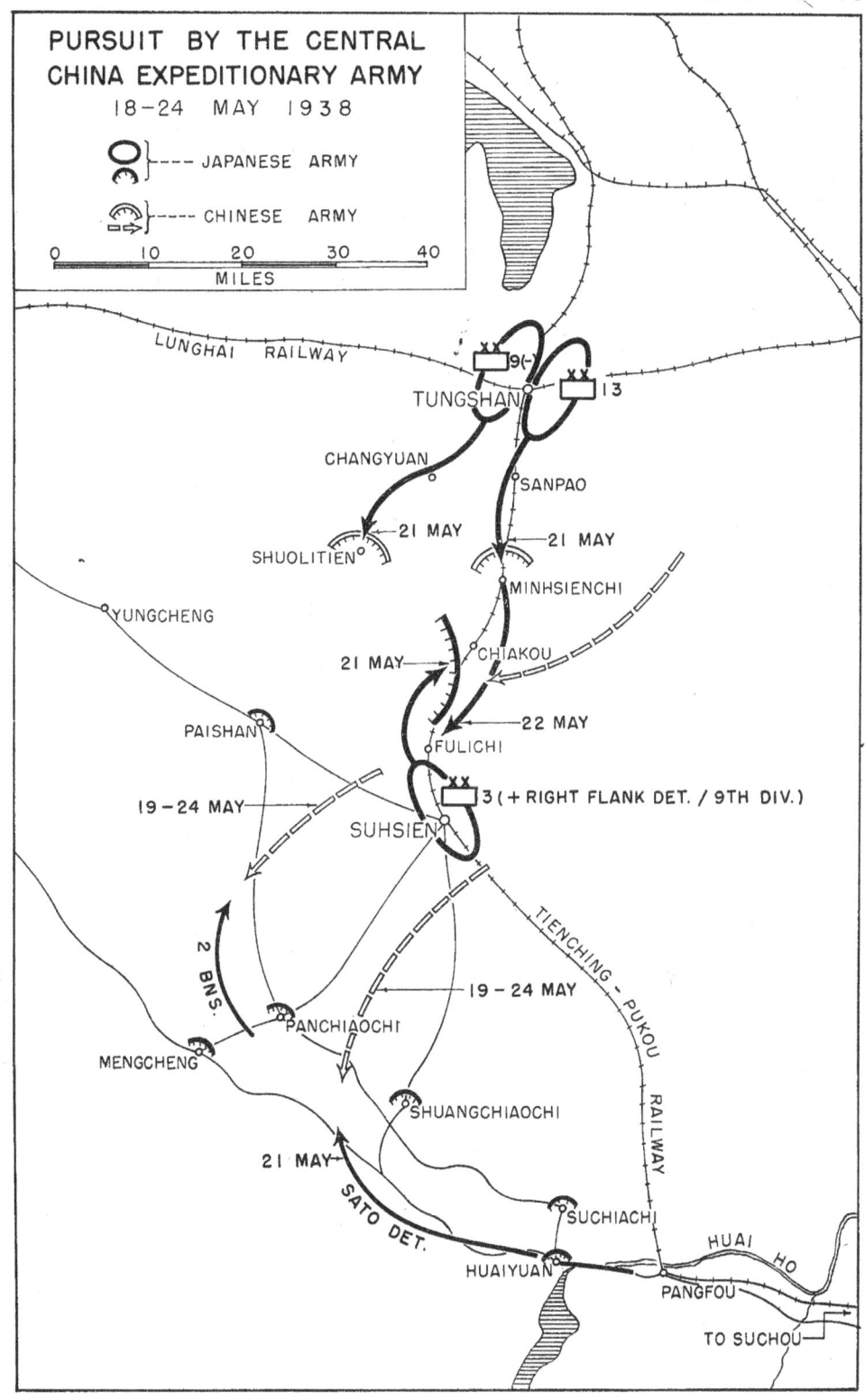

He assigned to the Army's Line of Communication Command two additional infantry battalions which had been following the main force of the 13th Division. This step was taken to cut off the enemy's escape routes by means of active operations by the Line of Communications units.[77]

On the 19th, he ordered the 3d Division to send powerful elements to the vicinity of Chiakou but to keep its main force between Suhsien and Fulichi to make preparations for pursuit.

The Army commander learned on the 20th that a powerful enemy force was likely to make a stand east of Tungshan and Shoulitien to cover the withdrawal of their main force to the west. Upon receipt of this information, he ordered the main force of the 9th and the 13th Divisions to advance to the vicinity of Changyuan and Sanpao, respectively, and destroy the enemy.

Thus, on the 21st, the 3d Division occupied various key points from the area north of Fulichi to the west of Chiakou, intercepting the enemy troops retreating westward. The same day, the 9th Division conducted mopping up operations against hostile remnants in the vicinity of Shoulitien. Also, the 13th Division advanced to the vicinity of Fulichi on the 22d, after mopping up hostile remnants in the vici-

---

77. At that time, the Army's Line of Communications Command had three major lines, with small units assigned to each key point. The three lines were the road from Huaiyuan to Yungcheng via Suchiachi, Panchiaochi and Paishan, the road from Huaiyuan to Mengcheng and the road from Shuangchiaochi to Suhsien.

nity of Minhsienchi on the 21st.

The enemy forces crossed the Japanese lines of communication in their southwestward withdrawal from the area north and south of Suhsien and the Army's Line of Communications Unit engaged powerful retiring units in several places from the 19th to the 24th. Therefore, on the 21st, the Army commander rushed the Sato Detachment to the area along the Huaiyuan - Mengcheng road to assist the Line of Communications Unit. The reinforcements were composed of half an infantry battalion and two field artillery batteries of the 3d Division, led by Major Sato.

The Central China Expeditionary Army commander, in accordance with instructions from the Imperial General Headquarters, ordered each unit which advanced northward on 21 May to concentrate gradually on the banks of the Huai Ho. Towards the end of May the main force had assembled in the vicinity of Pangfou while the 13th Division had assembled in the vicinity of Mengcheng. At the same time, the Expeditionary Army ordered the 9th Division returned to Suchou.

Garrisoning of Occupied Areas

As the 16th Division, which had been transferred to the 2d Army, and the 14th Division were both engaged in the Tungshan Operation, it became necessary for the 1st Army commander to change the disposition of troops in the garrison areas.

He, therefore, ordered the 108th Division to withdraw from the

Changchih Plain and to garrison the area in the vicinity of Chinyang, Huochia and Hsiuwu in place of the 14th Division. At the same time, he ordered the 4th Independent Mixed Brigade (less two infantry battalions) to garrison Hsinhsiang and Tangyin, while making the 3d Independent Mixed Brigade responsible for the area which had been garrisoned by the 16th Division.

The enemy operating in southern Shansi Province had been gradually reinforced after ealy May, and its strength in the operational area of the 20th Division (commanded by Lt Gen Bunzaburo Kawagishi until 23 June when Lt Gen Sanetsune Ushijima assumed command) was more than 20 divisions. The enemy was planning to recapture all of southern Shansi Province, and, in the meantime, frequently destroyed sections of the Tatung - Fenglingtu railway. On 12 June,[78] simultaneously with the diversion of the Huang Ho, Chuwu was attacked by hostile infantry and artillery forces while, at the same time, the Japanese garrison forces stationed in southern Shansi Province were attacked by a superior enemy force. Although the Division stubbornly resisted these attacks, it experienced difficulty in replenishing supplies, and was forced to withdraw its garrison forces from Yungchi, Juicheng and Pinglu in order to maintained Ani, Hoching, and Wenhsi. Meanwhile, the main force of the Division secured the areas in the vicinity of Chuwu, Houmachen, and Hsinchiang. At the same time, the garrison forces were faced with

---

78. The original Japanese manuscript gives this date as 12 May. This is an error.

a serious shortage of ammunition and provisions caused not only by the fact that they were faced by a superior enemy force but also by the interruption in communications by heavy rains.

The garrison forces, although compelled to subsist on dogs, cats and weeds, exerted every possible effort to resist the violent attacks of the enemy for two months and, at the same time, made preparations to launch an offensive.

The main strength of the 20th Division, having completed general preparations, launched an offensive against the enemy on 5 July, attacking and pursuing him southward, while the unit operating at Lishih in the garrison area of the 109th Division was attacked by a superior enemy force but succeeded in repulsing it.

Although enemy attacks against the 14th Division's supply route north of Chenliu became very frequent from the latter part of May, the 4th Independent Mixed Brigade charged with protecting this route destroyed the enemy at Changyuan and sectors south and secured the supply route after 1 June.

Before the Tungshan Operation, the area under the direct control of the North China Area Army was protected by the China Garrison Group (to which two infantry battalions of the 4th Independent Mixed Brigade had been attached) and the 114th Division. However, with the commencement of the campaign, on 8 April the main force of the 114th Division was transferred to the 2d Army and, during the latter part of April and early May, two infantry battalions, the Hirayama Detachment and the rest of the 114th Division (two infantry battalions) were also transferred to the 2d Army, greatly reducing the strength of the garrison forces.

Taking advantage of this situation, communist troops in the area northwest of Ihsien and west of Chingyuan carried out persistent guerrilla attacks. This was especially true after the garrison forces were withdrawn from the vicinity of Laiyuan.

In the Central China area, with the participation of the 9th and 13th Divisions in the Tungshan Operation, the Central China Expeditionary Army commander ordered the 101st Division and three infantry battalions of the 9th Division to secure the area previously garrisoned by the 9th Division while ordering the four infantry battalions of the 3d Division to secure the 13th Division's garrison area. However, with the participation of the main force of the 3d Division in the Tungshan Operation in the middle of May, the area south of the Yangtzu River within the 3d Division's garrison area was secured by approximately two and a half infantry battalions of the division, while the Chiangtu sector north of the river was garrisoned by one infantry battalion and a heavy artillery unit.

Thus, while the garrison force disposed to the south of the Yangtzu River was very small, it contained enemy guerrilla attacks encountered at Chiahsing, Sanchoushan Range, the sectors east and west of Taihu, the sectors northwest and west of Hangchou and also in the Ningkuo neighborhood, by repeated mopping-up operations against enemy troops.

Situation in the North China Area During the Wuchang - Hankou - Hanyang - Operation[79]

General Situation After the Tungshan Operation

Enemy Situation

After the Tungshan Operation the enemy's 1st War Sector Army retreated to the west of the Peiping - Hankou railway, and in order to defend the Wuchang - Hankou - Hanyang area, the 5th War Sector Army, which had been defeated in the Tungshan Operation, was disposed near the Tapiehshan Mountains lying north of the Wuchang - Hankou - Hanyang area where they constructed formidable fortifications along the Tapiehshan Range on a line stretching north-south of Juichang, and along the banks of the Yangtzu River. In June, the 9th War Sector Army was organized and gradually disposed around the Wuchang - Hankou - Hanyang area. During the initial phase of the operation (mid-July), enemy strength in the 5th and 9th War Sectors totalled over 60 divisions. In addition, in the 3d War Sector, Chinese troops were still near Hukou and in the area south of the Yangtzu River and were threatening the Japanese lines of communication.

Disposition of the North China Area Army

After the Tungshan Operation the main force of the 2d Army

---

79. The Wuchang - Hankou - Hanyang Operation (abbreviated title Wu-Han Operation) is described fully in Monograph No 179, <u>Central China Area Operations, Vol I</u>. This monograph simply gives details of the North China Area Army's support of the operation.

(14th and 16th Divisions) pursued the enemy westward, and, early in June, massed its forces near Chungmou and Yushih.[80] On 14 June, the 2d Army commander ordered the 16th Division to mass east of the area which had been inundated when the enemy had cut the dikes of the Huang Ho. Passage through the flooded areas was difficult because of the harassing actions of the enemy, but, on 7 July, the 2d Army succeeded in massing its force along the line connecting Kaifeng and Chihsien.

In July, when the 2d Army was transferred to the Central China Expeditionary Army, the North China Area Army commander divided the area formerly garrisoned by the 2d Army and the area under the direct control of the Area Army into three defense areas, and assigned the China Garrison Group[81] the defense of the Peiping - Tienching area, the 114th and 5th Divisions and 5th Independent Mixed Brigade the Shantung Province and the southern section of the Tienching - Pukou railway, and the 16th Division, which was later relieved by the Cavalry Group, the area east of the new Huang Ho.

From early June, the 10th Division massed near Hsiai and Yungcheng, and, from the middle of July, in accordance with an Area Army order, commenced movement to assemble near Hofei.

---

80. On 13 June, the 14th Division returned to the 1st Army.
81. On 15 July, the China Garrison Group was expanded into the 27th Division and transferred to the 11th Army. The 11th Army was organized to conduct the Wuchang - Hankou - Hanyang Operation.

In July, the 110th Division[82] was sent to the north China area and by the middle of the month had relieved the China Garrison Group in garrisoning the Peiping - Tienching area.

Imperial General Headquarters Orders Relative to the Drive Against the Wuchang - Hankou - Hanyang Area

After completion of the Nanching Operation, Imperial General Headquarters began to study the Wu - Han Operation and, capitalizing on the favorable situation during the Tungshan Operation, decided to prepare promptly for this operation.

Imperial General Headquarters, therefore, in accordance with the plan to "occupy Hankou as swiftly as possible this fall and drive the Chiang Government out of Central China, and, if the situation permits, drive on to Canton and sever the enemy's supply route," formulated a general plan for the conduct of the operation, which was as follows:

> The Central China Expeditionary Army will advance one army along the Huai Ho and another along the Yangtzu River in a drive on Hankou and will destroy as many of the enemy as possible.[83]

---

82. In accordance with an Imperial General Headquarters order, the 110th Division arrived from Japan in late June. It reached north China in early July.

83. The Chinese cut the dikes of the Huang Ho northeast of Chenghsien on 12 June and the course of the river was diverted to the southeast flooding great areas of land. Therefore, the 2d Army was ordered to advance overland south of the Huai Ho, instead of along the Huai Ho as previously ordered. Because of the rise of the Huai Ho, the 3d Division stationed around Shouhsien began to move toward Pangfou on 19 June and the 13th Division stationed around Chengyangkuan began to move toward Hofei on 21 June. The railway bridge across the Huai Ho, near Pangfou, was washed away by the flood on 13 July. The main area of battle of the Central China Expeditionary Army, therefore, shifted to the Yangtzu River area.

An element of the North China Area Army, prior to the commencement of the Central China Area Army's drive, will occupy the area in and around Chenghsien and contain the enemy in the north.

North China Area Army's Support of the Drive on the Wuchang - Hankou - Hanyang Area

As the North China Area Army commander planned to employ an element to contain the enemy to the north and thus support the Wu - Han Operation, on 9 August, he ordered the 1st Army to mop up enemy troops on the left bank of the Huang Ho as soon as possible, and, with an element, secure strategic points on the banks of the old river and, from early September, contain the enemy by employing aggressive action. The commander also ordered the Cavalry Group (commanded by Lt Gen Shoichi Naito and built around two cavalry brigades which were garrisoning the area east of the new Huang Ho) to employ, from early September, a powerful element near the flooded area of the Huang Ho and, by aggressive action, contain the enemy. On 27 September, he ordered the 12th Air Regiment to conduct interdiction bombing of strategic targets along the southern section of the Peiping - Hankou railway, north of but excluding Hsinyang, and along the western section of the Lunghai railway in order to contain the enemy in the north.[84]

Accordingly, the 14th, 20th and 109th Divisions of the 1st Army,

---

84. The North China Area Army Air Unit did not possess a heavy bomber unit, therefore, the 12th Air Regiment was attached to it on 22 September.

mopped up enemy troops on the left bank of the Huang Ho and carried out a show of force (mainly artillery bombardment) against the enemy on the opposite bank of the river. The 14th Division conducted its mopping-up operation in the Peiping - Hankou railway area from late August to early October, the 20th Division continued its mopping-up operation in southern Shansi Province until late October, and the 109th Division conducted mopping-up operations in the western area of Lishih from early September on through the middle part of September.

Early in September, the Cavalry Group occupied Taikang and Huaiyuan, advanced to a line on the east bank of the new Huang Ho and made a river crossing feint; between middle and late September, an element landed on the opposite bank and, early in October, another element attacked the northern and eastern part of Chouchiakou and threatened the enemy. On 14 October, the 4th Cavalry Brigade was transferred to the Central China Expeditionary Army, and then, on the 25th, by order of the North China Area Army, the show-of-force action was suspended.

Air Operations in North China Area During the
Wuchang - Hankou - Hanyang Area Campaign

After the Tungshan Operation, the North China Area Army was busy consolidating the occupied areas, but, early in August, when the

North China Area Army Air Unit[85] was organized, the Area Army commander ordered the main force of the Sudo Unit (one fighter squadron and two light bomber squadrons)[86] to Anyang and an element to Tungshan and assigned them the mission of supporting operations of the 1st Army garrison groups - the 5th and 114th Divisions and the 5th Independent Mixed Brigade, (garrisoning the Shantung Province and the sector near Tungshan), the 110th Division (garrisoning the Peiping - Tienching area), and the Cavalry Group (garrisoning the area in and around the east bank of the new Huang Ho). Further, it was assigned the mission of collecting intelligence material about the enemy air situation. The Area Army commander also ordered the main force of the Yamase Unit (two light bomber squadrons) to Yangchu and an element of it to Tatung and ordered them to support the operations of the 1st Army and of the Mongolia Garrison Army in that area.[87]

---

85. The Order of Battle of the North China Area Army Air Unit was issued on 2 August 1938. The unit was composed of the 3d Squadron of the 64th Air Regiment, 27th Air Regiment, 90th Air Regiment and two airfield battalions. At the same time, the Provisional Air Corps, then under the command of the North China Area Army, was renamed the Air Corps, transferred to Central China and assigned to the Central China Expeditionary Army.

86. The original Japanese manuscript states that the Sudo Unit was composed of three air reconnaissance squadrons. This is an error.

87. The North China Area Army commander divided the ground units of the Air Unit into the east and west groups: the east group was responsible for ground duties on airfields at Peiping, Tienching, Chinan, Tungshan and Shangchiu, and the west group on airfields at Shihchiachuang, Anyang, Hsinhsiang, Yangchu, Linfen and Ani.

In the middle of September, an element (one light bomber squadron[88] and an element of the airfield battalion) of the North China Area Army Air Unit, was transferred to the 21st Army,[89] and, on 22 September, an element of the Kwantung Army (the 15th Air Regiment, composed of two reconnaissance squadrons, the 12th Air Regiment, composed of two heavy bomber squadrons, and two airfield battalions) was placed under the tactical command of the North China Area Army commander. The Area Army commander ordered the North China Area Army Air Unit to support the operations of the 1st Army and the Mongolia Garrison Army, and the 15th Air Regiment (minus a squadron) to support the operations of the 114th and 21st Divisions,[90] the Cavalry Group and the 5th Independent Mixed Brigade. The 12th Air Regiment was disposed at Anyang, and ordered to attack the western section of the Lunghai railway and the southern section of the Peiping - Hankou railway.

In the Northern Shansi Province Operation carried out from late September, the main force of the North China Area Army Air Unit supported the 1st Army and the Mongolia Garrison Army operations, and the 15th Air Regiment, disposed in Nanyuan, supported mainly the 110th

---

88. The basic Japanese manuscript states that one air reconnaissance squadron was transferred. This is an error. It was a light bomber squadron.
89. The 21st Army was organized in the middle of September for the Canton Operation.
90. The 21st Division was organized in Japan on 15 July 1938 and placed in the Order of Battle of the North China Area Army the same day. The Division landed at Tangku in late August, and, in early September, was ordered by the North China Area Army commander to garrison around Tungshan.

Division's operation while the 12th Air Regiment supported the Wu-Han Operation by attacking the area along the Peiping - Hankou railway.

On 6 October, the 7th Air Brigade Headquarters, commanded by Maj Gen Hisao Hozoji of the Kwantung Army, was placed under the command of the North China Area Army commander, and the Area Army commander ordered air units in north China under the command of this headquarters to continue with their original missions.

Late in October, after the fall of the Wuchang - Hankou - Hanyang area, the 7th Air Brigade commander received a report that the main body of the hostile air force had retreated to the western regions and that the greater part of it was massed at Lanchow. He, therefore, in accordance with an Area Army order, decided to destroy enemy air strength in that area. He massed the brigade's main force at Paotou and Ani, and, from the middle to the end of November bombed Lanchow continuously. In addition to this, an element of the Air Brigade bombed Ningsia, Wuyuan, Changan and Fushih.

On 17 November, the 12th Air Regiment and an airfield battalion of the North China Area Army were placed under the tactical command of the Central China Expeditionary Army commander, and, at the same time, the former organization of the North China Area Army Air Unit was inactivated and its remaining units incorporated into the Order of Battle of the North China Area Army.[91]

---

91. These units were the 7th Air Brigade Headquarters 3/64th Air Regiment, 27th Air Regiment (minus one squadron), 90th Air Regiment, 15th Air Regiment and three airfield battalions (minus an element).

The main force of the 7th Air Brigade thenceforth supported the operations of the various units in North China.

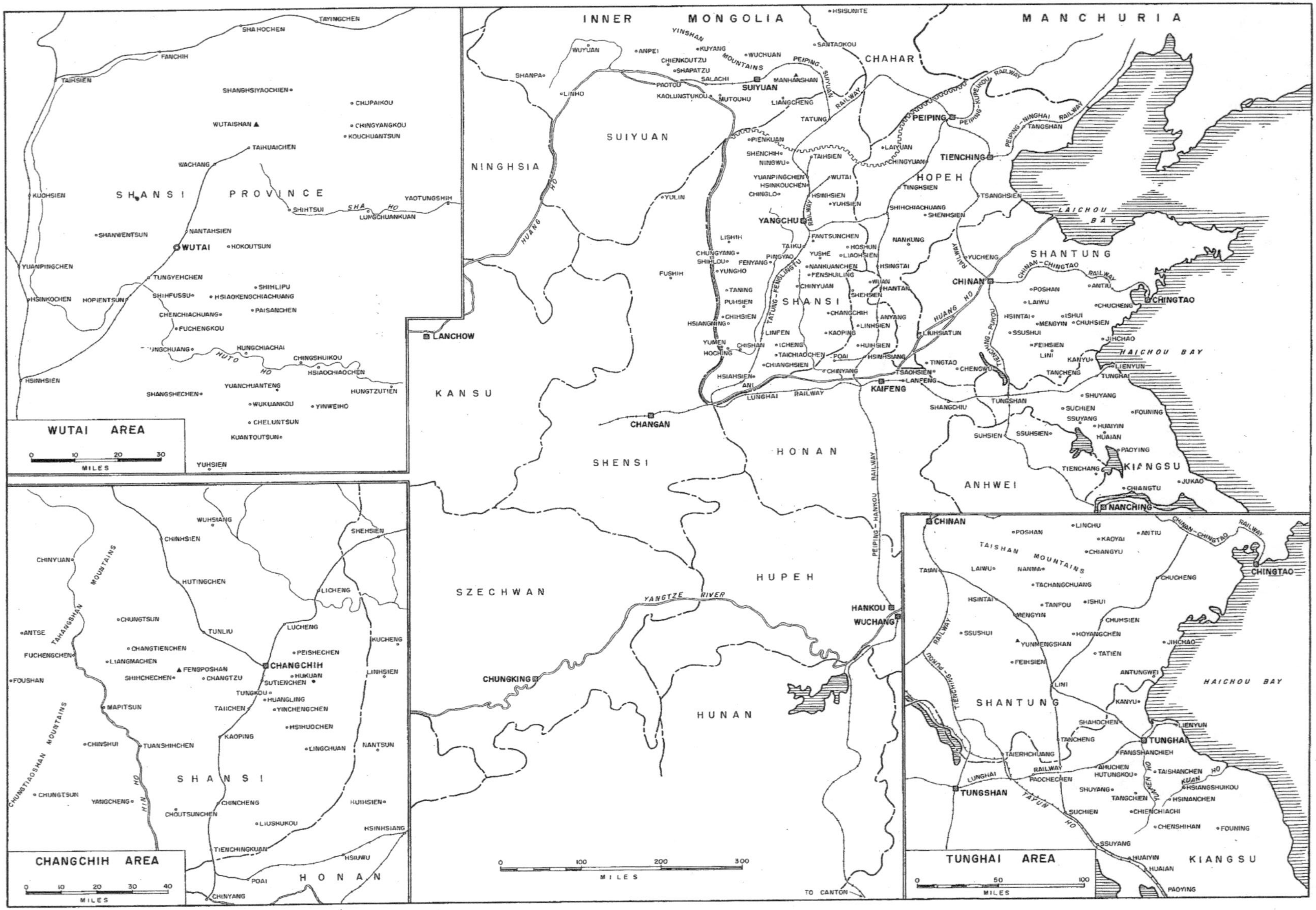

INNER MONGOLIA
MANCHURIA
CHAHAR
SUIYUAN
NINGHSIA
KANSU
SHENSI
SHANSI
HOPEH
SHANTUNG
HONAN
ANHWEI
KIANGSU
HUPEH
SZECHWAN
HUNAN
LAICHOU BAY
HAICHOU BAY
YINSHAN MOUNTAINS
HUANG HO
YANGTZE RIVER
PEIPING
TIENCHING
SUIYUAN
YANGCHU
CHINAN
CHINGTAO
KAIFENG
CHANGAN
LANCHOW
HANKOU
WUCHANG
CHUNGKING
NANCHING
PEIPING-SUIYUAN RAILWAY
PEIPING-KUPEIKOU RAILWAY
PEIPING-NINGHAI RAILWAY
TATUNG-FENGLINGTU RAILWAY
CHINAN-CHINGTAO RAILWAY
TIENCHING-PUKOU RAILWAY
LUNGHAI RAILWAY
PEIPING-HANKOU RAILWAY
TO CANTON
0 100 200 300 MILES
WUTAI AREA
0 10 20 30 MILES
SHANSI PROVINCE
WUTAI
WUTAISHAN
SHA HO
HUTO HO
CHANGCHIH AREA
0 10 20 30 40 MILES
CHANGCHIH
TAHANGSHAN MOUNTAINS
CHUNGTIAOSHAN MOUNTAINS
HIN HO
TUNGHAI AREA
0 50 100 MILES
TUNGHAI
TUNGSHAN
TAISHAN MOUNTAINS

CHAPTER III

Operations During 1939

Estimate of the Situation

In autumn 1938, Japan, in an endeavor to bring the war to a definite conclusion, had carried out aggressive operations and occupied Canton and the Wuchang - Hankou - Hanyang area.[92] The Chiang Kaishek regime, refusing to admit defeat, attempted to recover its military strength, while retreating to the remote western provinces of China. They strove to bring in supplies through newly established overland routes or through ports in French Indo-China, and continued to resist stubbornly.

Imperial General Headquarters estimated, however, that in spite of their efforts, Chiang Kaishek's forces had deteriorated to a mere local military power unable to carry out large-scale operations as they had lost all modes of transportation to the coast as well as the greater part of their resources and manpower by retreating to the remote interior.

Japan was now in a position to bring the war to a successful conclusion by political maneuvers. The next important step for the Army was to create conditions favorable to the sound development of the new central regime in China which then was being set up.

---

92. Canton was occupied by the 21st Army on 21 October 1938, while the Wuchang - Hankou - Hanyang area was occupied by the Central China Expeditionary Army on 27 October 1938.

It was not considered necessary to conduct a large-scale, prolonged war against the Chiang Kaishek regime, but rather to establish a new regime which would cooperate with Japan, at the same time maintaining sufficient Japanese strength in China to maintain peace and order.[93] Further, it was estimated that tremendous effort would be expended with little comparable results, should the Japanese Army continue to seek out the enemy's weak points and capture local strategic areas. At the same time, it was felt that it would be foolish to completely ignore the defeated Chiang Kaishek regime, as it might prove a source of trouble later. Therefore, appropriate steps, to include military operations, where necessary, were to be taken to destroy Chiang's regime.

Measures taken During 1939

In accordance with this estimate, the following essentials of tactical command were drawn up:

Purpose

Effort shall be exerted to secure the occupied areas, to maintain peace therein, and to suppress and destroy the remaining anti-Japanese forces through a strong prolonged siege.

Summary of General Guidance

a. Aid shall be given to the sound development of a pro-Japanese regime by securing important points in the Mongolian border area and the presently-occupied areas in north China and

---

93. A Provisional Government was established in Peiping on 14 December 1937 and in Nanching on 28 March 1938.

in the eastern part of central China by establishing peace and order therein.

In these areas garrison troops shall be stationed at permanent posts whenever possible and the density of garrison strength shall be as high as possible in order to accelerate the restoration of peace and order. In the same areas, guidance shall be given to Chinese armed organizations with the object of obtaining their cooperation in maintaining peace and order under the Japanese Army's control.

b. One powerful operational army shall be stationed in the Wuchang - Hankou - Hanyang area, for the purpose of restraining and intimidating the hostile main force in the Hupeh, Hunan and Kiangsi Provinces.

This army shall break the enemy's will to fight by counter-attacking hostile forces at appropriate times, but the expansion of the war area shall be avoided as much as possible.

c. Air operations shall be conducted as aggressively as before and efforts shall be exerted to neutralize enemy military and political strategic centers and to destroy enemy air strength.

The organization, disposition and installations of the air force in China shall be changed gradually so that the execution of prolonged aggressive operations may be facilitated.

d. Espionage and political activity organs shall be skilfully utilized to destroy the anti-Japanese forces.

According to the situation, small operations shall be executed in support of the above plan.

Enemy forces with pro-Japanese and anti-Communist inclinations outside the Japanese occupied areas shall be aided, and the areas occupied by these forces shall be maintained. At the same time, efforts shall be made to pacify these forces and at least make them non-partisan factions of the new regime.

Tactical Command in the Various Areas

a. North China Area

The security and stabilization of the occupied areas shall be the primary aim. The rapid restoration of peace and order in the strategic areas in the northern part of Hopeh Province, Shantung Province, northern part of Shansi Province, and in the Mongolian border area shall be planned while, at the same time, important lines of communication shall be secured.

Whenever necessary, large scale mopping-up operations shall be carried out in occupied areas.

b. Central and South China Areas

Omitted.

The Japanese Army, after capturing the Wuchang - Hankou - Hanyang area and Canton, diverted to north China the 27th and 10th Divisions from central China and the 5th Division[94] from south China.

The strength of the Japanese Army in China at the beginning of 1939 was approximately 1,000,000 men comprising 11 divisions, four mixed brigades and one cavalry brigade in north China, 10 divisions and one cavalry brigade in central China, and two divisions and one detachment in south China, as well as various line of communication units.[95]

It was also planned to reorganize the second reserve units into nine mixed brigades in the near future and to station these brigades in north and central China.

Japanese air strength at the beginning of 1939 was 270 Army and 250 Navy planes, the main air strength of the Army being disposed in central China with elements in north and south China, while naval air strength was disposed mainly in central and south China.

Air operations for strategic and political purposes were to be carried out by both the Army and Navy, with the Army air strength con-

---

94. The 5th Division had been assigned to the 21st Army on 19 September 1938 and had taken part in the Canton Operation.
95. It was estimated that the fighting strength of the Japanese Army at that time was approximately 550,000, while the various line of communications units totalled approximately 450,000 men.

ducting strikes against key points mainly in central and north China and the Navy air strength mainly in central and south China. The main force of the Army air strength planned to raid the enemy's Supreme Command Headquarters in Chungking as well as other important places in the interior of China. However, lingering unfavorable weather conditions caused this plan to be postponed.

At the outbreak of hostilities the strength of the Chinese Army was about 200 divisions of 2,000,000 men; but it suffered great losses in the successive battles, especially during the Wu-Han Operation and was reduced to approximately one-half of its former strength. At the beginning of 1939 its actual strength was estimated to be about 210 divisions totalling 900,000 men with gradually deteriorating equipment.[96]

The enemy's air strength of first-line airplanes was approximately 200, but the air force seemed to lose its fighting spirit after the fall of Canton and the Wuchang - Hankou - Hanyang area. The enemy disposed its main strength, especially that of the Kuomintang Army, in the area south of the Yangtzu River with elements stationed in northwest and southwest China. The enemy also appeared to be endeavoring to place under its command the Communist and Kwangsi armies. Further, attempts

---

96. Although there were 210 divisions at the beginning of 1939 as compared with 200 at the beginning of hostilities, as the Chinese Army had suffered very heavy casualties these divisions were all very much under-strength.

were being made to reinforce the Army by forcibly recruiting new soldiers and by reorienting and training bandits and surviving soldiers. This was found to be a difficult task as both the supply of arms and the replenishment of manpower were insufficient. The reformation and reinforcement of units seemed to be done only in the directly affiliated Army units. Therefore, it was estimated that the enemy would be unable to take the offensive until April or May at the earliest.

Although public peace and order in north China began to improve from October 1938 and many bandits submitted to Japanese control, the enemy continued to bring in arms from the Soviet Union via Lanchow and Changan, while the Communist Army using Fushih and Changan as bases, began to extend its influence over the area from Wutai and central Shansi Province to Hopeh and southern Shantung Provinces. To suppress these activities, the North China Area Army had been carrying out operations since the fall of 1938 in northern Hopeh Province and the Wutai area and had succeeded in mopping up some enemy elements. Actually, the Japanese Army was fighting in Shansi Province against Yen Hsishan's Army and in Shantung Province against Shih Yusan's Army. It was believed that the Chinese Army was preparing to counterattack in an endeavor to prevent the reinforced Japanese Army[97] from attacking Changan and Lanchow.

---

97. The North China Area Army had been reinforced by the 5th, 10th and 27th Divisions.

In the middle of September 1939, the Imperial General Headquarters, recognizing the need for swiftness, diplomacy, and coordination in military and political operations throughout China, decided to establish the China Expeditionary Army General Headquarters in Nanching. The authority of the commander-in-chief of this headquarters was the same as an Area Army commander over the 11th and 13th Armies[98] in Central China, while his authority over the North China Area Army and the 21st Army consisted of ruling only on fundamental issues and policy on military operations and administrative affairs. The details were left to the commander of the North China Area Army and the 21st Army.

Toward the end of September, the Imperial General Headquarters dissolved the Central China Expeditionary Army's Order of Battle, and ordered the formation of the China Expeditionary Army's Order of Battle.[99]

With the changing situation the Order of Battle of the North China Area Army changed from time to time and, on 23 September 1939, it was as follows:

Commander of the North China Area Army: Lt Gen Hayao Tada

---

98. The Order of Battle of the 13th Army was issued on 23 September 1939.
99. The Order of Battle of the China Expeditionary Army was issued on 23 September 1939, but the Army did not assume command responsibilities until 1 October 1939.

Headquarters of North China Area Army

The 1st Army

    Commander of the 1st Army: Lt Gen Yoshio Shinozuka

    Headquarters of the 1st Army

    The 20th Division

    The 36th Division

    The 37th Division

    The 108th Division

    The 109th Division

    The 3d Independent Mixed Brigade

    The 4th Independent Mixed Brigade

    The 9th Independent Mixed Brigade

Mongolia Garrison Army

    Commander of Mongolia Garrison Army: Lt Gen Naosaburo Okabe

    Headquarters of Mongolia Garrison Army

    The 26th Division

    Cavalry Group (without the 4th Cavalry Brigade)

    The 2d Independent Mixed Brigade

The 12th Army

    Commander of the 12th Army: Lt Gen Sadakata Iida

    Headquarters of the 12th Army

    The 21st Division

    The 32d Division

    The 5th Independent Mixed Brigade

The 6th Independent Mixed Brigade

The 10th Independent Mixed Brigade

The 27th Division

The 35th Division

The 110th Division

The 1st Independent Mixed Brigade

The 7th Independent Mixed Brigade

The 8th Independent Mixed Brigade

The 15th Independent Mixed Brigade

The 4th Cavalry Brigade

Summary of Mopping-up Operation

Early in December 1938 the Imperial General Headquarters planned to secure and promote stability in the occupied areas, and also by establishing a steady, protracted siege, to control and destroy the surviving anti-Japanese faction. Therefore, orders were issued stating:

> The commander of the North China Area Army shall be responsible for the maintenance of security and stability in the presently-occupied areas, and especially he shall strive for the rapid restoration of peace and order in the strategic areas in northern Hopeh Province, Shantung Province, northern Shansi Province and the Mongolian border area. At the same time, he shall secure the main lines of communication.

In compliance with this order, the North China Area Army not only conducted offensive air operations against the interior, but also ordered its air force to cooperate closely with the ground forces which were carrying out mopping-up operations against enemy bandits in the occupied areas. In the spring of 1939, the bandit forces near Shenhsien and Nankung in central Hopeh Province, in northeastern Shansi Province, especially in the vicinity of Wutai, and in Tunghai and Huaiyin in northern Kiangsu Province were destroyed. In the summer, the powerful enemy base near Changchih in eastern Shansi Province was attacked and destroyed. Japanese forces then were stationed in these areas in order to expand the occupied areas.

Mopping-up operations during 1939 were divided by the North China Area Army into three phases: The following is a summary of these operations.

First Phase of the Mopping up Operation (From January to May 1939)

In order to carry out the first phase of the mopping-up operations, in the middle of December 1938, the North China Area Army ordered the disposition of units to be changed as follows:

> The operational area of the 1st Army shall be limited to the Shansi Province. Its strength shall be organized around three divisions and three independent mixed brigades. (The 10th and 14th Divisions, which hitherto have been attached to the 1st Army, shall be directly attached to the Area Army.)
> Hopeh Province and Honan Province north of the Huang Ho shall be under the direct control of the Area Army. Four divisions and two independent mixed brigades will be responsible for the mopping-up operations in this area as follows:
>
> The 27th Division (one independent mixed brigade attached):
> Area on both sides of the Peiping - Ninghai and Tienching - Pukou railways.
>
> The 110th Division:
> Area on both sides of the Peiping - Hankou railway north of Tinghsien and the Peiping - Kupeikou railway.

The 10th Division (one independent mixed brigade attached):
   Area on both sides of the Peiping - Hankou railway between Tinghsien and Anyang.

The 14th Division:
   Most of Honan Province north of Huang Ho.

The operational area of the 12th Army remains unchanged.[100]
Its strength shall be composed mainly of three divisions and three independent mixed brigades. The Cavalry Group (minus one brigade) shall be attached to the Mongolia Garrison Army. Also the 5th Division, in compliance with the Imperial General Headquarters orders, shall dispatch the mixed brigade attached to the division to the vicinity of Chingtao for special training.

The operational area of the Mongolia Garrison Army remains unaltered.[101] Its strength shall be composed mainly of one division, one cavalry group (minus one brigade), and one independent mixed brigade.

This re-adjustment was completed by the beginning of February while the organization of new mixed brigades was concluded about the middle of February.

As a result of the changes the disposition of the Area Army units was generally as follows:

The Mongolia Garrison Army, to which the Cavalry Group (minus one brigade) was attached, disposed its force in the Paotou - Kuyang area.

The 1st Army transferred the 3d Independent Mixed Brigade stationed along the Peiping - Hankou railway to the area east and

---

100. This area consisted of the area bounded by the operational boundary of the Central China Expeditionary Army area, the area north of the New Huang Ho, the northern boundary of Shantung Province, and the area south of the Huang Ho line upstream from Liuhsiatun.
101. This area included the area north of the Inner Great Wall and Inner Mongolia east of the Hsisunite - Paotou line.

west of Ningwu, and north of Hsinkouchen (not included), and placed the newly attached 9th Independent Mixed Brigade which was charged with the defense of the area surrounding Yangchu, under the command of the 109th Division commander.

The operational areas of other units remained unchanged.

The 12th Army ordered the 5th Division to attach its elements to the 114th Division and the 5th Independent Mixed Brigade. Accordingly, the Oikawa Detachment (commanded by Maj Gen Genshichi Oikawa and consisting of about one infantry and one cavalry regiment and one field artillery battalion) was attached to the 114th Division while the Sakata Detachment (commanded by Col Genichi Sakata and mainly composed of one infantry regiment and one field artillery battalion) was attached to the 5th Independent Mixed Brigade for the purpose of mopping up northern Shantung Province. Further, it ordered the 21st Division simultaneously with the transfer of the Cavalry Group, to be responsible for the Group's guard area. The newly attached independent mixed brigades were stationed one each with the 114th and 21st Divisions.

In the latter part of February, the Area Army gave the following missions for the first phase of the mopping-up operations to the units under its command:

> The Mongolia Garrison Army shall continue with its present duty, be responsible for the maintenance of peace and order in its operational area, and, especially by securing the strategic areas in southern Chahar Province, prevent bandits from approaching the Peiping - Tienching area by following the mountain range of the Tahangshan Mountains.

The 1st Army shall attack the remnants of the enemy regulars in northern Shansi Province, and, at the same time, mop up as great an area as possible on both sides of the Tatung - Fenglingtu and Shihchiachuang - Yangchu railways. As for the mountainous region east of the Tatung - Fenglingtu railway, the 1st Army shall seize and secure strategic points used by the enemy from the west and south for liaison and supply purposes, in order to isolate the bandits in that area.

The 110th and 10th Divisions, directly commanded by the Area Army, shall mop up the area east of the Peiping - Hankou railway with its main force and secure and control strategic points leading to the mountainous area west of this railway with a part of its forces in order to cooperate in the 1st Army's blockade of the mountainous region. The 14th Division shall mop up its own operational area, as well as secure the boundary of Shansi Province with part of its troops.

The 27th Division shall mop up the area west of the Peiping - Ninghai and Tienching - Pukou railways with its main force, at the same time, it shall dispatch part of its troops to the area east of the Tienching - Pukou railway in the southern part of Chinghaitao (southeast district of Hopeh Province) in order to cooperate with the 12th Army operating in that area.

The 12th Army shall mop up the Lupeitao district (the northwest district of Shantung Province) and as great an area as possible on both sides of the Chinan - Chingtao and Tienching - Pukou railways, and, with part of its troops, occupy strategic points in Laichou and Haichou Bays, in order to intercept the bandits' land and sea supply and communication lines.

Each group shall disperse its own main strength at some distance from the railway lines.

Simultaneously with the assignment of missions the Area Army planned to envelop and destroy enemy bandits in the vicinity of Shenhsien and Nankung, and ordered the forces (approximately 10 infantry battalions of the 27th, 110th and 10th Divisions and the 12th Army) to advance simultaneously from all directions to seize and destroy them. The groups commenced operations on 8 March and attacked as directed. The enemy broke through the Japanese lines and dispersed in all directions. Each group then returned to its former position after mopping up the remnants of the enemy.

Earlier, during the latter part of February, the 12th Army attacked and drove out enemy regulars entrenched in northern Kiangsu Province. It then disposed its own troops in the area.

The 1st Army, which planned to wipe out the Nationalist Army and Communist Army entrenched in northern Shansi Province, dispersed the enemy by continuing operations throughout March, and expanded its occupied area in the vicinity of Chinglo and Shenchih.

During May and June, the 1st Army mopped up Communist bandits around Wutaishan and stationed troops at strategic points in order to control the movement of enemy troops. Meantime the enemy had planned an April offensive, but, taking the initiative from the enemy, the Japanese Army carried out counterattacks in the following manner:

As it was ascertained that the enemy was planning to take the offensive in the Suiyuan - Kuyang - Paotou area, the Mongolia Garrison Army turned to the offensive and destroyed the enemy before it could take the initiative.

In the Shansi Province area elements of the enemy made several attacks from the eastern mountainous region against the 20th and the 108th Divisions during the period from 10 to 16 April, but every assault was beaten off by the Japanese troops.

In the middle of March, an enemy force attacked the vicinity of Kaifeng, after crossing the New Huang Ho, but was hurled back by the 12th Army.

Second Phase of the Mopping up Operations
(June to September 1939)

Four newly-organized divisions were sent to north China in April and May. They were the 35th Division, which arrived at Chinan late in April under the command of Lt Gen Osamu Maeda; the 36th Division, which arrived at Yangchu late in April under the command of Lt Gen Tsutao Mai; the 37th Division, which arrived at Ani in the middle of May under the command of Lt Gen Kenkichi Hirata; and the 32d Division, which arrived at Chinan in the middle of May under the command of Lt Gen Heitaro Kimura. The 35th Division, by order of the Area Army, took over the defense of the vicinity of Hsinhsiang and a part of Honan Province west of Hsinhsiang from the 14th Division, which was commanded by Lt Gen Takamasa Izeki and which was then delegated the defense of the sector east of Hsinhsiang and that part of Honan Province north of the New Huang Ho. The 36th and the 37th Divisions, by order of the 1st Army, took over the defense of the operational sectors of the 109th and 20th Divisions respectively, and by order of the 12th Army, the 32d Division took over the defense of the operational sector of the 114th Division.

Towards the end of May the Area Army published its plan for the second phase of the mopping-up operations. This plan, calling for the continuation of the dispersed disposition of troops, was designed to destroy the bases from which the enemy conducted persistent operations against the strategic areas in north China. Those units which had been temporarily held in reserve during the change in disposition were to be employed to mop up hostile bandits still active in the Changchih Plain and in the western plains of Shantung Province. In accordance with this operational plan, on 10 June the Area Army commander ordered the 10th and 35th Divisions and the 1st Army to mop up hostile remnants in the vicinity of Changchih. On the same day he ordered the 12th Army and the 14th Division to mop up hostile remnants in the vicinity of Tsaohsien in the western part of Shantung Province. These operations were commenced late in June and early in July respectively, and carried on until the enemy's major bases were destroyed and peace and order restored (These two operations were known as Changchih or Eastern Shansi Province Operation and the Western Shantung Province Operation.)

The Third Phase of the Mopping-up Operations
(October - December 1939)

The Area Army, in an effort to extend the results attained in the preceding phase, published its plan for the third phase of the mopping-up operations at the beginning of October. To carry out this plan it was necessary to make certain changes in the disposition of troops as some divisions had already been ordered to return to Japan.

In July Imperial General Headquarters had ordered the return of the 114th Division and in August, ordered the return of the 10th Division. It issued a similar order to the 14th and 109th Divisions in September and to the 20th and 108th Divisions in November. Later, the return of the 14th Division was postponed until after the middle of November.[102] In September the Imperial General Headquarters ordered the 5th Division to Manchuria.[103]

Meanwhile, the 1st and 15th Independent Mixed Brigades were incorporated into the Area Army late in July, and the 41st Division and 16th Independent Mixed Brigade into the 1st Army in October and November respectively. Also, the 4th Cavalry Brigade was brought back under the command of the North China Area Army in August.

As a result of these changes, the Area Army ordered the 15th Independent Mixed Brigade to defend Peiping and its vicinity, the Mongolia Garrison Army to take over additionally the defense of Laiyuan and its vicinity from the 110th Division, and the 110th Division to take over the defense of the operational sector of the 10th Division. At the same time, the 8th Independent Mixed Brigade, a part of the 109th Division, and other units were removed from the command of the 10th Division and brought under that of the 110th Division. The 1st Independent Mixed Brigade also was assigned to

---

102. It was first planned that the 14th Division would be returned to Japan in September upon the completion of the mopping-up operation in the western sector of the Shantung Province in July. However, the enemy in the western sector of the Peiping - Hankou railway, south of the Huang Ho, became very active and the North China Area Army in mid-September ordered the 14th Division, together with the 35th Division, to mop-up the enemy in this area.

103. On 5 September the 5th Division of the 12th Army was assigned to the Kwantung Army and proceeded to Manchuria. On 29 September it was placed under the direct command of Imperial General Headquarters. On 16 October, the Division was assigned to the 21st Army in south China.

the 110th Division. The 4th Cavalry Brigade was ordered to defend Shangchiu and its vicinity and to enter the command of the 35th Division commander.

Meanwhile, the 1st Army ordered the 41st Division, which had arrived at Linfen on 23 October and which was under the command of Lt Gen Morie Tanabe, to take over the defense of the operational sector of the 108th Division. It also ordered the 16th Independent Mixed Brigade to defend an area embracing Pingyao, Fenyang and Lishih, and the 36th Division to defend the southeastern part of Shansi Province around Changchih, after the departure of the 20th and 108th Divisions for Korea and Japan Proper.

With this series of transfers of the Japanese forces there was a sudden increase in enemy activity in the western sector of the Peiping - Hankou railway, south of the Huang Ho and the New Huang Ho. To meet this situation, the Area Army, in the middle of September, ordered the 35th and 14th Divisions to intercept and destroy the enemy forces infiltrating across the Huang Ho and the New Huang Ho and then mop up their remnants.

The operations were commenced late in September. The 14th Division successfully completed its operation in a few days, but it took the 35th Division about one month to destroy the enemy infiltrating into the Chinyang area.

The Tahangshan Mountain Range, rising west of Peiping, was a base of operations for the hostile Communist forces, threatening the

Peiping - Tienching area. Although the Japanese forces had been carrying out a series of operations for a considerable time in this area they had achieved little success. Therefore, the Area Army, in November, ordered the Mongolia Garrison Army, the 110th Division and the 1st Army to combine their efforts to mop up these communist guerrillas.

In accordance with this order, the Japanese forces, with their combined strength equal to about 12 infantry battalions, commenced their operations in the middle of November and destroyed the enemy's bases by the beginning of December.

The enemy launched a winter offensive in December, and in the Mongolian border area between 6,000 and 7,000 hostile troops of the Eighth War Sector Army made an attack against Paotou and vicinity. To meet the situation, the Mongolia Garrison Army reinforced its Cavalry Group with elements from the 26th Division and, by the end of the month, had hurled back the enemy attacks.

From the beginning of December, in the southwestern part of Shansi Province, the 37th Division had been making a series of attacks against the enemy forces entrenched in the Chungtiaoshan Mountain Range, east of Hsiahsien, and had severely damaged this stronghold and inflicted considerable casualties on the enemy. However, with the enemy's winter offensive being under way, the 1st Army ordered the 37th Division to destroy in mid-December an enemy force which had advanced to the area east of Chianghsien and Icheng. This was successfully accomplished.

In the Honan Province area, the enemy operating as guerrillas along the Lunghai railway line was destroyed by the 35th Division.

The destruction of railway and communication lines was the most annoying part of the guerrilla activities. Besides cutting railway and communication lines with tools and instruments, the guerrillas frequently blew them up and, as they became more and more skilful in the use of explosives, many trains were blown up by land mines. Such tactics rendered ineffective various protective measures which had been employed in the past, such as observation patrols. Therefore, the 110th Division built screening trenches parallel with the Peiping - Hankou railway line to protect it from guerrillas. It also made efforts to mop up the occupied areas by searching every private house for guerrillas.

Security Measures

The North China Area Army, while carrying out subjugation and mopping-up operations worked out a security maintenance program which was divided into several phases and ordered each unit under its command to put this program into effect. The outline of the first phase of the program was as follows:

> Each force will complete dispersion of its troops at a distance from railway lines by the end of February.
> Efforts will be made to improve the people's livelihood by expediting economic recovery and by improving transportation facilities which have a direct influence upon public peace and order.

Special service agencies will enter the command of each local commander, guide local administration machinery, and strive for the speedy realization of security measures.

Guerrillas who pledge allegiance to the new administration will be made to give up their arms if they cannot be reorganized into a garrison unit of the provisional government. However, such guerrilla forces as the Shansi Army, which could be used for political purposes, will be pacified and kept away from areas occupied by Japanese forces.

Toward the end of May, when the Area Army mapped out a plan for the second phase of the mopping-up operations it gave the following instructions concerning security measures:

The present policy of wide dispersal of troops will be maintained.

Dispersed forces will carry out subjugation and pacification operations in close cooperation with measures for the promotion of public welfare in each locality, especially economic measures.

Various Chinese agencies will be reorganized and expanded, laying the greatest stress on the maintenance of public peace.

Self-defense organizations will be strengthened and expanded, and every effort will be made to strengthen the police force.

Preparations for the organization of a security force will be expedited so that eight security regiments can be organized by November. For this purpose, personnel will be drafted and equipment requisitioned.

Economic and transportation measures taken in the first phase will be continued on a large scale, especially the repair of blocked or interrupted roads of strategic importance. Every effort will be made to complete the repair of these roads by the end of the year.

Economic blockade against regions still infested with guerrillas will be tightened. The recovery of local industry will be hastened by encouraging the propertied class to return to their homes and by the disposition of factories under military control.

The inhabitants will be informed by means of propaganda of the facts concerning the results of Japanese mopping-up operations and the progress of its security program. For this purpose, the radio, in particular, will be made more available to the populace.

The Area Army published its plan for the third phase of the mopping up operations on 1 October. At that time the section devoted to security measures was, in the main, an extension of the previous phase, except for the addition of the following items:

> An area will be designated as a model area and the achievements and merits of this area will be spread to other areas.
> Railway defense agencies will be strengthened to ease the Army of its burden of guarding railways.
> The construction of roads, whether for guard purposes or planned by the Construction Agency,[104] will be directed, excepting those otherwise specified, generally by each force within the frame work of the fundamental program mapped out by the Agency. The main roads are as follows:
> The Hsingtai - Yucheng road, the Shihchiachuang - Tsanghsien road, and the Chingyuan - Tienching road (these three roads serve as links between the Tienching - Pukou and the Peiping - Hankou railway lines) and the Peiping - Tangshan road.

Thus, the above series of mopping-up operations and security measures gradually restored peace and order in north China, but the situation was not completely satisfactory, because of the failure to wipe out hostile guerrillas. This was mainly because they evaded outright combat whenever possible and confined their activities to disrupting communications and generally disturbing the peace. Their practice of hiding when a Japanese unit approached proved most effective during the Wutai Operations in June. The guerrillas took to flight or hid as soon as they got word of the Japanese approach. In consequence, the Japanese forces were unable to meet the enemy

---

104. Roads built specifically to be used for guard purposes were constructed by the Army. New roads or repairs to existing roads to be used for communications or transportation were the responsibility of the Construction Agency. This was a Chinese Government agency set up to assist the Japanese Army.

guerrillas in combat and the results of the operations were regarded as disappointing. Accordingly, mopping-up procedures were changed to surrounding and destroying hostile guerrillas, sector by sector.

Mopping-up Operation in Shansi Province Area

The Shansi Army and Communist troops, which had suffered severe losses in the Chihsien, Yungho and Shihlou areas during the Hopeh Operation carried out in the early spring of 1938, had fled into the mountainous area in western Shansi, penetrated deeply into Shansi Province and disturbed the peace by taking advantage of the unfavorable situation resulting from the diminished strength of the 1st Army about May of that year[105] and the diminished garrison area under the 1st Army.[106] The 1st Army, for the purpose of cleaning up Shansi Province, mopped-up the Southern and Northern Shansi Armies and the Communist troops from the end of 1938 to the latter part of March 1939.

Mopping-up Operation Against the Southern Shansi Army

The Shansi Army gradually pushed forward and finally entrenched itself in the mountainous district in the vicinity of Linfen and began disturbing the peace. The 1st Army commander, therefore, at

---

105. The diminished strength of the 1st Army was caused by a powerful element being detached to cooperate in the Tungshan operation.
106. The garrison area of the 1st Army had been contracted into a narrow area along the Tatung - Fenglingtu railway.

the end of 1938 determined to crush this Army and destroy its bases. He ordered the 108th Division to destroy the enemy in the vicinity of Puhsien and Taning and the 20th Division to crush the enemy in the Chihsien sector. At the same time, he ordered the 109th Division to advance elements toward the sector south of Chungyang and make a show of force.

On 25 December 1938, all forces began moving simultaneously. The 108th Division, in accordance with the order, attacked and occupied Puhsien and Taning from the direction of Linfen, while elements of the 20th Division advanced from the Chishan sector toward Hsiangning. At the same time, the main force of the 20th Division attacked strong enemy positions at Yumen and, after making a breakthrough, captured Chihsien. Thereafter, the two divisions engaged in mopping up the enemy in their respective areas. On 10 January 1939, they returned to Linfen and Hoching respectively, dealing crushing blows to the remnants of the enemy on the way back.

Meanwhile, elements of the 109th Division advanced from Lishih to the sector south of Chungyang and cooperated in the operation.

Mopping-up Operation Against the Northern Shansi Army

Enemy bandits, scattered in groups along the fringes of the area occupied by the 1st Army, had begun organized underground activities, and, at the same time, the Communists forces were very active.

Therefore, the 1st Army, in accordance with an order of the North China Area Army, established a plan for a thorough mopping-up operation in Shansi Province, especially in the strategic northern area. First the Army recognized the necessity for mopping up irregulars mainly composed of the Chao Chengshou Army and the 8th Route Army, which were entrenched in the sector northwest of Yangchu. It also considered it necessary to station garrison forces in the vicinity of Chinglo and Shenchih, in order to establish peace and order in the Yangchu and Hsinhsien Plains. Further, the Army recognized the necessity for securing the sector north of the Tatung - Fenglingtu railway in order to cut the route used by enemy guerrillas infiltrating into Hopeh Province via Wutaishan from Shensi Province. Accordingly, the 1st Army issued the following orders to the units under its command:

    1. The 3d Independent Mixed Brigade shall initiate operations on 1 March to crush the enemy in the sector south of Ningwu and also in the vicinity of Shenchih, while elements of the Brigade shall be stationed at Shenchih.
    2. On 1 March, the main force of the 109th Division shall start moving from the vicinity of Hsinhsien and Yangchu in order to capture Chinglo, and, after mopping up the area surrounding Chinglo, the Division shall establish a Chinglo Garrison Force in the area.
    3. During this operation, the 4th Independent Mixed Brigade shall annihilate the communists troops operating in the vicinity of the Huto Ho.

On 1 March 1939, as ordered, the 1st Army units launched operations simultaneously. The 3d Independent Mixed Brigade, in compliance with the order, moved forward and captured Shenchih on the 9th, and mopped up the enemy in the vicinity. The 109th Division occupied Chinglo on the 5th and crushed the enemy in the vicinity. In addition, the Division dispatched elements from the vicinity of Lishih and Yangchu in order to contain the enemy in that area. Meanwhile the 4th Independent Mixed Brigade, in concert with elements of the 109th Division, mopped up the sector north and west of Menghsien.

The operation in Shansi Province area was completed on 22 March.

Wutaishan Operation

Situation Before the Operation

Japanese troops had not been stationed at Wutaishan and the mountainous area to its east, which extend approximately 150 kilometers from east to west and about 100 kilometers from north to south, due not only to difficult terrain features (there were no real roads through the mountains and it would have been necessary to bring supplies in by pack horse) but also because the strong guerrilla bands in the area had indocrinated the natives with strong anti-Japanese feelings. Therefore, if the area were to be garrisoned at all, a large force would have had to be used and the 1st Army could not afford the necessary strength at this time. Therefore, bandits were strongly entrenched in this region.

Although the 1st Army had conducted mopping-up operations during the autumn of 1938 in the mountainous district near Wutaishan, after the beginning of 1939 three Communist divisions as well as guerrilla units gradually began to assemble in the Wutaishan sector and to establish a base for guerrilla attacks against the Peiping - Tienching area.

The Wutaishan sector was in the operational sector of the 109th

Division of the 1st Army. Therefore, in the autumn of 1938, the Division disposed one infantry battalion at Wutai and another at Tungyehchen. The 3d Independent Mixed Brigade, after shifting to the area adjacent to the 109th Division in the spring of 1939, disposed one infantry battalion each in the area between Tayingchen and Fanchih, the area between Kuohsien and Taihsien, and in the Yuanpingchen section. At the same time, the 4th Independent Mixed Brigade[107] stationed one infantry battalion in the sector north of the Shihchiachuang - Yangchu railway (the railway excluded) in the Shansi Province.

The 10th Division on the east of the 1st Army disposed approximately one infantry battalion and one cavalry regiment in the sector west of the Peiping - Hankou railway and north of the Shihchiachuang - Yangchu railway but south of Tinghsien in the Hopeh Province, while the 110th Division placed approximately two infantry battalions in the area west of the Peiping - Hankou railway, but north of Tinghsien in the Hopeh Province.

The 36th Division, which had been newly incorporated into the command of the 1st Army, arrived in Yangchu in the latter part of April. The Army, in order to relieve the 109th Division of garrison duty, ordered the 36th Division to prepare to mass in the operational sector of the 109th Division, and, at the same time, the Army detached

---

107. Although the basic Japanese manuscript states that this was the 2d Independent Mixed Brigade, it was the 4th. The 2d IMB was under the command of the Mongolia Garrison Army.

elements from the 109th Division to be used by the Army. During the Wutaishan Operation, the 36th Division assumed responsibility for garrisoning this sector.

Tactical Command

The 1st Army drew up a plan in accordance with an order directing it to mop up enemy troops in the Wutaishan mountainous area around Taihuaichen and Hungchiachai with elements from its force during the period extending from the beginning of May to the latter part of June, and to station garrison forces at strategic points and thus effect a thorough mopping up of the Wutaishan mountainous district. Under this plan, the operation was divided into four phases, and on 18 April an order was issued to prepare for the operation.

Chart No 2 gives a summary of the operational plan.

The Army issued orders for the commencement of operations on 1 May. A summary of the progress of the operation in each phase is given below:

The First Phase (Mopping up of Taihuaichen and vicinity)

The Sasaki Detachment of the 109th Division (composed of approximately four infantry battalions and one mountain artillery battalion) commenced moving from Wutai on 8 May and the Kanoh Unit of the 3d Independent Mixed Brigade (composed primarily of one infantry battalion) from Tayingchen on 9 May, and, gaining control of both the Wutai - Hokoutsun - Shihtsui road and the Tayingchen - Chupaikou - Kouchuantsun road, cut the enemy's eastward retreat route near Taihuaichen. On 10

Chart No 2

Summary of 1st Army's Operational Plan for Mopping Up the Wutaishan Mountainous District

Phase Classification	1st Phase (about 5 days from 8 May)	2d Phase (about 24 days from 13 May)	3d Phase (about 8 days from 7 June)	4th Phase (about 12 days from 14 June)
Aim of Operation	Mopping up Taihuaichen and vicinity	Mopping up Western Wutaishan	Mopping up Lungchuankuan and vicinity	Mopping up Hungchiachai and vicinity
Strength — 109th Div	Approximately 4 inf bns and 1 mt arty bn	Same		
Strength — 3d Ind Mixed Brigade	Approximately 1 inf bn	About 6 inf cos		
Strength — 36th Div			Approximately 2 inf bns and 1 mt arty bn	About 2½ inf bns and 4 mt arty btrys
Strength — 4th Ind Mixed Brigade				About 1 inf bn
Gist of Order	After encircling the enemy in the vicinity of Taihuaichen along the roads connecting Wutai, Hokoutsun, Shihtsui, Kouchuantsun, Tayingchen, and Shahochen, crush the enemy. Then station garrison forces at the strategic points.	Attack the enemy from both flanks at the same time from the Wutai - Taihuaichen line and the Yuanping-chen - Taihsien - Shahochen line, and thereafter station garrison forces at the key points. Subsequently carry out the reorganization of the 109th Div and disposition of the rear troops.	Prepare to advance in the vicinity of Shihtsui and Taihuaichen and mop up the enemy along the line extending from north to south of Lungchuankuan. During this engagement, cooperate with elements of the 110th Div operating in the valley of Sha Ho.	Prepare to advance in the vicinity of Yuhsien, Shangchechen, Tsungchuang, Tungyehchen and Wutai and then advance downstream from Hungchiachai to the valley of Huttu Ho in order to destroy the enemy. During this engagement, cooperate with elements of the 10th Div operating in the same area.

May, the Sasaki Detachment and Kanoh Unit advanced to Shihtsui and Kouchuantsun respectively, while elements proceeded to Taihuaichen separately, tightening the encirclement but without encountering any large enemy force. Taihuaichen was occupied on the 11th. The Sasaki Detachment subsequently stationed its troops at strategic points along the Wutai - Taihuaichen road, while the main force of the Kanoh Unit, on its way back from Tayingchen by the same course it had taken on its way out, encountered enemy troops which offered stubborn resistance between Kouchuanchen and Chingyangkou. Therefore it changed its course to the direction of Shanghsiyaochien. However, it again encountered a large enemy force in the vicinity of Shanghsiyaochien and suffered heavy casualties. Upon the arrival of reinforcements from Shahochen on the 14th it broke through, and returned to Tayingchen on the 15th. (Map 19)

The Second Phase (Mopping up of Western Wutaishan)

The Army decided, on 15 May, to continue operations according to the designated plan, and ordered the 109th Division and 3d Independent Mixed Brigade to conduct operations in accordance with the plan for the second phase of the operations.

On 18 May,[108] the 109th Division, with a strength of about six

---

108. As the 1st phase of the operation took several days longer than planned, the second phase was not begun until 18 May.

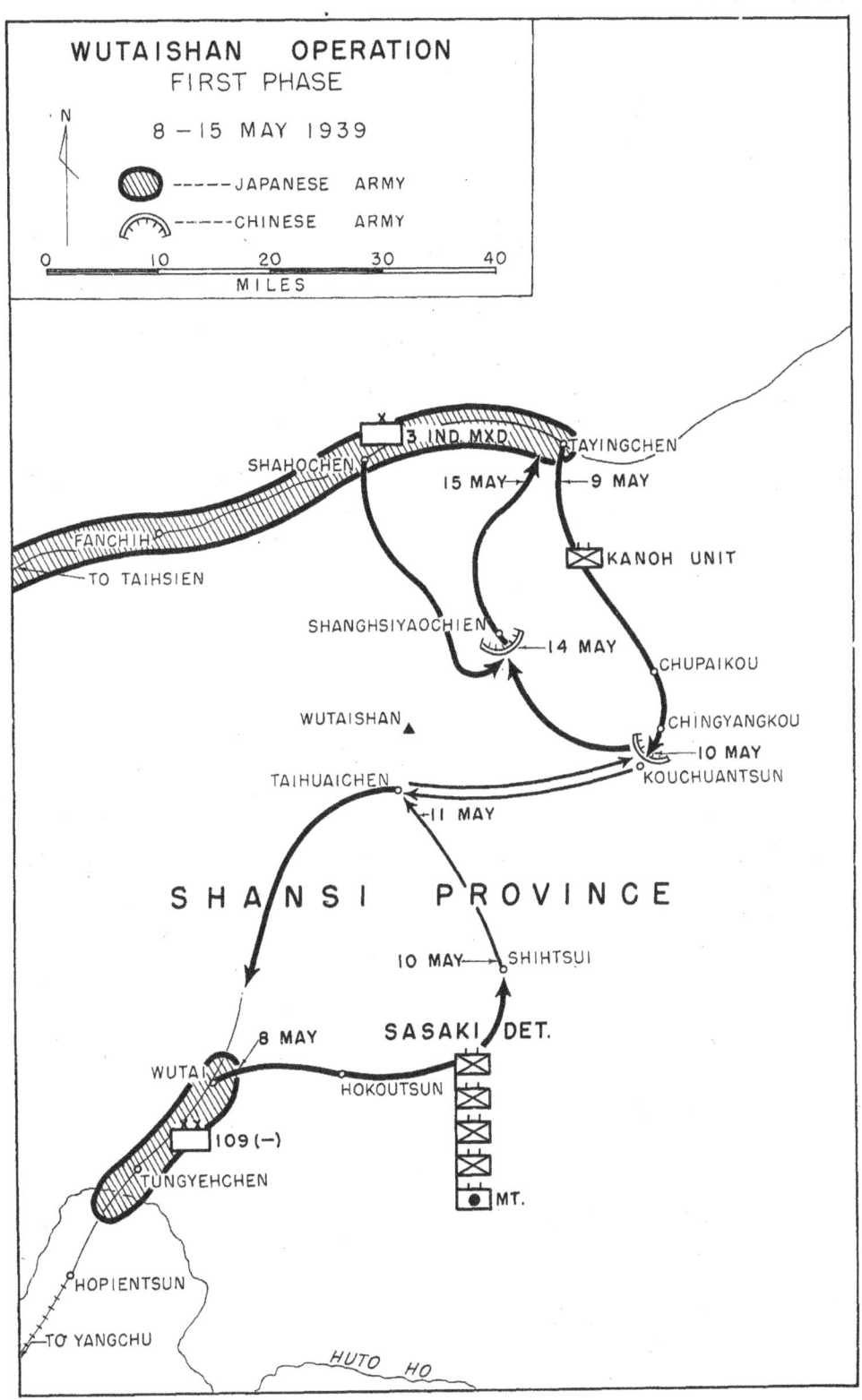

and a half infantry companies,[109] went into action from such points as Hopientsun, Tungyehchen, Wachang and Taihuaichen while the 3d Independent Mixed Brigade commenced operations from Yuanpingchen, Taihsien and Fanchih, by dispatching units composed of approximately two infantry companies from each of these places. They carried out simultaneous mopping-up operations from all directions, but they did not encounter any large enemy forces. Therefore, the units of the 3d Independent Mixed Brigade returned to their home bases on the 20th, while the 109th Division stationed a part of its force at Shanwentsun and completed its scheduled actions on the 21st.[110] (Map 20)

The transfer of the operational sector of the 109th Division to the 36th Division was concluded on 22 May.

The Third Phase (Mopping up of Lungchuankuan and Vicinity)

The Army ordered the 36th Division, on 22 May, to carry out the the third phase of the operation. The Kasahara Detachment (mainly composed of two infantry battalions and one mountain artillery battalion, and commanded by Colonel Kasahara) of the 36th Division

---

109. Although the original plan called for four infantry battalions and one mountain artillery battalion of the 109th Division to be used in this phase of the operation, actually only about six and a half infantry companies were used in actual combat. The remainder of the strength was used to garrison the area between Wutai and Taihuaichen.

110. Although it was originally planned that the second phase of this operation would last 24 days, the objective was attained in a much shorter period of time as no large enemy force was encountered.

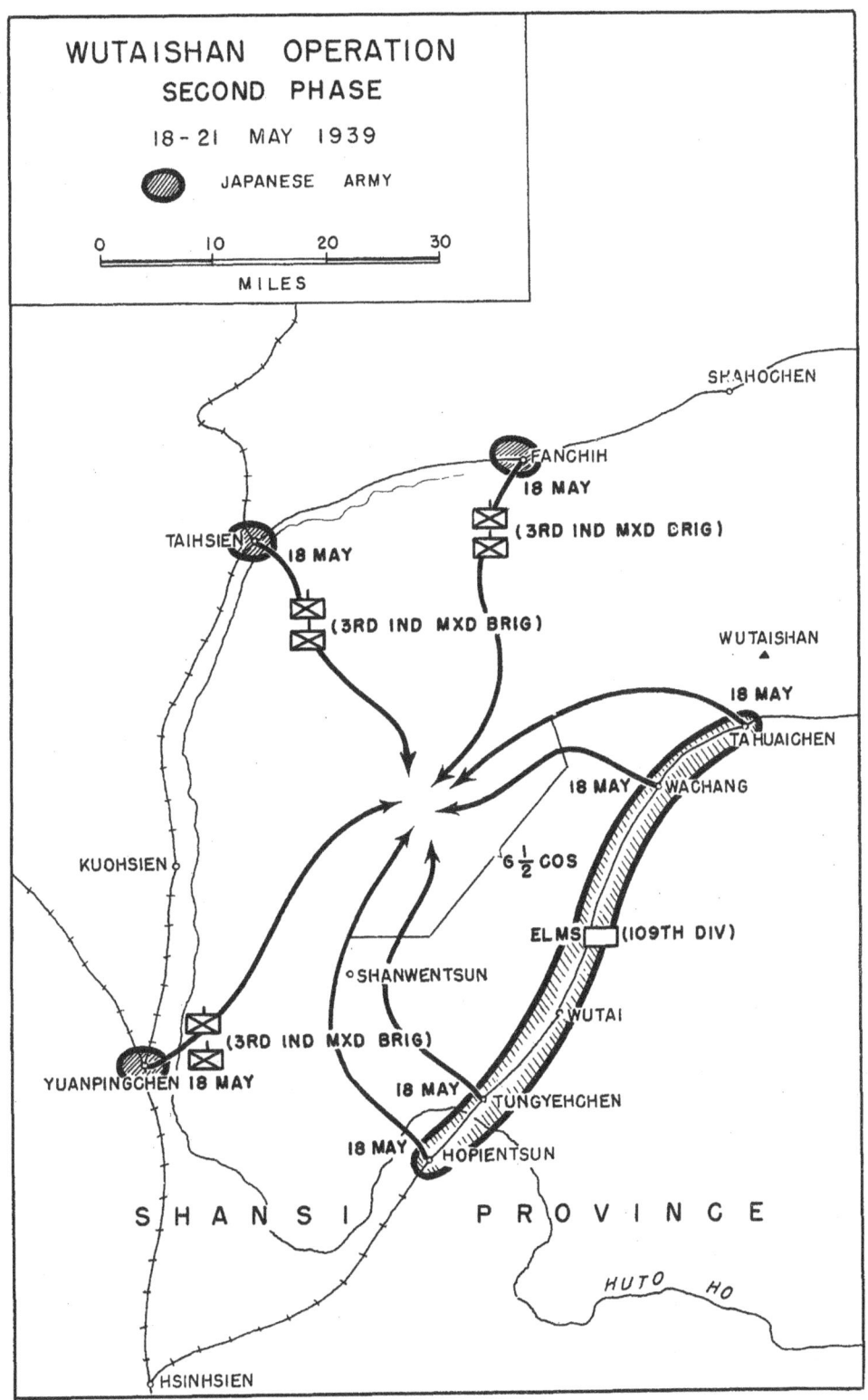

left Taihuaichen on the night of 4 June, and on 5 July destroyed some enemy troops. The same day it arrived at Shihtsui. Subsequently, it formed into three columns and attacked Lungchuankuan, while sending a part of its force to Yaotungshih to cut off the enemy's retreat, but the main force of the enemy had already fled far to the east.[111] The punitive force, after having mopped up the immediate area, returned to Shihtsui on the 8th. (Map 21)

The Fourth Phase (Mopping up Hungchiachai and Vicinity)

It was planned that the 10th Division would cooperate in the 1st Army operation by advancing a unit composed of approximately one infantry battalion to the vicinity of Hsiaochiaochen via the Huto Ho valley. On 16 June, the Army, in accordance with the plan, ordered the commanders of the 36th Division and the 4th Independent Mixed Brigade to carry out the fourth phase of the operation. At the same time the Army specified their advance routes. The 36th Division was assigned the Tungyehchen - Fuchengkou - Tsungchuang - Hungchiachai road, the Shihfussu - Hungchiachai road and Wutai - Shihfussu - Shihlipu road while the 4th Independent Mixed Brigade was assigned the Kuantoutsun - Yinweiho - Hsiaochiaochen road and the Cheluntsun - Chingshuikou - Hungchiachai road. The Army also stated that the departure from Tungyehchen and Wutai would be on the 19 June, from Kuantoutsun and

---

111. As the operation was conducted earlier than planned, elements of the 110th Division were not in position in the Sha Ho valley and the main force of the enemy escaped to the east.

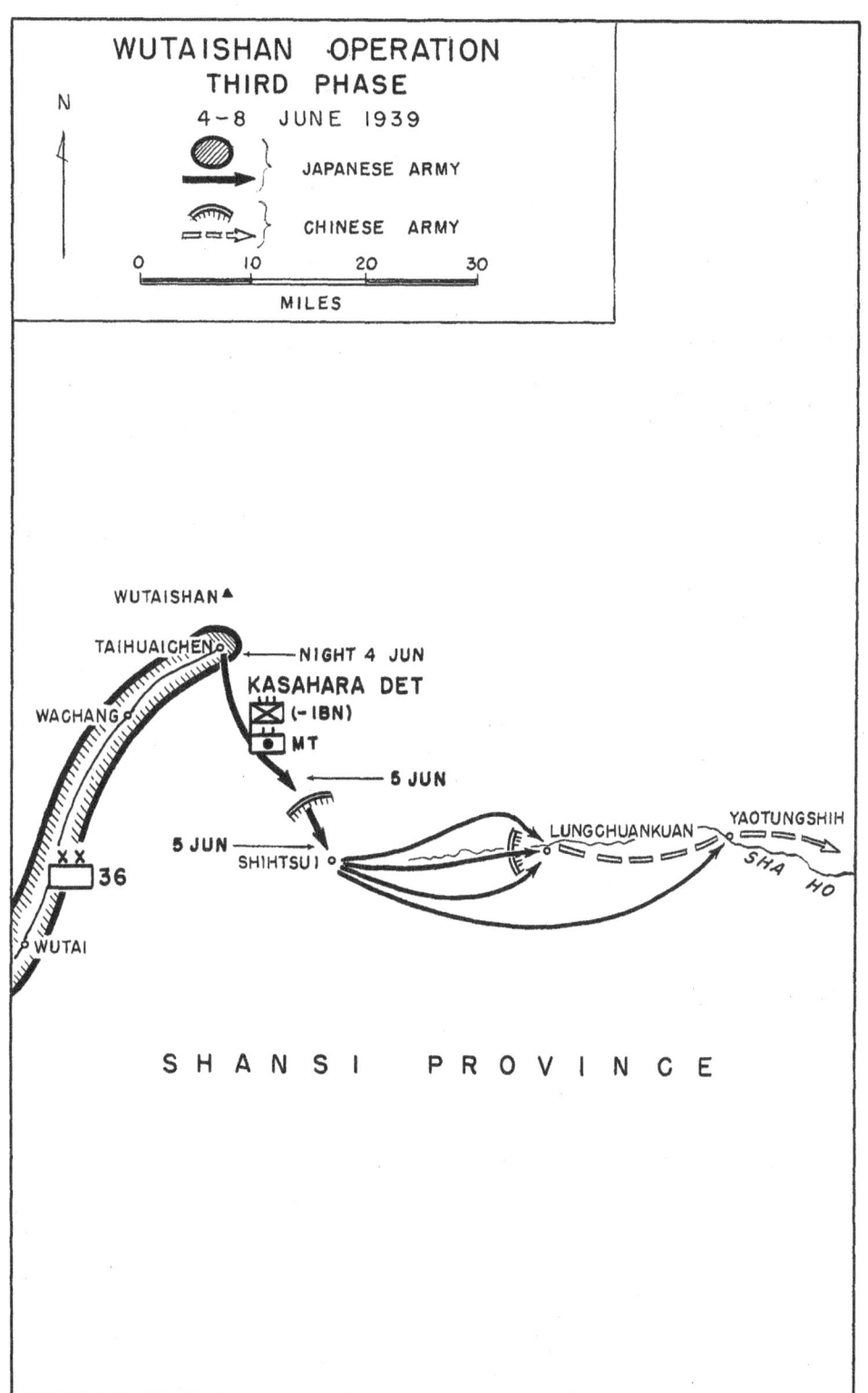

Cheluntsun on the 20th and from Tsungchuang on the 21st.

The 36th Division formed three columns on 19 June and proceeded to Hungchiachai; the right column (mainly composed of two infantry companies and one mountain artillery battery) taking the Tungyehchen - Fuchengkou - Tsungchuang road, the central column (mainly composed of six infantry companies and two mountain artillery batteries) taking the Wutai - Shihfussu road, and the left column (mainly composed of one infantry company and one mountain artillery section) taking the Nantahsien - Hsiaokengchiachuang - Paisanchen road. They converged at Hungchiachai on the 22d. In the meantime, in the vicinity of Chenchiachuang the central and left columns attacked the enemy forces holding out in the hills extending from north to south of the area, and put them to flight eastward. The 4th Independent Mixed Brigade formed two columns on 20 June, and proceeded to Chingshuikou. The right column (mainly composed of two infantry companies) took the Kuantoutsun - Yinweiho - Hsiaochiaochen road, and the left column (approximately the same strength) took the Wukuankou - Yuanchuanteng road. On the 21st they made a combined assault against approximately 200 enemy troops in the hills north of Chingshuikou and defeated them.

A part of the 10th Division reached the line crossing Hungtzutien from north to south on the 17th, and later advanced in two columns (each column composed of two infantry companies), destroying a small number of enemy troops. It arrived at Hsiaochiaochen on the 22d and made contact with the 4th Independent Mixed Brigade there. (Map 22)

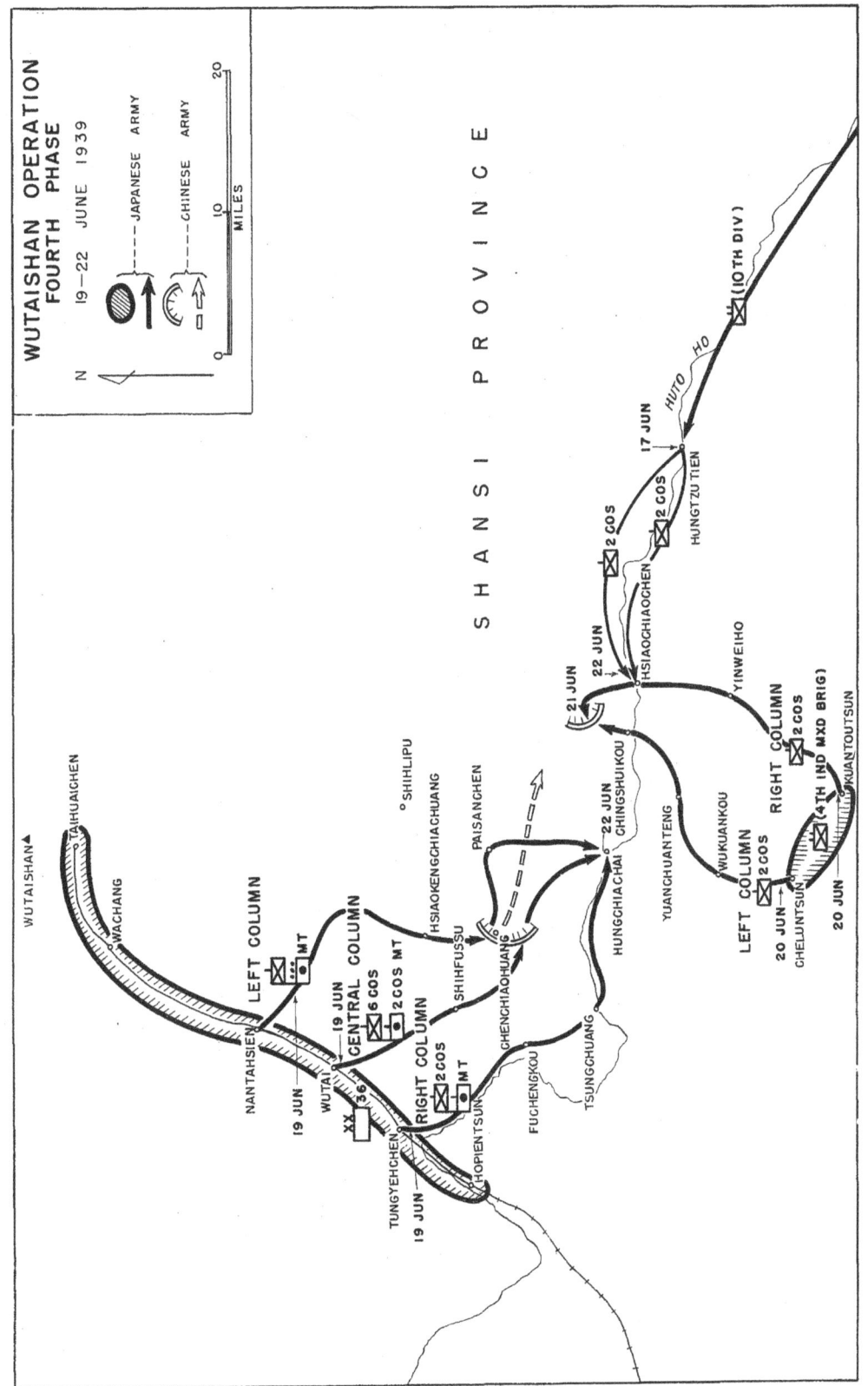

Eastern Shansi Province Operation

Situation Prior to the Operation

Since the 1st Army had detached an element of its units for the Tungshan Operation, enemy troops, after the 108th Division guarding the Changchih area had moved to the sector along the Tatung - Fenglingtu railway gradually assembled in the southeastern part of Shansi Province centering about Changchih, making the area a base for enemy activities to disturb the peace along the Tatung - Fenglingtu and the Peiping - Hankou railways. This enemy force consisted of about 80,000 Nationalist Army troops commanded by Wei Lihuang and Pang Pinghsun and about 20,000 Communist troops commanded by Chu Te.

The 36th and 37th Divisions newly assigned to the command of the 1st Army in April had taken over the defense missions of the 109th and 20th Divisions, and completed the change-over by the end of June, thus releasing the 20th and 109th Divisions to prepare for the next operation.

Tactical Command

The North China Area Army, in accordance with the plan for the second phase of the mopping-up operation, planned to launch a mopping-up operation in the southeastern sector of Shansi Province when the newly assigned units arrive in April and May to take over the garrison and guard duties of the old units. Therefore, on 30 May four infantry battalions, one mountain artillery battalion (less one battery) and one engineer company were detached from the 1st Army and dispatched to Hsingtai to enter the command of the 10th Division commander. Subsequently, on 10 June, the Area Army issued the following orders:

    1. The 1st Army, with as large a force as possible, shall start on 5 July from the Antse - Nankuanchen - Hoshun line and on 7 July from the Tachiaochen - Icheng line and shall destroy the enemy in the Changchih Plain and the nearby mountainous regions.

    The 10th Division, with the units sent as reinforcements from the 1st Army constituting its main force, and with as large a force as possibly can be detached from the various units of the Division, shall advance on 5 July from the vicinity of Wuan and cooperate with the 1st Army's operation.

    The 35th Division, with three infantry battalions and one mountain artillery battalion, shall launch its operation on 12 July from the vicinity of Poai and, advancing to the vicinity of Chincheng, in cooperation with the 1st Army shall destroy the enemy.

    2. In order to check the possible escape of enemy units to the east during the operation in the vicinity of Changchih, the 10th Division shall leave a roving element on the road connecting Shehsien and Linhsien, and the 35th Division shall take similar measures in the vicinity of Nantsun.

    3. For the maintenance of the 1st Army units advancing to the vicinity of Changchih and Chincheng, the 10th Division shall secure the road connecting Wuan, Shehsien, Lucheng and Changchih and will be responsible for supply to the 1st Army, while the 35th Division shall assist in the logistics of the 1st Army by stockpiling munitions and provisions in the vicinity of Chincheng.

    4. Once the mopping-up operation is completed, the 1st Army shall occupy limited strategic points on the Changchih Plain and, by conducting mobile operations covering as wide an area as possible in the vicinity, shall prevent the enemy from entering the plain and using it as a base to conduct assaults against other regions.

Tactical command of the various units in accordance with the above disposition was roughly as follows:

<u>1st Army</u>

The 1st Army laid down its plan of operations on 12 June with the idea of dividing the Army's operational sector into two fronts, the south and north. The north front was to commence action on 5 July with 11½ infantry battalions and about 4 artillery battalions from the northwest toward the vicinity of Changchih, and the south front, with about 9 infantry battalions and 3 artillery battalions, was to commence movement on 7 July from the west toward Changchih.

Units and their strength in this operation were planned as follows:

On the north front: An element of the 108th Division (approximately three infantry battalions plus one artillery battalion), the 109th Division (plus one heavy field artillery battery, but minus five infantry battalions and two mountain artillery batteries), and an element of the 4th Independent Mixed Brigade (one and one half infantry battalions, one mountain artillery battery and one mountain artillery section.)

On the south front: The 20th Division (plus two mountain artillery battalions and one heavy field artillery battery, but minus three infantry battalions, and two artillery battalions).[112]

The 1st Army's operational plan was divided into three phases on the north front and into two phases on the south front as follows:

---

112. Actually, during the initial phase of the operation, almost all the main strength of the 20th Division and an element of the 36th Division (approximately one infantry battalion) participated in the operation and on 10 July an element of the 108th Division (approximately two and one-half infantry battalions) was ordered to take part in the operation.

First Phase on the North Front (about six days).

The 108th Division was to make preparations for an operation in the vicinity of Antse, the 109th Division in the vicinity of Nankuanchen and the 4th Independent Mixed Brigade in the vicinity of Hoshun. Action was to be launched by the 108th and 109th Divisions on 5 July, and the 4th Independent Mixed Brigade on 3 July. The 108th Division was to advance to the vicinity of Liangmacheng, the 109th Division to the line connecting Chinhsien and Wuhsiang and the 4th Independent Mixed Brigade to the vicinity of Liaohsien and Yushe. The 4th Independent Mixed Brigade was to return to its original base after mopping-up the area in the vicinity of Liaohsien and Yushe.

Second Phase on the North Front (about seven days).

The 108th and 109th Divisions were to start from the line connecting Liangmacheng and Wuhsiang and attack the enemy in the vicinity of Changchih and Tunliu.

During this time, the 36th Division was to guard the area north of and including Fenshuiling.

First Phase on the South Front (about 11 days).

The southern front units were to make preparations for an operation in the vicinity of Chianghsien, start on 7 July from the vicinity of Tachaochen and Icheng and advance to a line on the Chin Ho in the vicinity of Yangcheng and Tuanshihchen.

Third Phase on the North Front and Second Phase on the South Front (about seven days).

The Army, with the two groups operating on both the north and south fronts planned to seize and destroy the enemy in the vicinity of Changchih and Tunliu and the sector to the south. With the advance of the 20th Division to the line connecting Changchih and Tunliu, the 108th Division was to return to its original base and the 109th Division to move to the sector north of Hutingchen.

After completion of the advance operation, the Army planned to occupy strategic key points north of Changchih and prevent enemy forces from venturing into the area by mopping up as wide an area as possible. To this end, the 20th Division was to garrison the Changchih Plain and the 109th Division the Chinhsien Plain.

The 10th Division

The 10th Division, with the Taniguchi Unit (the Taniguchi Mixed Brigade [comprising four infantry battalions, two mountain artillery batteries, and one engineer company detached from the 109th Division] plus one and a half infantry battalions and one artillery battery from the 10th Division) planned to make preparations for the operation in the vicinity of Wuan, and was to start moving on 5 July and advance to the vicinity of Shehsien about 10 July[113] and then advance to the vicinity of Lucheng and Changchih.[114]

---

113. This period corresponds to the first phase of the operation on the north front of the 1st Army.
114. This period corresponds to the second phase of operation on the north front of the 1st Army.

During this period, the Division was to secure the road connecting Wuan, Shehsien and Changchih and to instruct the Murozumi Unit (comprising nine lines of communications motor transport companies) to supply the 20th, 108th and 109th Divisions in the vicinity of Changchih.

Further, the 10th Division planned to dispatch from its south front about half an infantry battalion to the vicinity of Linhsien and one infantry company to the vicinity of Kucheng to check possible flight of the enemy to the east.

The 35th Division

The 35th Division realized that, in view of the enemy situation along the Chincheng road, it would be impossible to arrive in the vicinity of Chincheng on or about 16 July and carry out the supply of the 1st Army if it were to leave the vicinity of Poai on 12 July in accordance with the Area Army order. Therefore, it decided to start moving on 6 July. With its main body (consisting of five infantry battalions, six artillery batteries and one mountain artillery battalion) the division planned to proceed northward along the Chincheng road to Chincheng[115] and near Chincheng, in co-operation with the 20th Division, to contact the enemy and, after the 20th Division advanced into Chincheng, to return to its original station, withdrawing from the area. However, it also planned to continue maintaining the

---

115. This period corresponds to the second phase of the operation on the south front of the 1st Army.

security of the Chincheng road to prepare for the operation of supplying the 1st Army.

With an element (about half an infantry battalion) the division planned to advance to Nantsun from Huihsien and prevent the enemy from escaping to the east.

Outline of the Operation

A little more strength than that stipulated in the plan participated in the operation.

An element (consisting of about one and one-half infantry battalions, one mountain artillery battery and one mountain artillery section) of the 4th Independent Mixed Brigade on the north front of the 1st Army, started moving on 3 July while an element (consisting of about one infantry battalion) of the 36th Division and the 109th Division started moving on 5 July. The element of the 4th Independent Mixed Brigade defeating the enemy on its front, occupied Liaohsien on the 4th and, in cooperation with elements of the 36th and 109th Divisions, occupied Yushe on the 8th. The element of the 36th Division returned to its original station on the 10th, while the element of the 4th Independent Mixed Brigade returned to Hoshun on the 14th, both forces mopping up the enemy on their return routes.

The 109th Division advanced in columns sweeping away the enemy confronting it, and, on the 5th, occupied Wuhsiang and Chinhsien without meeting strong enemy resistance. It then began to prepare for the next operation.

The Yano Detachment of the 108th Division, taking into consideration the rise in the level of the Chin Ho, occupied, with its advance party, the crossing point at Fuchengchen on the 3d. The main body of the Detachment left the vicinity of Antse on the 5th, and occupied Liangmachen on the 7th and Changtienchen on the 9th, after sweeping away the confronting enemy. It then prepared for the next operation.

An element of the 108th Division (consisting of about two and one-half infantry battalions) started moving from the vicinity of Foushan on the 10th and, after mopping up the enemy in the east sector, returned to Foushan on the 12th.

On the south front, the 20th Division started an assault on 7 July against strong enemy positions east of Chianghsien (on the right flank, the assault was started on 5 July), and broke through after a fierce battle. It advanced to Chungtsun on the 8th and Chinshui on the 9th. However, rain made the advance of vehicle units difficult, so the Division decided to remain at Chungtsun and Chinshui for the time being and prepare for future operations.

The Taniguchi Unit in the 10th Division sector started moving from the vicinity of Wuan on 5 July and occupied Shehsien on the 8th. However, this unit found it impossible to advance further because bridges had been washed away by a flood brought about by heavy rain beginning the night of the 8th. The unit therefore decided to wait and advance when the weather cleared.

An element of the 10th Division advancing from the south sector, occupied Kucheng on the 16th and Linhsien on the 19th.

The 35th Division left the vicinity of Poai on 5 July and broke through the provincial border on the 11th, after overcoming considerable enemy resistance. An element of the same Division left Huihsien on the 5th and advanced as far as Hantsun by the 8th.

The 108th and 109th Divisions on the north front of the 1st Army resumed the advance on 11 July, and the 109th Division, sweeping away any confronting enemy, captured Changchih on the 13th, while the 108th Division captured Changtzu on the 14th.

Subsequently, the commander of the 1st Army, in view of the difficulty experienced by the 20th Division in advancing because of the heavy rain and in view of the weak enemy resistance on the north front, planned to catch and destroy the enemy near Chincheng, and, on 15 July gave the 108th and 109th Divisions the following order:

> The 109th Division shall, if possible, advance to the area of Kaoping and cooperate with the 20th Division. The 108th Division shall reinforce the 109th Division when the latter advances toward Kaoping. At the same time, both Divisions shall execute the third phase of the operation in cooperation with the 20th Division.

The Area Army commander also issued the following order to the 35th Division on 17 July:

> The 35th Division shall advance with as great strength as possible to the vicinity of Chincheng, contact and destroy the enemy in cooperation with the 1st Army, and, if necessary, advance an element to Choutsunchen, thus facilitating the advance of the 20th Division to the left bank of the Chin Ho.[116]

---

116. According to an order of the Area Army commander dated the 13 July approximately one infantry battalion of the 14th Division was placed under the 35th Division command.

The 35th Division, even after occupying the provincial border, continued advancing and occupied Tienchingkuan on the 18th and Chincheng on the 19th, repeatedly defeating a stubbornly resisting enemy. Immediately after occupying these places, an element of the Division advanced to Choutsunchen while another element reached Hsiuwu from Chincheng via Liushukou.

The main body of the 35th Division met the 20th Division, which arrived in the vicinity of Chincheng on the 20th, and, after transferring the garrisoning of the Chincheng area to the 20th Division in accordance with an Area Army order, the 35th Division withdrew from Chincheng on the 24th and secured the Chincheng - Poai road in order to carry out the supply of the 20th Division.

From 13 to 15 July, the 20th Division resumed action from Chungtsun and Chinshui, and, on the 19th, elements of the Division crossed the Chin Ho at Yangcheng and Tuanshihchen. The Division advanced to Chincheng on the 20th and to Kaoping on the 21st, destroying the enemy on the way. However, the main body of the right column encountered a strong enemy force west of Yangcheng but defeated it before crossing the Chin Ho on the 25th and arriving at Chincheng on the 27th.

The 108th and 109th Divisions began the third phase of the operation on the 17th and, in order to cooperate with the 20th Division, advanced into the Chincheng area. On the 18th they occupied Kaoping and on the 20th advanced into Chincheng, defeating the enemy on the way.

The Taniguchi Unit of the 10th Division, stayed in the vicinity of Shehsien until 6 August as heavy rain had washed away bridges and made the roads practically unusable. From the end of July the weather improved, therefore, the unit left Shehsien on 7 August and advanced to Licheng on the 8th. On 21 August it finally opened the road between Hantan and Changchih. (Map 23)

The 1st Army commander decided to station strong units in Chincheng with the idea of conducting mopping-up operations against the enemy in the south-eastern part of Shansi Province. Thus on 21 July the commander stationed the 20th Division in the Chincheng - Kaoping area and the 109th Division in the Changchih - Chinhsien area to mop-up the enemy in their respective districts. He also assigned to an element of the 108th Division the duty of mopping up enemy remnants on the right bank of Chin Ho near Chinyuan. This element returned to its original station after successfully completing the mission.

From 6 to 8 August the 109th Division swept away one and one-half enemy divisions near Peishechen and from 7 to 12 August the 108th Division attacked and dealt a crushing blow to an enemy of approximately two divisions plus 1,500 men near Chungtsun.

From 9 to 11 August, the 20th Division mopped up approximately 2,000 enemy soldiers stationed near Tienchingkuan. Also from 10 to 13 August the division encircled and destroyed an enemy of approxi-

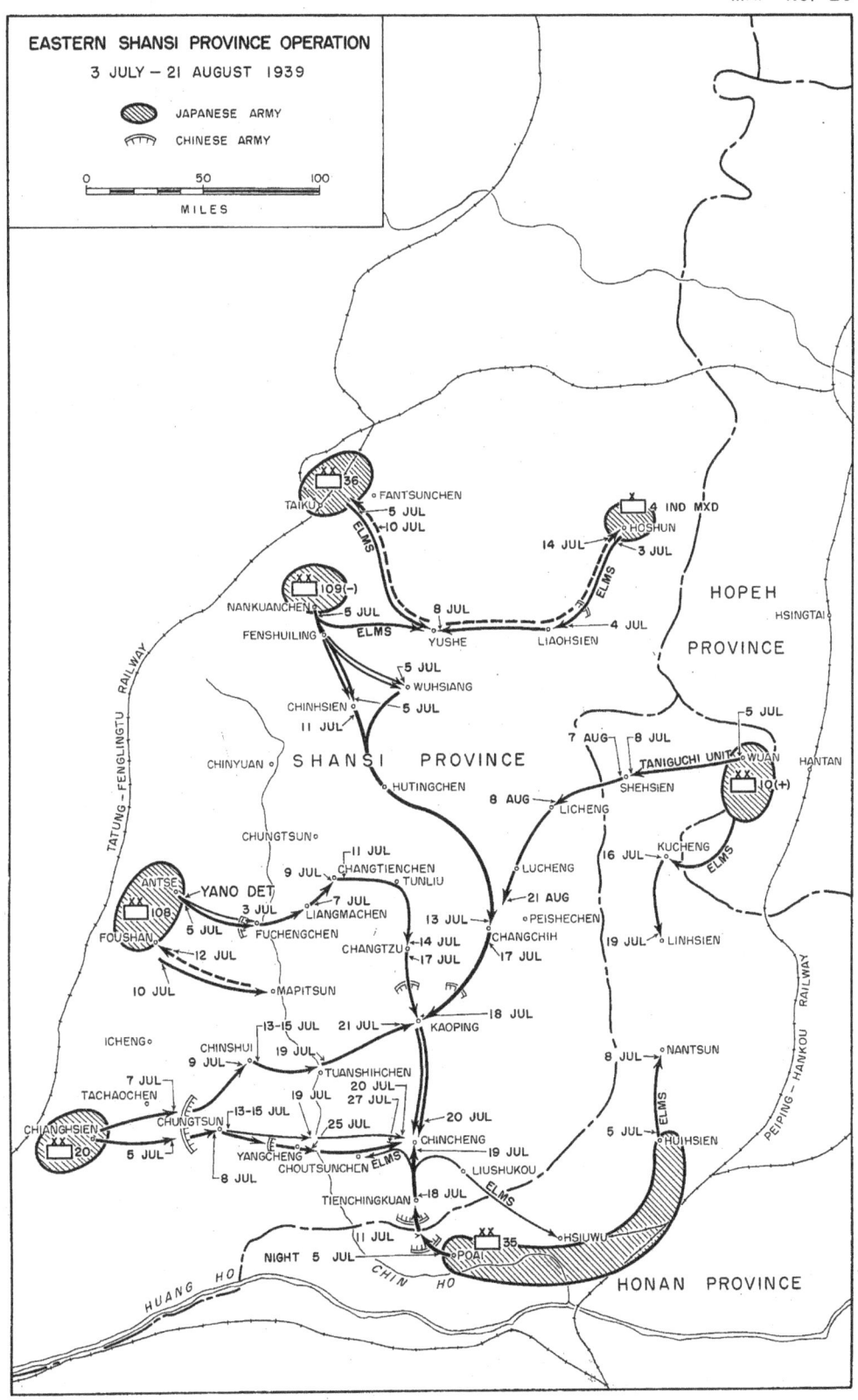

mately 10,000 massed northwest of Chincheng. The 109th, 36th and 108th Divisions caused heavy casualties to approximately two enemy divisions around Chinhsien in a mopping-up operation on 7 and 8 August.

On 10 August the 1st Army commander, with a view to establishing permanent stations at strategic points in the Changchih and Chinhsien areas, ordered the 20th Division to leave Chincheng between 16 to 18 August and advance northward to Changchih and Chinhsien to mop up enemy remnants there.

On 9 September, the Army ordered the 109th Division to relieve the 20th Division in the area around Licheng and Lucheng, which the latter division had been temporarily defending from the latter part of August, as it planned to use the main strength of the 20th Division for mopping-up operations in the Changchih Plain. (Map 24)

After the completion of the Eastern Shansi Operation at the end of August, approximately six enemy divisions remained massed near Changchih apparently still planning to attack despite the heavy losses they had already sustained. Their fighting spirit was high and it seemed very likely that they would attempt to invade the Changchih Plain.

At the end of September, the 1st Army decided to destroy this force, and accordingly published the following plan:

Operational Plan

    a. The 20th Division shall employ an element to capture

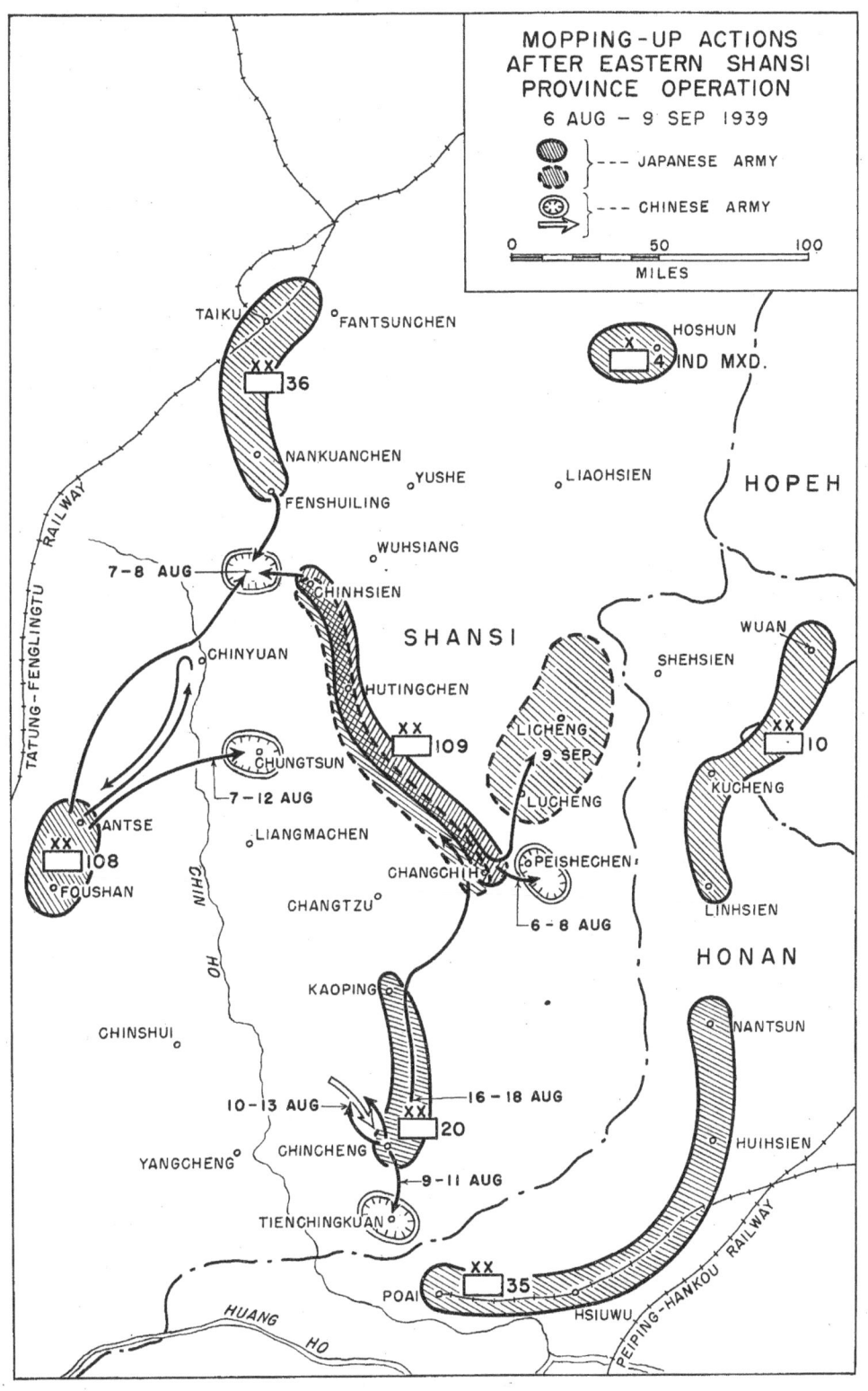

Changtzu and another to capture Hukuan: The main body of the Division (consisting of approximately five infantry battalions) shall concentrate secretly near Changchih and prepare for the next attack.

    b. The 109th Division shall complete by 5 October the concentration of a force near Changchih consisting of approximately three infantry battalions.

    c. The 20th Division and elements of the 109th Division shall commence action on 7 October. The 20th Division shall search out, encircle and destroy the enemy in front of Changtzu while the 109th Division elements shall destroy the enemy on their front.
    The attack on Taiichen shall be the mission of the 20th Division, and the attack on Yinchengchen, the mission of the 109th Division elements.

    d. The field for this operation shall be the area north of the heights north of Kaoping. After the completion of this operation, the 20th Division shall assume its position for the next operation while the 109th Division elements shall return to their original station.

    e. The 36th Division and the 4th Independent Mixed Brigade shall each transfer approximately half an infantry battalion to the command of the 20th Division commander.

In the middle of September the 109th Division, in accordance with Army orders, relieved the 20th Division in garrisoning the Lucheng and Licheng sectors. At the end of September, the disposition of the 20th Division strength was: on the front line in the Changtzu sector approximately two infantry battalions; at Sutienchen, approximately half an infantry battalion; at Hukuan, approximately one infantry battalion; and near Changchih, approximately four infantry battalions, four infantry companies and the main force of other line branch units. The lines of communication in the rear were garrisoned by approximately four infantry battalions. The Army commander issued the necessary orders according to the operational plan.

Changchih Area Operation

The 20th Division decided to attack the enemy near Shihchechen from the north and south with a powerful force (three infantry battalions and one mountain artillery battery from the north and four infantry battalions, one artillery battalion and one cavalry regiment (with half an infantry battalion attached) from the south). In the meantime, the Division, seizing the opportunity, assigned another element (Division Headquarters, two infantry battalions and the main body of an artillery unit) stationed near Changtzu to proceed to Shihchechen. The north and south units started action simultaneously at midnight of 7 October. They went forward in columns, overcoming the enemy on the way. On the morning of the 8th, the Division commander, taking advantage of the fact that units of the southern force had advanced to Fengposhan, ordered the unit stationed at Changtzu to attack. The coordinated attack by the three columns inflicted heavy casualties on the enemy. These attacks lasted from the afternoon of the 8th to the 9th, and, on the 10th, the Division returned to its original station after having mopped up enemy remnants in the area.

In accordance with the 1st Army order that two infantry battalions of the 109th Division were to advance to the vicinity of Hsihuochen from the vicinity of Sutienchen via Yinchengchen, this force started to advance in columns on the evening of 7 October.[117] On the 8th, the two battalions defeated a strong enemy force in position on the line connecting Tungkou and Huangling, before occupying Yinchengchen on the same day. Later, they massed near Changchih, after mopping up the enemy in the area south of Hukuan. (Map 25)

Operations on the Mongolian Border

Spring Counterattack Operation

During the April offensive, it gradually became clear that in the Mongolian border area, the enemy was employing the Ho Chukuo Army to assume the offensive against the Suiyuan area from the south and the Men Pingyueh Army and others against the Kuyang - Paotou area from the west in an attempt to regain Suiyuan.

The Japanese Mongolia Garrison Army (commanded by Lt Gen Shigeru Hasunuma, and formed around the 26th Division, the Cavalry Group (minus the 4th Brigade) and the 2d Independent Mixed Brigade) was preparing for action in order to take the initiative and defeat the enemy, when, on 10 April signs of an enemy offensive became markedly conspicuous in the sector east of Pienkuan and Wuyuan.

Therefore, the Army resolved to take the initiative immediately and directed each force to seek out and attack the enemy stationed near its operational sector.

---

117. Although the plan called for three infantry battalions to be used in the operation, only two were used. The third battalion remained to garrison around Changchih.

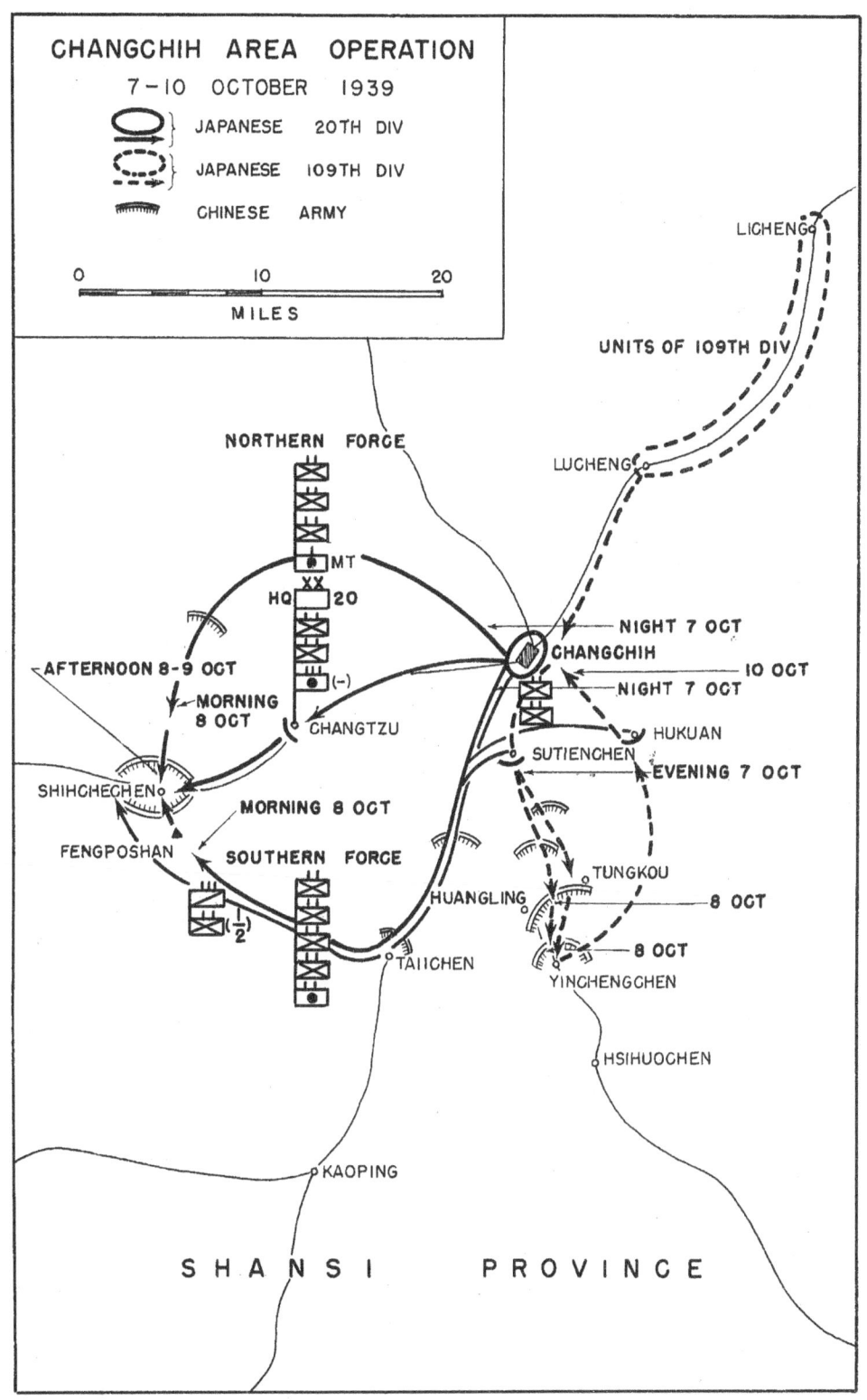

The Cavalry Group, starting its movement on 10 April, occupied Anpei and mopped up this sector as well as the area surrounding Kuyang; and then, turning to the south, it destroyed an enemy force moving northward in the vicinity of Salachi. Further, it destroyed enemy troops successively at Mutouhu, Kaolungtukou and the sector northeast of Anpei.

The 26th Division, meanwhile, destroyed enemy troops massing at Pienkuan, Yulin, the vicinity of Santaokou, north of Suiyuan, the Yinshan Mountain Range, the sector south of the Peiping - Suiyuan railway and in the vicinity of Manhanshan. The Mongolian Garrison Army then returned its units to their original stations, while leaving behind a force at Anpei to provide against future enemy attacks. (Map 26)

This operation ended on 31 May, having succeeded in frustrating the Eighth War Sector Army's offensive plan.

Elements of the 10th and 15th Air Regiments and the Mongolian Army cooperated in this operation.

Enemy's Winter Offensive and Japanese Counterattack

In the winter offensive assumed by the enemy in December throughout the whole line, there was no major offensive in north China, but in the Mongolian border area, there was a fairly strong attack. The enemy seemed to be planning an attack against the Paotou area, as the Ma Chanshan Army, about 1,000 strong, cut off communications between Suiyuan and Paotou from the sector south of Salachi, while the

MAP NO. 26

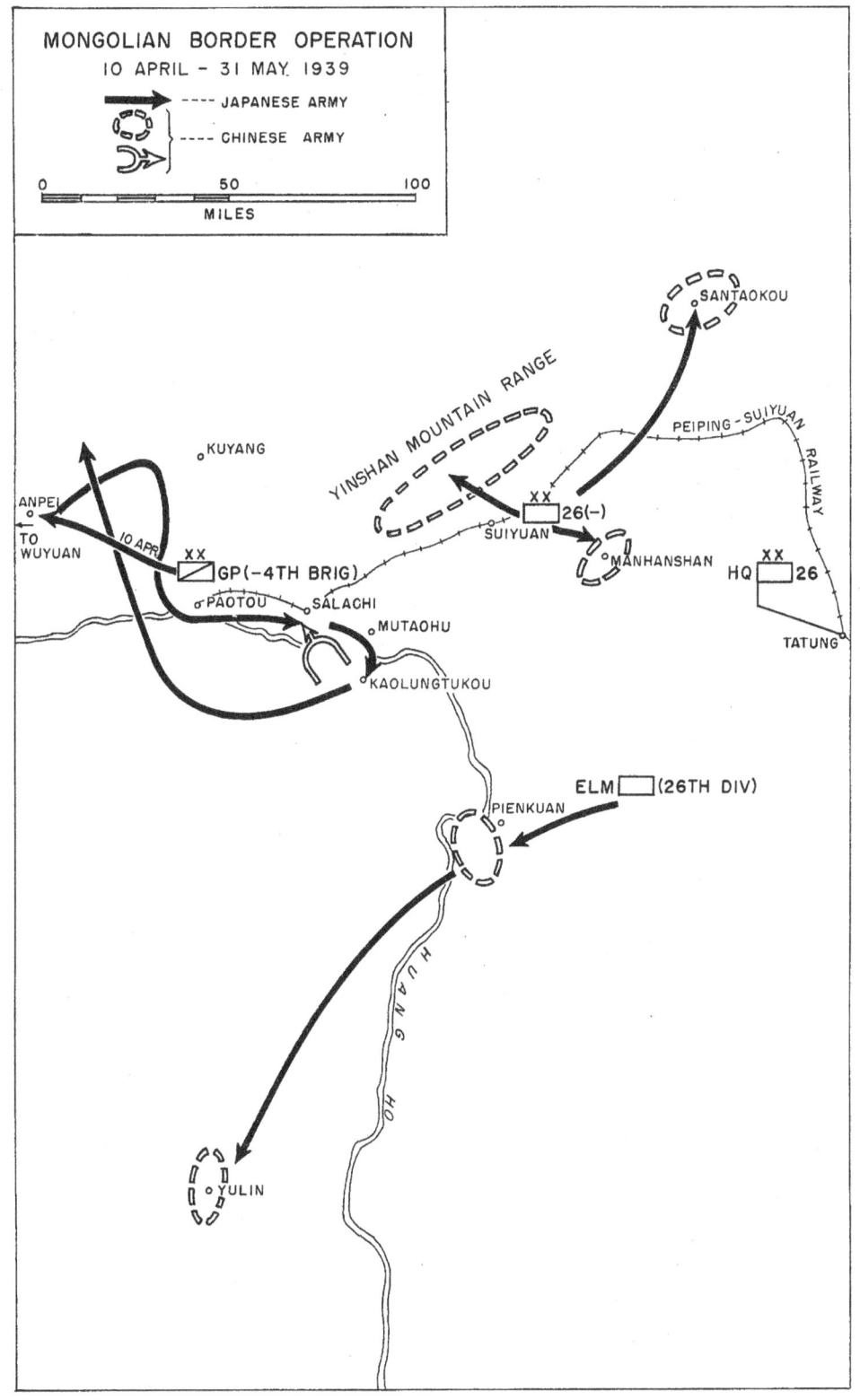

main force of the Fu Tsoi Army gradually pushed forward from early December in order to attack Paotou from the south and west.

To meet this offensive, the Mongolia Garrison Army took action to reinforce the infantry regiment of the 26th Division and the Cavalry Group.

From 11 December, the Cavalry Group took the initiative and repulsed the Ma Chanshan Army south of Salachi and further, from the 18th, beat back the Men Pingyueh Army, about 2,000 strong, which had invaded the sector south of Paotou.

On the morning of the 20th, a hostile force, 6,000 to 7,000 strong, attacked the northwest and northeast gates of Paotou but the small garrison unit fought off the attacks. On the same day, the Kobayashi Unit, stationed at Salachi, decided to relieve Paotou, and a part of the unit launched a counterattack at 1400 hours on the 21st. During the afternoon of the 22d, the main force of the unit pursued the enemy to the northwest while another element pursued the enemy northward. The main force of the Kobayashi Unit continued to advance westward from north of Paotou and, on the way, fought against a superior enemy force in the vicinity of Shapatzu and Chienkoutzu. It forced the enemy to retreat and, when the enemy near Paotou also began to retreat, the Unit attacked the flanks of the fleeing enemy before massing near Paotou on the evening of the same day. (Map 27)

Subsequently, from 28 December 1939 to 4 January 1940, Japanese

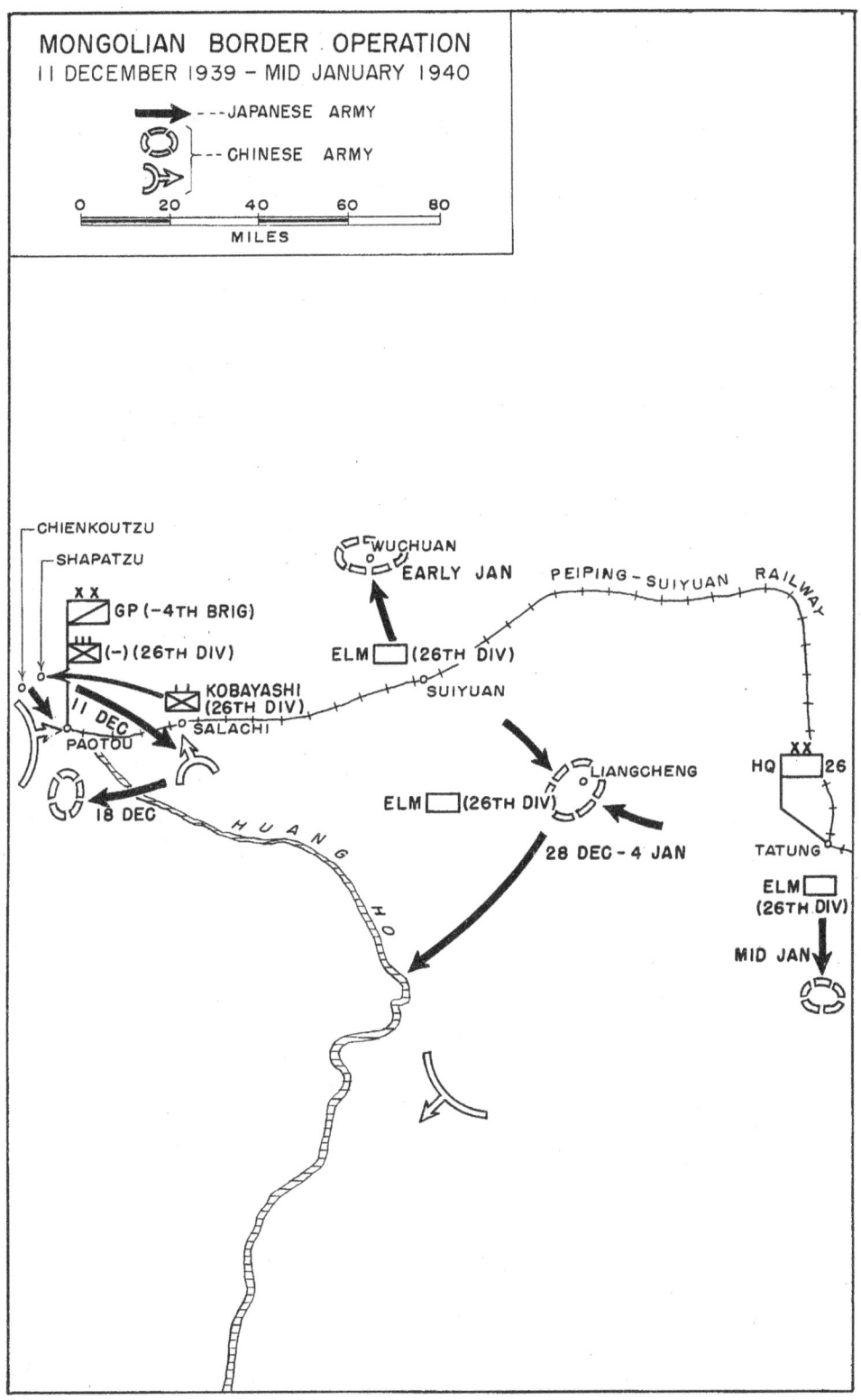

forces encircled and attacked infiltrating enemy troops near Liangcheng, and beat them back to the left bank of the Huang Ho.

In early January, the Japanese Army destroyed the enemy active near Wuchuan and those in the sector south of Tatung in the middle of the month, thus frustrating the enemy's winter offensive plan.

The Northern Kiangsu Province Operation

Situation Prior to the Operation

The enemy in northern Kiangsu Province was from 35,000 to 50,000 strong. It was composed of the regular army's 57th and 89th Armies, elements of the 51st Army, guerrillas and the security units. Indications were that its main force was deployed in the Huaiyin and Ssuyang areas and elements in Tunghai and the sector to the west. In early February, irregulars advanced to reconnoiter.

The 21st Division under the command of the Japanese 12th Army was responsible for the defense of the northern Kiangsu Province area and on its eastern front, occupied the line connecting Ssuhsien, Suchien and Paochechen, where it constantly conducted mopping-up operations.

Southern Shantung Province was defended by the Japanese 114th Division which was garrisoned in Taierhchuang and Lini.[118]

For protection against the enemy from the north, the Central China Expeditionary Army garrisoned the line connecting Tienchang,

---

118. No troops were disposed in the area from Lini to Chingtao.

Chiangtu and Jukao. At the same time, a special naval landing force held the port of Lienyun.

The North China Area Army had long desired to occupy northern Kiangsu Province, especially the area near Tunghai, the supply and communication center for enemy bandits. On 7 February, Imperial General Headquarters ordered the North China Area Army to dispose the main strength of the 5th Division at Chingtao and its vicinity and elements in the Tunghai district. The North China Area Army, therefore, decided to occupy the town of Tunghai as well as the strategic enemy base of Huaiyin and ordered the 12th Army to carry out mopping-up operations from late February against enemy bandits in the Hsuhaitao district (northern district of Kiangsu Province), and to garrison the necessary strength in Huaiyin, Hsinanchen and Tunghai districts. At the same time, a force chiefly composed of an infantry regiment and an artillery battalion of the 5th Division stationed in Chingtao was attached to the 12th Army by the Area Army for this operation. It also ordered the 7th Air Brigade to support the 12th Army.

The Army - Navy Agreement concerning this operation was concluded between the 12th Army and the 4th Fleet, and, in regard to air operations, an agreement was concluded between the Area Army and the 4th Fleet's Air Unit. The Army was to be responsible mainly for the occupation of Tunghai, and the Navy was to support a landing operation against the Antungwei district and a force going up the Kuan Ho.

Based on the Area Army order, the 12th Army prepared its plan to commence action late in February. In cooperation with the 7th Air Brigade and the Navy it planned first to occupy the Huaiyin district, thus intercepting the enemy's retreat route, and then to capture Tunghai. Subsequently, in accordance with this plan, it disposed its troops as shown on Chart 3.

Summary of Operational Progress

The main force of the 21st Division assembled in the vicinity of Suchien while elements of the Division assembled in and around Paochechen before launching operations on 24 February. They advanced to the line connecting Ssuyang, Shuyang, and Ahuchen on 27 and 28 February. However, the enemy in the vicinity of Ssuyang, contrary to expectations, made no resistance and showed signs of retreating toward the south of Huaiyin. The Army, therefore, decided to attack Huaiyin immediately, without awaiting the massing of its whole strength, and, at the same time, to crush the enemy in the sector north of the narrow area in the vicinity of Paoying. Thereupon, the Army ordered the main strength of the 21st Division and the Division's Azuma Raiding Unit, organized around two infantry companies, immediately to pursue and attack the enemy and to advance toward the Huaiyin area.

The main force of the 21st Division advanced rapidly to Huaiyin from the sector south of Tayun Ho despite the bad roads and occupied the town on 2 March. Subsequently, pursuing the enemy southward, the Division captured Huaian on the 3d, and Paoying on the 5th.

Meanwhile, the Army, in concert with the bombing by the air unit,

Chart No 3

Plan for Disposition of 12th Army troops, Northern Kiangsu Province Operation

Unit Name	Strength Employed	Departure point	Summary
21st Div	Unit chiefly composed of about 5 inf bns and 2 arty bns.	To be in Ssuyang, Shuyang and Ahuchen by 1 March	With the view to making a combined assault on Tunghai an element (approximately 1 inf bn), will prepare to drive to the line connecting Hutungkou and Fangshachieh. The main force will prepare to advance to Huaiyin.
5th Div	Unit chiefly composed of about 3 inf bns and 1 arty bn.	In order to concentrate troops in Hsinanchen and its vicinity the unit will commence going up the Kuan Ho on 1 March.	The unit will prepare to drive to Taishanchen district so that it may make an assault on Tunghai at any time with an element (1 inf bn). Its main force will prepare for a drive to Huaiyin. A unit, chiefly composed of half an inf bn and 1 arty btry will be dispatched to Kanyu on the 27 February to prepare for a drive against the enemy in the Tunghai area.
114th Div	Unit chiefly composed of about 1 inf bn and 1 arty btry.	To be in the vicinity of the border of Shantung Province along the Lini - Tunghai road by 26 February.	The unit will occupy Tancheng and its vicinity by 27 February with 1 inf co to secure the left flank rear of the 21st Div. The unit will prepare for a drive against the enemy in the Tunghai area after advancing to Shahochen on 3 March.
Total	About 9 inf bns and 3 arty bns and 1 arty btry		
Remarks		The Army headquarters will establish its command post in Tungshan on 26 February.	

inflicted a crushing blow against the enemy around Huaiyin and in the southeastern area.

Elements of the 5th Division sailed from Chingtao on 25 February, and landed in the vicinity of Antungwei on the 26th. Meanwhile, another force of the Division, which left Chingtao on the 28th, sailed up the Kuan Ho on 1 March and arrived in the vicinity of Hsinanchen and Hsiangshuikou the same day.

At that time it was estimated that the main force of the enemy troops operating in the Huaiyin area had retreated southward. On 1 March, therefore, the Army decided to order the 5th Division to attack Tunghai, and ordered the troops to be employed for the attack, consisting of one infantry battalion and one artillery battery of the 114th Division and one infantry battalion of the 21st Division, to enter the command of the 5th Division.

The 5th Division carried out an attack against Tunghai and captured it on 4 March.

Inasmuch as Founing was the key point through which a Third Power could send supplies and communications to the bandit groups in northern Kiangsu, the Army issued an order to the 21st Division on 3 March to attack Founing after the conclusion of the battle in the Huaiyin area. The 21st Division diverted the Azuma Raiding Unit from Huaian to Founing, and captured Founing on the 7th.

Since 5 March a powerful enemy force had been advancing northward from the sector east of Shuyang via Fangshachieh, the Army planned to catch and crush this force. It, therefore, ordered the 114th Division unit and one infantry battalion of the 21st Division operating along the Lunghai railway,[119] as well as elements of the 5th Division, to advance toward Fangshachieh from the direction of Taishanchen and from the sector north of the Lunghai railway. As these forces began an encircling movement on the 10th, the enemy retreated to the vicinity of Tangchien. Thereupon, the Army ordered troops of the 5th Division to advance southward, while troops of the 21st Division were ordered to attack from the Chienchiachi and Chenshihan areas. Thus, on or about 13 March, each unit pursued and engaged the enemy in combat. As a result, the enemy suffered heavy losses, and his main force retreated eastward and southeastward in confusion. The Japanese units continued to pursue and destroy the hostile troops retreating toward the Yunyen Ho. (Map 28) After this operation, the Army ordered the 5th Division to dispose a force, organized around one infantry regiment and one artillery battalion at such strategic points as Tunghai, Taishanchen, Hsinanchen and Founing and to charge them with the mopping up of the eastern sector of northern Kiangsu Province. At the same time, the Army placed the 21st Division in charge of the mopping-up operation in the western sector of northern Kiangsu Province. The two divisions disposed their elements as ordered.

---

119. These units, in accordance with orders from 1st Army, were on their way back to their original stations.

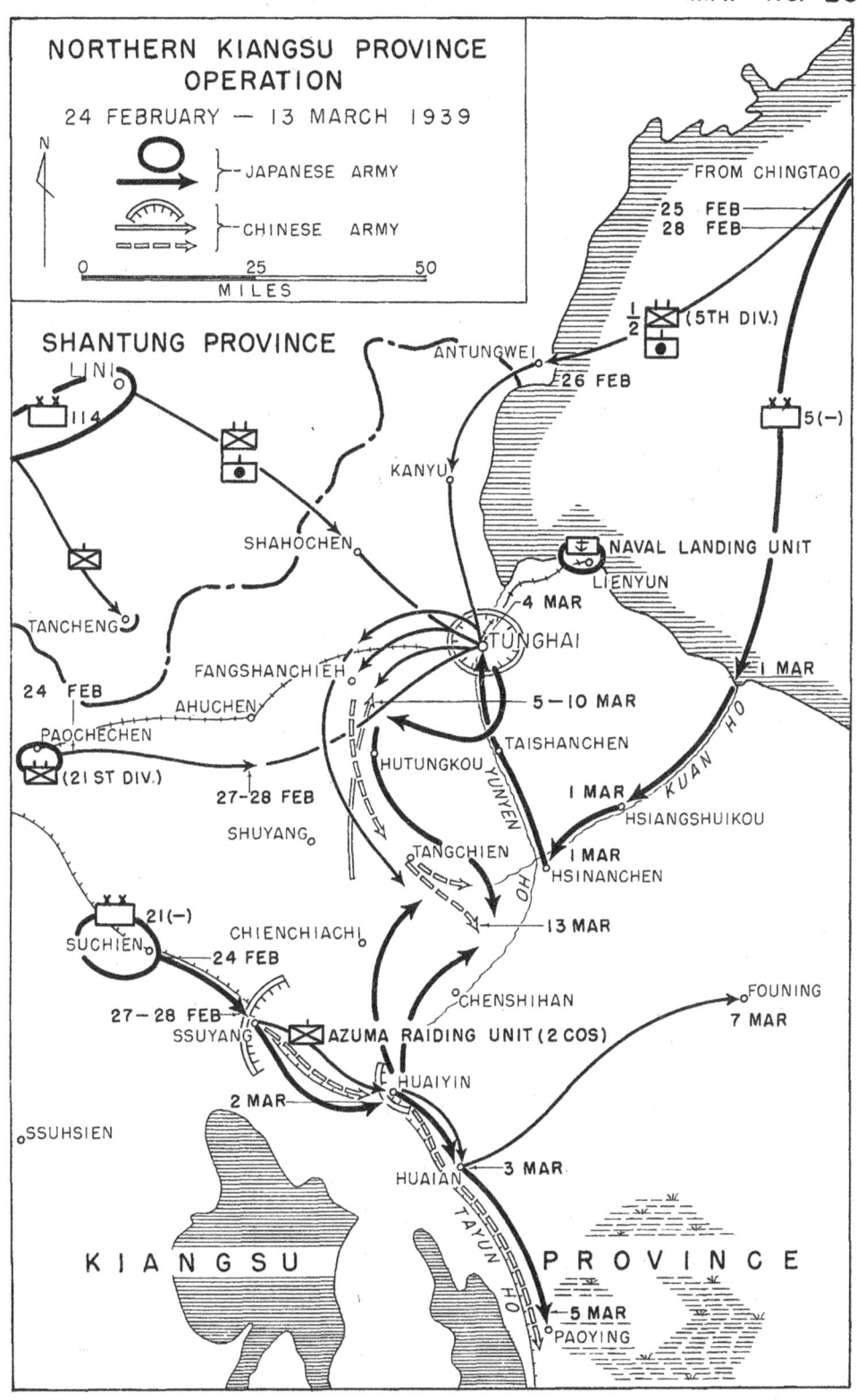

Southern Shantung Province Operation

Since Japanese troops had not been stationed in southern Shantung Province despite the fact that the 5th Division operated in this area before the Tungshan Operation, hostile Shih Yusan and Shen Hunglieh troops had gradually assembled in the area. After Yu Hsuehchung was appointed commander of the Shantung - Kiangsu War Sector, in cooperation with the Communist Army, he made this area a base for guerrilla activities in north China.

Early in April the enemy's 51st Army separated into small units and passed through the Japanese guard lines and assembled in the sector west of Ishui.

Furthermore, it appeared that this Army had disposed troops, which had begun arriving at Ishui about the latter part of April, in the vicinity of Kaoyai and Chiangyu, and also in the area between Chuhsien and Chucheng. Meanwhile, the 57th Army, which had been defeated in the northern Kiangsu Province Operation and which had retreated to the sector southwest of Chucheng had gradually advanced to Mengyin and the sector north of Lini. Also, the security units and the newly-organized divisions under the command of Shen Hunglieh were disposed along the perimeter of the positions of the regular Army forces, especially in the vicinity of Hsintai and Laiwu, while the Shantung Communist column was concentrated around the Ssushui area.

The strength of the enemy troops operating in the Taishan Mountain Range was estimated at between 50,000 to 70,000. The regular army, security units and the Communist guerrilla units constituted a joint front under the command of Yu Hsuehchung, who had undertaken the reorganization of the force.

Thereupon, the 12th Army decided to mop up this area, and ordered a force formed around the 5th Division, reinforced by elements of the 21st and 32d Divisions and 5th Independent Mixed Brigade, to launch operations on 4 June.

The First Air Brigade cooperated in this operation.

Summary of Operational Progress

On 4 June, the punitive forces of each unit simultaneously began moving from the vicinity of Lini, Feihsien, Hsintai, Laiwu, Poshan, Linchu, Antiu and Chucheng, and, in spite of intense heat, penetrated the steep Taishan Mountain Range where they destroyed the confronting enemy and advanced directly toward the Chuhsien and Ishui areas. On the 9th, the forces which had advanced from the north, occupied Ishui and Chuhsien, and the troops which attacked from the west and south, advanced to the line connecting Tatien, Hoyangchen, Tanfou and Nanma, tightened the encirclement and destroyed the enemy's main strength. Elements of the enemy sought to avoid contact with the Japanese troops by escaping to the mountainous area northwest of Ishui, to the vicinity of Jihchao, and also to the vicinity of Yunmengshan south of Mengyin. However, the Japanese Army continued to pursue the retreating enemy and to inflict heavy casualties.

From 15 June, Japanese reinforced troops attacked the enemy assembling in the mountainous district north of Ishui. At the same time, elements attacked the enemy in the vicinity of Yunmengshan and drove them into disorderly retreat.

Furthermore, from the 25th, an encircling operation was conducted from the vicinity of Nanma, Tanfou, Hsintai and Laiwu against the enemy assembling in the vicinity of Tachangchuang and several thousand enemy troops were destroyed.

Western Shantung Province Operation

Although western Shantung Province was frequently cleared by the Japanese mopping-up operations after the Tungshan Operation. Japanese troops were not stationed there, so that public peace could not be restored fully in this area. Communist troops infiltrated the area and their unceasing activities constituted a definite menace.

The North China Area Army, with a view to extending the area in which public peace had been established, decided to crush the bandit groups and destroy their bases in the area. The Area Army, therefore, ordered the 12th Army and groups directly attached to the Area Army to mop up the area.

The strength which participated in this operation was as given below:

Groups directly attached to the North China Area Army:

    The main force of the 14th Division

    Elements of the 10th Division

    Elements of the 35th Division

The 12th Army:

    Elements of the 32d Division

    Elements of the 114th Division

The main force, left the vicinity of Shangchiu and Lanfeng on 29 June and captured enemy bases at Chengwu and Tingtao. Then, in concert with the other units, mopped up enemy remnants in western Shantung Province.

Realignment of Troop Strength in China

Japan, in order to cope with the critical international situation and at the same time, to establish a foundation for a prolonged war in China, relieved the greater part of her standing and special divisions with garrison divisions. Further, it was planned to reorganize the second reserve unit into more than ten independent mixed brigades and use them to garrison the rear areas. This plan was carried out gradually.

The number of groups dispatched to China or organized in China in 1939, was 10 divisions, 14 independent mixed brigades, one mixed brigade, and one independent infantry unit.

During the year, ten divisions which had been fighting in China were returned to either Japan Proper or to Korea. Of these, the 9th 10th, 14th and 16th Divisions upon return to Japan Proper were reduced to peacetime strength, with the men whose term of service was completed being demobilized. The 20th Division returned to Korea where it was reduced to peacetime strength and the 101st, 106th, 108th 109th and

114th were ordered to be returned to Japan Proper to be deactivated and the men demobilized. The return of the 106th Division was delayed, however, until spring 1940, as it was considered necessary to attach this division to the 21st Army in the Canton area for a time.

The Air Corps conducted air operations from the operational area of the Central China Expeditionary Army during the early stages of the operations, but, on 28 April, Imperial General Headquarters ordered that it be incorporated into the Order of Battle of the North China Area Army and carry out operations from the operational area of the Area Army. On the same day, the 2d Squadron of the 10th Air Regiment was transferred to the Air Corps from the Kwantung Army and the 7th Air Brigade, consisting of the 7th Air Brigade Headquarters, 12th Air Regiment and the 15th Air Regiment, was returned to the Kwantung Army from north and central China. On 1 September, the Imperial General Headquarters disbanded the Air Corps and transferred the Air Corps Headquarters, the 27th Air Regiment and the 98th Air Regiment to the Kwantung Army, while at the same time ordering the formation of the 3d Air Group and putting this group in the North China Area Army's Order of Battle.[120] The 3d Air Brigade of the Air Corps was assigned

---

120. The organization of the 3d Air Group was as follows: Commander: Lt Gen Satoshi Kinoshita. 3d Air Group Hqs, 16th Independent Air Squadron, 60th Air Regiment and 1st Air Brigade (consisting of Hqs, 10th Independent Air Squadron, 83d Independent Air Squadron and 90th Air Regiment).

to the Central China Expeditionary Army. The 4th Air Brigade[121] was disbanded and the 21st Independent Air Unit (organized about two air squadrons) was formed. This new unit was placed in the Order of Battle of the 21st Army. With the formation of the China Expeditionary Army General Headquarters on 1 October the 3d Air Group was placed in the China Expeditionary Army's Order of Battle, and in November the headquarters of this Group was transferred to Nanching.

Thereafter, the commander of the 3d Air Group commanded the 1st and 3d Air Brigades, as well as other air units, in north and central China.

---

121. The 4th Air Brigade had been placed in the Order of Battle of the 21st Army in early October 1938 and was stationed in the Canton area from about the middle of October.

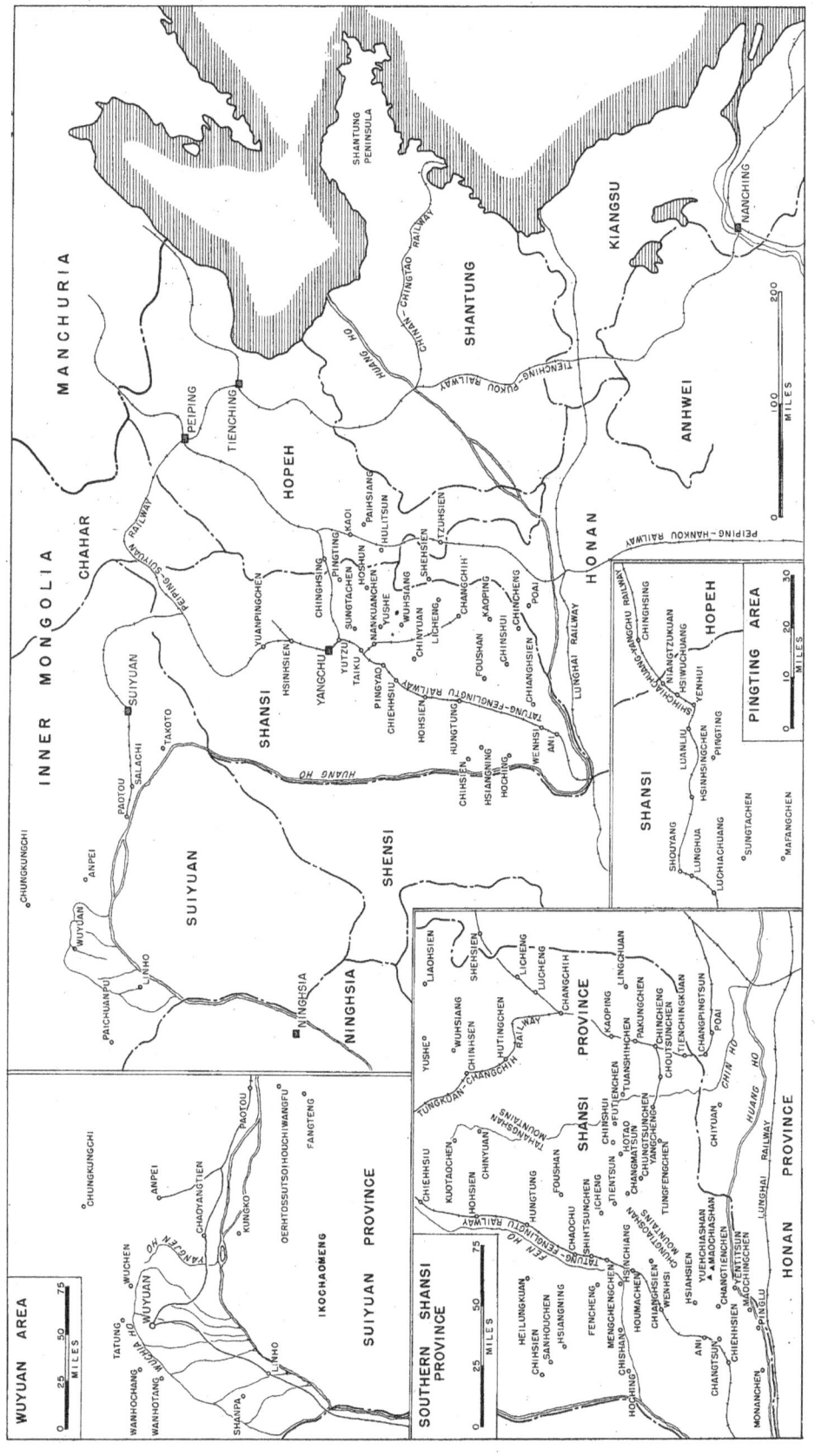

CHAPTER IV

Mopping-Up Operations During 1940

During 1940, the North China Area Army concentrated on the achievement of the security program it had worked out the year before. Its troops were dispersed widely to prevent enemy guerrillas from infiltrating into areas where public peace and order had been restored, and, at the same time, mopping-up operations were carried out against a powerful enemy force which had driven a wedge into the occupied areas.

The infiltrating enemy, after crossing the Shansi - Honan border, had penetrated deeply into Shansi Province. There were also stubborn communist forces and elements of the Nationalist Army still in the mountainous districts of Shansi Province as well as in the mountainous districts west of Peiping along the borders of Hopeh, Shansi and Chahar Provinces, in the mountains west of the Shantung Peninsula, and the plains of southern Shansi and Hopeh Provinces.

In the Mongolian border area, the operation to counter the enemy's winter offensive toward the end of the previous year, was followed by the Houtao Operation, which continued until spring. In the Shansi Province area, the 1st Army carried out the Southern Shansi Province Operation in spring in an endeavor to destroy the hostile Kuomintang Army south of Changchih. While engaged in this operation, however, the 1st Army received information that an enemy force had advanced to the area west of the Tatung - Fenglingtu railway line, after crossing the Huang Ho from the west. Therefore, it commenced the Hsiangning Operation immediately and compelled the enemy forces near Hsiangning, as well as in the southern part of Shansi Province, to withdraw. Enemy remnants in southern Shansi Province however regrouped for another assault, and the Army attempted to mop them up in May and June by carrying out what was known as the "Southern Shansi Province Counterattack Operation." Such efforts however, served only to drive the enemy away temporarily from southern Shansi Province and constituted a source of future trouble.

The pacification program was making steady progress in north China when the Communist forces carried out a surprise attack against the Shihchiachuang - Yangchu railway line on 20 August, inflicting heavy losses upon the Japanese forces stationed there.

To meet this situation, the 1st Army carried out two Central Shansi Province operations in an effort to catch and wipe out these forces, but failed to obtain satisfactory results. Meanwhile, the Area Army also carried out mopping-up operations against the forces entrenched in the mountainous districts west of Peiping along the borders of Shansi, Chahar and Hopeh Province from the middle of October to the beginning of December, but the clever tactics employed by the Communists in taking cover prevented the Area Army from attaining its objective before the year ended.

Mongolian Border Area Operation

Early 1940

Towards the end of 1939 Fu Tsoi's Army attacked Paotou, but was beaten back by the Japanese forces. However, he made a false report that the attack had been very successful, and Chiang Kaishek not only commended Fu but ordered him to make another attack against Paotou. As a result, an estimated 10,000 enemy troops, led by Han Hsihou,[122] advanced eastward along the south bank of the Huang Ho via Shanpa and Wuyuan in the middle of January. Also around 15 January, elements of Ma Chanshan's Army and Pai Fenghsiang's Army (both guerrilla forces) commenced operations in an attempt to cut the railway line between Suiyuan and Paotou. Further, there were some 30,000 enemy troops operating north of the Huang Ho and west of Paotou, which were believed to belong to the 35th Army, the 6th Cavalry Army and other guerrilla units. It seemed that their main forces were in positions east of Wuyuan. At that time, the Huang Ho was frozen over with ice thick enough to allow the passage of troops.

Upon receipt of this information, the Mongolia Garrison Army requested that it be allowed to destroy the enemy's base of operations in the Houtao area.[123] Accordingly, on 16 January, Imperial General Headquarters authorized the China Expeditionary Army commander to advance his troops to the area west of Anpei[124] in January or February.

---

122. Han Hsihou was a division commander in Fu Tsoi's Army.
123. The area around Wuyuan was known as the Houtao area.
124. At that time the area west of Anpei was excluded from the operational area of the China Expeditionary Army and it was necessary for the Army to obtain approval from Imperial General Headquarters for operations in this area.

As a result, the North China Area Army commander drew up a new operational plan to cope with the situation. According to this plan, the Mongolia Garrison Army commander was to muster as many troops as possible to first destroy the hostile forces in the Ikochaomeng area and then, turning westward, advance to the Houtao area to find and destroy the enemy's main strength.

By order of the Mongolia Garrison Army commander, the Cavalry Group, the main force of the 26th Division and elements of the 2d Independent Mixed Brigade were assembled between Salachi and Paotou.

Operations in the Ikochaomeng Area (21 - 25 January)

The Mongolia Garrison Army began preparations for the counteroffensive around 15 January and commenced its operations on 21 January, as it received information that the enemy's 86th Division was retreating to the south. The 26th Division left the vicinity of Salachi, and, with its main force, destroyed the enemy forces at Oerhtossutsoihouchiwangfu and Fangteng, while elements crushed an enemy force in the sector between Takoto and Paotou, on the south bank of the Huang Ho. On 25 January, the Division assembled its troops near Paotou and began preparations for an attack against the enemy forces in the Houtao area.

The First Houtao Operation (28 January - end of February)

The Mongolia Garrison Army disposed its troops so that the main force of the Army would advance towards Wuyuan along the Paotou - Anpei - Wanhochang - Wuyuan road while its elements would advance toward the same destination by following the Huang Ho. The advance force of the 26th Division left Anpei and the area north thereof on the evening of the 30th and the main force left Paotou the following day. On the 31st, the advance force attacked an enemy position northeast of Wuchen breaking through their lines on 1 February. The next day it captured another enemy position near Wanhotang. On 3 February it surged into Wuyuan after a flanking movement from the west.

The main force of the Cavalry Group left Paotou on 28 January and advanced in two columns toward the west along both banks of the Huang Ho. On the 31st, the right column attacked and drove to the west an estimated 4,000 enemy troops occupying positions southeast of Chaoyangtien. The same day the left column also attacked and drove to the west an estimated 1,000 enemy troops occupying positions near Kungko. Both columns then advanced to the Yangjen Ho on 2 February and assembled in the vicinity of Wuyuan on the 4th. The main force of the Group then conducted mopping-up operations against hostile remnants around Wuyuan.

The Army concentrated the units under its command in the vicinity of Wuyuan on the 4th, before ordering elements to pursue the enemy towards Linho, while ordering the main force to leave on 5 February for Shanpa in pursuit of the enemy forces. The Left Pursuit Unit captured Linho on the evening of the 4th and sent elements in further pursuit of the enemy into Ninghsia Province. The Right Pursuit Unit captured Shanpa on the night of the 5th and then carried out mopping-up operations against the enemy remnants in the area.

Meanwhile, an element of the Inner Mongolian Army left the vicinity of Chungkungchi about 2 February and advanced to the vicinity of Paichuanpu to cut off the enemy's escape to the west.

Some of the enemy troops fled into Ninghsia Province and others into the Ikochaomeng area on the south bank of the Huang Ho. (Map 29)

Having attained its objective, the Army began to withdraw from the Wuyuan Plain in the middle of February and by 1 March had returned to the positions which it had held before the operation.

The Second Houtao Operation (21 - 29 March)

Upon receipt of the report concerning the defeat of Fu Tsoi's forces near Wuyuan, Chu Shaoliang, Eighth War Sector commander, personnally went to Ninghsia and ordered Fu to reorganize his forces immediately and counterattack. Fu declared that the full force of his army would attack again and destroy the Japanese forces as soon as the thawing season set in. This was not an idle boast. An enemy force, believed to be the 35th Army, made a pre-dawn attack against Wuyuan on 21 March. Despite Japanese stubborn resistance, the inner castle of Wuyuan finally fell into enemy hands that night. Among the forces that tried to fight off the invading enemy were the special service agency,[125] three divisions

---

125. This special service agency was the Wuyuan branch of the Special Intelligence Agency of the Japanese Mongolian Garrison Army with its headquarters at Wanchuan.

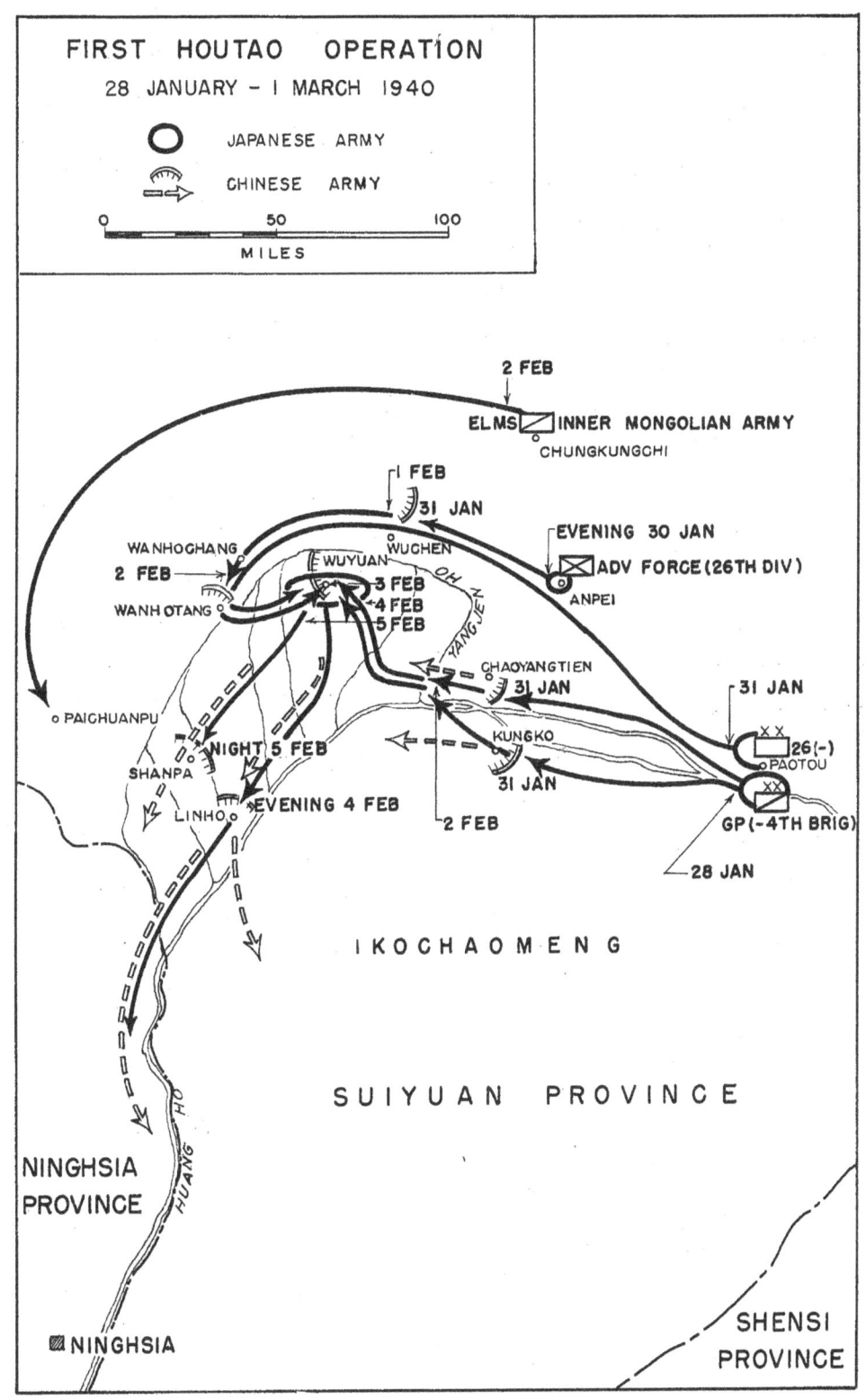

MAP NO. 29

of the Inner Mongolian Army[126] and the Suiyuan Garrison Force[127] stationed at Wuyuan.

To alleviate the situation, the Anpei Garrison Force, the main force of the Cavalry Group and part of the 26th Division were rushed to the Wuyuan area as reinforcements. These forces reached the vicinity of Tatung, north of Wuyuan, on the evening of 22 March. There they made preparations to cross the Wuchia Ho. On the evening of the 25th, assisted by friendly aircraft, they succeeded in crossing the river under enemy fire and entered Wuyuan the following day. However, the enemy broke the banks of the Wuchia Ho and caused a flood which spread more and more widely, until at last the Army had to give up pursuing the enemy. After mopping-up hostile remnants in the area, the Japanese forces left Wuyuan on 29 March and returned to their respective original stations. (Map 30)

Southern Shansi Province Operation

As a result of the Eastern Shansi Province Operation and the

---

126. These divisions were composed of poorly-equipped Inner Mongolian Army troops. The strength of each division was approximately 1,000 to 1,200 men. The reasons for this limited strength were that there were no supporting branch units, such as artillery, engineer and transportation units; almost no rear service units, such as medical and supply, and no organization of battalions or brigades. For political reasons, many of the high positions in the Inner Mongolian Army were held by Japanese officers of the Japanese Advisory Group attached to the Inner Mongolian Army.

127. This force, which was commanded by retired Japanese Army officers, was composed of poorly-equipped Inner Mongolian troops. It was sent from Wanchuan to assist in the defense of Wuyuan. Its strength was approximately 350 men.

MAP NO. 30

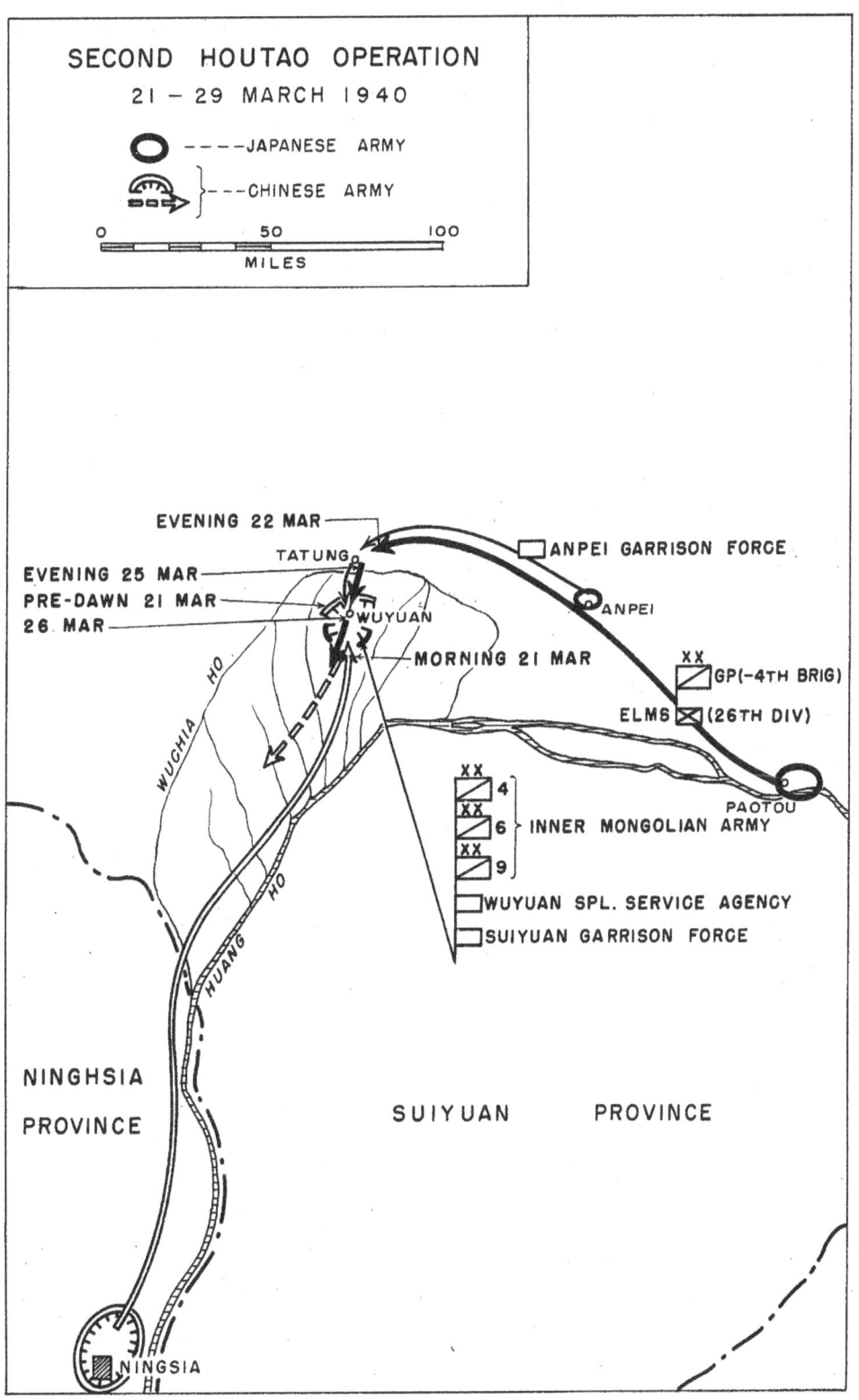

Changchih Mopping-Up Operation carried out in the summer and autumn of 1939, the Changchih area was occupied by Japanese forces. However, the rest of southern Shansi Province, especially the Tahangshan and Chungtiao mountain areas, was still in the hands of the Kuomintang Army and was the enemy's largest base of operations in north China.

The mountainous area north of Changchih also served as a base of operations for communist forces under Chu Te, who tried to extend his sphere of influence to the Changchih Plain. This caused political friction with the Kuomintang Army in southern Shansi Province.

In the southwestern part of Shansi Province, the hostile Shansi Army, led by Yen Hsishan, still held strong positions, but it was suffering from internal troubles. To prevent the spread of this internal conflict, four divisions of the Kuomintang Army under the command of Li Wen advanced from Shensi Province to the vicinity of Hsiangning to act as a surveillance force.

The fighting spirit of the Kuomintang Army in southern Shansi Province was very high and, about the middle of March, it ordered a force to advance from the south bank of the Huang Ho to the vicinity of Kaoping. At the same time, the enemy changed its troop disposition, laying new emphasis on the sector south of Changchih to meet the possible attack by Japanese forces from the Changchih area. The nucleus of this force was about 20 divisions of the Kuomintang Army under the command of Wei Lihuang and about 10 other divisions. With the change in the disposition of the Kuomintang Army, the Communist forces in the Changchih Plain retired to the north of Changchih.

The Japanese 1st Army, charged with the mission of defending Shansi Province, had been reinforced the previous year by the 36th, 37th and 41st Divisions as well as by two independent mixed brigades. However, with such garrison forces as the 20th, 108th and 109th Divisions being ordered to return to Japan Proper and Korea in the summer and autumn, the strength of the 1st Army in Shansi Province dwindled to three divisions and four independent mixed brigades. Thus, the 37th and 41st Divisions were jointly responsible for the defense of the area along the southern section of the Tatung - Fenglingtu railway, while the 36th Division was charged with the defense of the Changchih sector. The area north of these sectors was defended by the independent mixed brigades.

In view of the fact that southern Shansi Province, especially the sector south of Changchih, constituted the greatest base of operations for enemy forces in north China, the North China Area Army ordered that the Southern Shansi Province Operation be started in the middle of April and ordered the 35th Division to cooperate with the 1st Army in the operation.

The outline of the 1st Army's operational plan was as follows:

1. Purpose of the Operation

To destroy enemy forces throughout southern Shansi Province and paralyze their activities at their source, thus crippling the fighting power of Chiang's Government, and, at the same time, extending the Japanese occupied area in order to expedite the creation of a peaceful and orderly north China.

2. Forces to be Employed in the Operation

The 36th, 37th and 41st Divisions.

The 37th Division completed massing its troops by the evening of

15 April. The main force of the Division was assembled south and southeast of Ani while an element assembled in the vicinity of Chiehhsien. A second element of the Division occupied the vicinity of the watershed of the Chungtiao Mountain Range.

At dawn on 17 April, under cover of friendly aircraft, the units launched an attack from Chiehhsien, Changtsun and Changtienchen and, between 1500 and 1700 hours, reached the north bank of the Huang Ho near Monanchen, Pinglu and Maochingchen.

The Japanese forces which had occupied Maochingchen veered to the left and attacked enemy positions to the northeast on the 18th. They recaptured Yentitsun, one of the enemy strongholds, the following day and continued to advance and mop up the remnants of the enemy 17th Division of the 4th Army Group in the Maochiashan - Yuehchiashan area until the 25th.

Meanwhile, the 37th Division, by order of the 1st Army, organized a detachment to be sent as reinforcements for the 41st Division. The detachment left the battlefront on the 19th and went by train from Ani to Icheng.

The 36th and the 41st Divisions commenced an attack against the area south of Changchih on 20 April.

Prior to the commencement of the attack by the main force of the 41st Division on the 20th, elements of the Division had staged a dawn attack against a hostile force southeast of Icheng on the 17th so as to divert the enemy's attention and thus facilitate subsequent operations. They destroyed the enemy force in this area around 0800 hours that morning.

They made another dawn attack against another hostile position southeast of Tientsun on the 18th, advanced to the vicinity of Changmatsun on the 19th and commenced an attack against strong enemy positions near Chungtsunchen on the 20th.

The main force of the Division assembled east of Foushan on the 19th and launched a southward drive in four columns toward Chinshui, Futienchen and Hotao early the following morning. Brushing aside enemy resistance on the way, it captured these positions on the 21st. It then changed its formation to three columns and continued to advance, crushing the enemy force that occupied the steep mountain positions. After capturing Yangcheng on the 24th, it advanced towards Choutsunchen on the 25th, and captured this town the following day. Elements were sent to the Tienchingkuan area to cut off the enemy's escape route.

The right column of the Division had been attacking enemy positions near Chungtsunchen since the 20th, but little progress was made and the situation became a stalemate. It was not until the 26th that Chungtsunchen was occupied after defeating the hostile 14th Army which had clung stubbornly to its position. As soon as the right column took Chungtsunchen, it began to pursue the retiring enemy towards Yangcheng. Meanwhile, the detachment sent as reinforcements from the 37th Division, arrived at Icheng and began to advance rapidly along the Icheng - Chinshui road. It captured Tuanshihchen on the 26th, and mopped up enemy remnants in the area the following day.

The 36th Division assembled its troops south of Changchih on the 19th. Early the following morning the main force of the Division began to advance in three columns towards Lingchuan, which was regarded as the enemy's base of operation for the 27th Army, while an element advanced in two columns towards Kaoping.

The two columns marching towards Kaoping drove back the Chinese 88th Division in an encounter north of their objective and then broke through strong enemy positions near Kaoping on the 21st. Next, they captured strong enemy positions west and southwest of Kaoping, one after another. On the night of the 23d, the left column left the battlefield and moved to the sector east of the Kaoping - Chincheng road. On the morning of the 25th, it captured positions near Pakungchen and pursued the enemy towards Chincheng.

The main force of the Division, after its advance to the vicinity of Lingchuan, launched an attack against enemy positions to the north on the afternoon of the 20th. However, the enemy resisted stubbornly and the situation did not turn in favor of the Japanese until the night of the 21st when the right column made a flanking attack and Lingchuan fell. Enemy casualties were heavy.

An element of the Division was left at Lingchuan to conduct mopping-up operations, while the main force advanced further to the southwest and captured Chincheng on the afternoon of the 25th. On the 27th, a powerful element of the Division drove towards Tienchingkuan in hot pursuit of the enemy, while another element wheeled to the north to mop up hostile remnants southwest of Kaoping.

A powerful element of the 35th Division launched an attack against enemy positions near Changpingtsun, northwest of Poai, on the morning of the 25th and broke through the line the same day. The following morning it started to pursue the enemy towards Chincheng and advanced to Tienchingkuan, where it established contact with elements of the 36th Division. Later, information was received that the enemy was falling back to the vicinity of Chiyuan, and the 35th Division moved its troops in that direction.

Subsequently, the Army garrisoned such places as Pinglu, Changmatsun, Chinshui, Yangcheng and Chincheng and ordered these troops to carry out mopping-up operations in an effort to establish public peace and order.

Early in May, before its main force returned to its original station, the 41st Division mopped up remnants of the enemy around Tungfengchen. (Map 31)

Following this operation, the Army carried out the Hsiangning Operation to destroy those enemy forces in the southwestern part of the province which, taking advantage of the thin ranks of Japanese rear echelon troops, had become active during the Southern Shansi Province Operation.

Hsiangning Operation

A surveillance unit of the Kuomintang Army, led by Li Wen, had made its way into the Hsiangning area to prevent the demoralization and retreat of the Shansi Army. Spurred on by Li, the Shansi Army gradually advanced into the Fen Ho Plain and stepped up its activities, taking advantage of the thinned strength of the Japanese garrison force caused by the Southern Shansi Province Operation. At the beginning of May it commenced an attack against the Japanese garrison forces in the

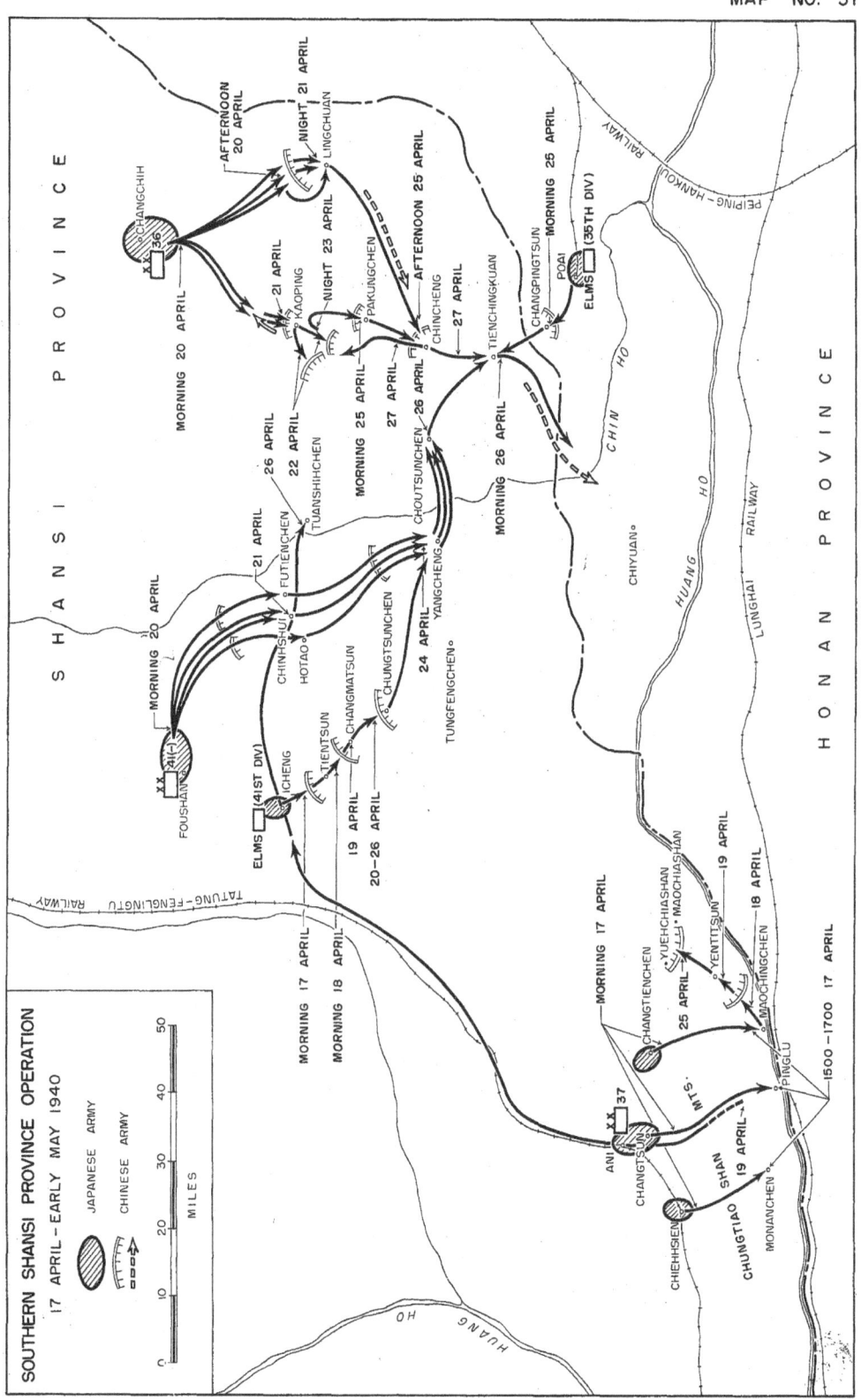

plain country.

On the Japanese 41st Division front, the enemy gradually approached Fencheng, and, on 1 May, a hostile force, believed to be the 53d Division, staged an attack upon Fencheng. That evening another hostile force, believed to be an element of the 61st Division, attacked Houmachen. Also, in the Heilungkuan area and the area west of Linfen, enemy activities showed a gradual increase. The Division bravely fought against these attacks, and, by order of the Army gradually assembled its troops between Chaochu, Shihtsunchen and Mengchengchen in preparation for a full scale offensive.

On 2 May the 37th Division made an attack against elements of the hostile 109th Division in the vicinity of Hoching and Chishan, where the enemy had not had time to establish strong positions. A part of the 37th Division made a rear attack against 500 enemy troops who were attacking the Houmachen area. Surprised from the rear, the enemy retreated in a rout. Then, by order of the Army, the main strength of the Division was concentrated in the vicinity of Chishan and Hoching while an element assembled near Hsinchiang.

The 1st Army decided that the enemy forces in the southwestern part of Shansi Province should be engaged and destroyed on the north bank of the Huang Ho before they took the initiative. Accordingly, it ordered the 37th and 41st Divisions to make operational preparations. At the same time, it ordered elements of the two divisions which had taken part in the Southern Shansi Province Operation to return quickly to their original command.

On 10 May, the Army ordered the 37th and 41st Divisions to commence operations to capture Hsiangning.

Therefore, on 10 May, the 37th Division, in cooperation with the 41st Division, launched an offensive from the sector north of Hoching, and, after defeating a stubbornly resisting enemy, pursued the retreating forces and advanced to the vicinity of Sanhouchen, northwest of Hsiangning, thus cutting off the enemy's escape route to Chihsien. Despite a series of persistent attacks by the enemy, the 37th Division reached and occupied Hsiangning on 15 May. Also, on 10 May, elements of the 37th Division left Hsinchiang and advanced to the northwest, while the 41st Division left Chaochu and Mengchengchen and advanced to the west. Fighting a daring pursuit action, they drove towards Hsiangning against stubborn resistance offered by the enemy from steep mountain positions. On the 16th, they reached the sector east of Hsiangning and, in conjunction with the main force of the 37th Division, attacked and defeated the enemy troops retreating northward.

Having completed their mission, the Army ordered the units to begin returning to their original stations from the 17th.

In accordance with this order, the two divisions wheeled around and began heading back toward their original posts about the 17th, conducting mopping-up operations on the way back. They returned to the Fen Ho Plain around the 20th. (Map 32)

While the Hsiangning Operation was still under way, remnants of

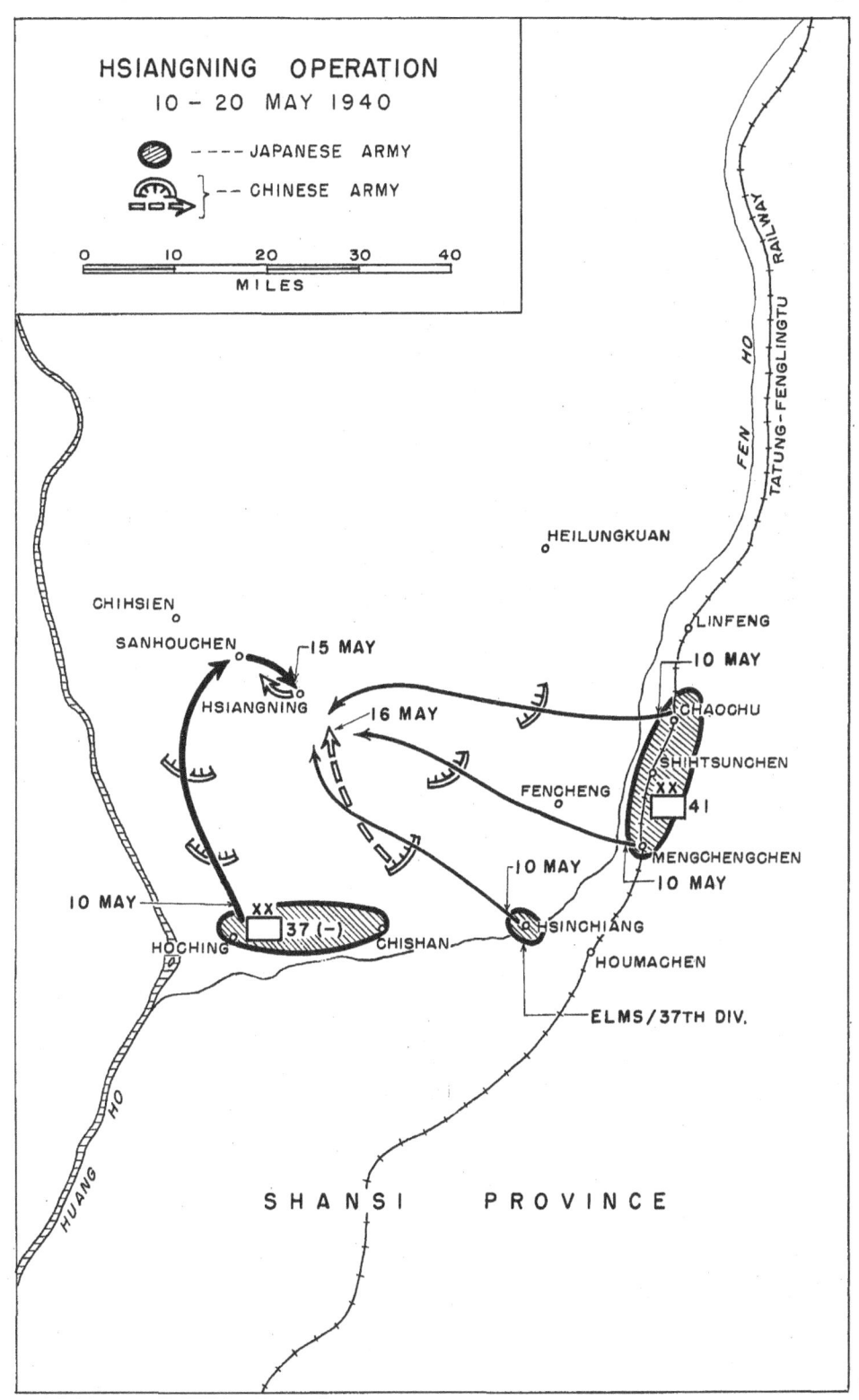

MAP NO. 32

the enemy in southern Shansi Province regrouped and again became active. Toward the end of May, they began a second counteroffensive, which the Japanese forces crushed in what was known as the "Repulsing Operation in Southern Shansi Province."

Repulsing Operation in Southern Shansi Province

As a result of the Southern Shansi Province Operation in spring, the Japanese forces were disposed at such places in Southern Shansi Province as Pinglu, Changmatsun, Chinshui, Yangcheng and Chincheng. However, the enemy seemed to be planning the recapture of these points, particularly as the Hsiangning Operation had resulted in a considerable decrease in the strength of the Japanese garrison forces in southern Shansi Province. The enemy began to increase his activities and, the First War Sector Army commander, Wei Lihuang, issued an order to launch a coordinated counteroffensive throughout Southern Shansi at 2400 hours on 20 May.

The Japanese 1st Army also decided to take advantage of the results attained in the Southern Shansi Province Operation and destroy the enemy and ordered every unit under its command to engage and destroy all enemy forces.

The 36th Division beat back the assaulting enemy on every front. Especially in the sectors west of Chincheng and southwest of Tienchingkuan, the Division organized several new detachments and repulsed the enemy's offensive.

On the 41st Division front, the Yangcheng Garrison Force, supported by 41st Division reinforcement units previously employed in the Hsiangning Operation, attacked from the southeast of Yangcheng enemy forces holding positions west and south of Yangcheng and threw them back to the southwest. Then the garrison force, in cooperation with other friendly units from Chinshui, drove the enemy to the north.

The 37th Division organized a striking force with troops detached from its subordinate units. This force first destroyed the enemy east of Chianghsien, while elements beat back with mobile operations a part of the hostile 98th Army east of Wenhsi. Also in the sector east of Hsiahsien the Division encircled and annihilated the enemy, after luring him out into flat country.

Thus, each Japanese force, despite its numerical inferiority, successfully fought off the enemy's offensive.

Central Shansi Province Operation

On the night of 20 August 1940, Chu Te, commander of the 18th Army Group, ordered the Chinese communist forces then concentrated in North China to simultaneously carry out surprise attacks on transportation lines and industrial areas (principally mines). They attacked the garrison troops along the Shihchiachuang - Yangchu railway and the northern section of Tatung - Fenglingtu railway and, at the same time, blasted and destroyed railroads and communication facilities.

The Chinghsing coal mine in the garrison area of the 8th Independent Mixed Brigade was attacked suddenly on the same night and its facilities were completely destroyed. These totally unexpected attacks caused serious damage, and it was necessary to expend much time and money in restoration work.

It was estimated that the enemy troops which carried out the surprise attack on the Shihchiachuang - Yangchu railway consisted of approximately 6,000 men of the 129th Division, 2d and 19th Regiments of the Shansi - Chahar - Hopeh Area Army, and students of the anti-Japanese Military Administrative College. Also, on the night of 20 August, Japanese garrison troops at Niangtzukuan, Hsiwuchuang, Yenhui, Luanliu, and in the sector between Hsinhsingchen and Luchiachuang were suddenly attacked. It was impossible to send them any relief as roads and railroads had been destroyed by previous attacks. However, the units finally repulsed the enemy.

The garrison unit at Lunghua to the south of Shouyang was attacked by a Chinese force of approximately 500 on 23 August, but was finally able to repulse the attack on the 26th.

The northern section of the Tatung - Fenglingtu railway also was subjected to surprise enemy attacks from midnight of 20 August. The garrison forces along the Tatung - Fenglingtu railway and in the area west of the railroad repulsed the enemy attacks, but the railroad suffered heavy damage. The 9th Independent Mixed Brigade advanced and mopped up the enemy to the west of Yangchu and Hsinhsien, and the 3d Independent Mixed Brigade mopped up the enemy forces to the west of Yuanpingchen. On the 29th, both brigades returned to their respective original stations.

In the southern section of the Tatung - Fenglingtu railway, the enemy attacked Chiehhsiu, Hohsien and other places along the railroad, but the 41st Division repulsed all the attacks.

On 20 and 21 August, enemy forces approximately 1,500 strong of the 3d Column[128] simultaneously attacked the Tungkuan - Changchih railway but were repelled.

A force of 8,000 to 10,000 consisting of an element of the Southern Hopeh Army belonging to the Shansi - Chahar - Hopeh Area Army and an element of the 129th Division carried out raids in the Peiping - Hankou railway area. The Japanese 110th Division destroyed an enemy force of approximately 1,000 near Kaoi on the 23d, and another force of approximately 2,000 south of Paihsiang on the 25th. Also on the 25th, it destroyed a force of approximately 1,000 at Hulitsun, while the 1st Independent Mixed Brigade successfully suppressed the newly organized Communist Army 1st Brigade which had been active south of Tzuhsien.

The 1st Army ordered the 4th Independent Mixed Brigade, consisting of four infantry battalions and the 9th Independent Mixed Brigade, consisting of three infantry battalions, to engage and destroy the 129th Communist Division, which had attacked the Shihchiachuang - Yangchu railway.

---

128. The Communist Army had organized this 3d Column to be used as a suicide unit as a last resort.

On 30 August, the 9th Independent Mixed Brigade began to move from the area between Taku and Yutzu and, on 1 September, the 4th Independent Mixed Brigade moved from areas near Pingting, Hoshun, Liaohsien and Yushe. The Brigades crushed enemy resistance in their way and pressed on to areas near Sungtachen and Mafangchen. There they swept away the enemy and destroyed his rear facilities. On 4 September, having completed their mission, they began to return to their respective places of departure, arriving on the 7th.

Although the Brigades had defeated the enemy whenever they had encountered him, strong enemy units were still hiding in the area. Therefore, on 9 September, the 1st Army ordered the Brigades to begin again operations to destroy the enemy in this mountainous area. The Japanese units continued to mop-up the enemy with considerable success until 18 September.

After their defeat in the first phase of the Central Shansi Province Operation, the main strength of Chinese Communist force organized around the 129th Division took refuge in the mountainous region between the section east of Wuhsiang and the section north of Licheng while an element retired to near Chingyuan. The enemy seemed to be planning fresh attacks against the road connecting Liaohsien, Yushe and Wuhsiang as well as the Tungkuan - Changchih railway.

On 11 October, therefore, the 1st Army, in order to destroy the enemy's main strength and to wipe out their bases, ordered the 4th Independent Mixed Brigade to start moving from the vicinity of

Liaohsien and an element of the 36th Division from the vicinity of Lucheng. The north and south forces, in coordination with each other, mopped up the enemy in the area extending from Liaohsien, Shehsien and Lucheng to Wuhsiang, and destroyed his bases. They completed their mission by 14 November. On 19 November, the 36th Division started from the vicinity of Hutingchen, Chinhsien and Nankuanchen, the 16th Independent Mixed Brigade, from Pingyao, Chiehhsiu and Hohsien, and an infantry battalion of the 41st Division, from the area east of Hungtung. They all converged upon Kuotaochen and Chingyuan destroying Communist bases in the Chin Ho area without encountering any strong enemy force. The operation was completed on 3 December.

The heavy blow suffered by the Communist forces and their bases during this operation forced them to resort to guerrilla warfare and thereafter they offered very little resistance in this area.

Disposition of Chinese Forces in Hopeh, Shantung and Northern Kiangsu Province areas

Upon completion of the offensive phase of the operations, the Japanese Army began the task of establishing peace and order in the occupied areas, which were too large for the garrison forces. Taking advantage of this situation, Nationalist and Communist forces infiltrated into the Japanese occupied area and frequently disturbed the peace. The Nationalist Army disposed the Shantung - Kiangsu War Sector Army, headed by Yu Hsuehchung, in Shantung and northern Kiangsu Provinces, and the Shih Yusan, Chu Huaiyung and Sun Tienying Armies in southern Hopeh, western Shantung, and northern Honan Provinces. The First War Sector Army was stationed in southeast Shansi Province while Communist forces, entrenched in the mountainous region of Shantung Province, northern Anhwei Province, the whole northern region of Shansi Province and districts west of Peiping extending over Shansi, Chahar and Hopeh Provinces, presented a threat to the Japanese garrison areas. The Kuomintang forces and the Communist Army found it impossible to reconcile their ideological differences and set out to expand their respective spheres of influence, with the result that the hostility between the two forces gradually became increasingly bitter. This was especially so in Shantung Province, northern Kiangsu, and the Kuang-Hua area (northern Kiangsu and northern Anhwei Provinces).

As the operations of the Communist Army became active after it had driven off the Nationalist force, the North China Area Army found it necessary to carry out punitive operations against the Communist troops in the various areas.

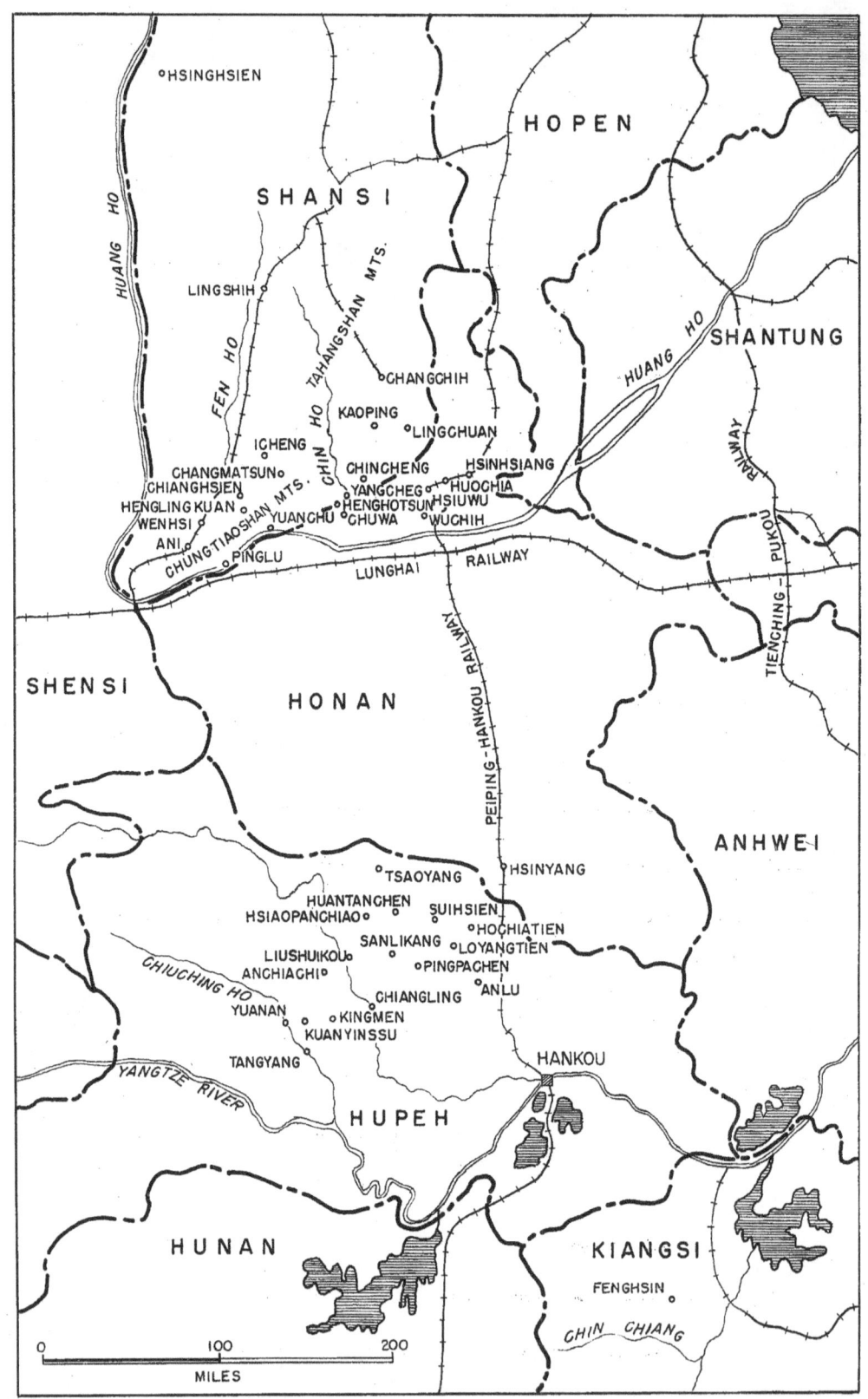

CHAPTER V

Mopping-up Operations in the Shansi Province Area During 1941

Western Shansi Province Operation

The Communist troops, which had been entrenched in the mountainous region north of Central Shansi Province had been hard hit by the Central Shansi Province Operation and the mopping-up operations in the districts west of Peiping, extending over Shansi, Chahar and Hopeh Provinces, which had been carried out by the 1st Army, the Mongolia Garrison Army and the units under the direct control of the North China Area Army during the autumn of 1940. However, the Communist 120th Division, which had entrenched itself in the area south of Hsinghsien in December 1940, was again gradually becoming active.

The 1st Army, therefore, decided to take the initiative and destroy the 120th Division's base using the main force of the 9th and 16th Independent Mixed Brigades and elements of the 36th, 37th and 41st Divisions, in cooperation with the 3d Independent Mixed Brigade and an element of the 1st Air Brigade.

On 13 December, the 1st Army units began to move but failed to engage the 120th Division in any major battle as the 120th Division gradually retreated from its lightly defended positions on the east bank of the Huang Ho to the west of the river. After mopping up along the east bank of the Huang Ho and destroying guerrilla bases in the district south of Hsinghsien, the 1st Army units returned to their original stations around 22 January 1941.[129]

In view of the above situation and also the fact that there appeared to be constant friction between the Kuomintang Army and the Shansi Army and, further, since the morale of the Shansi Army was known to be low, it was felt that it would take some time for the Communist forces west of the Tatung - Fenglingtu railway in Shansi Province to recover their fighting strength.

Although the 1st Army had defeated the Kuomintang Army in southern Shansi Province in the spring of 1940, a strong enemy force continued to secure strategic points along the Chungtiao Range. In cooperation with the enemy 93d Army in the western Tahangshan Range and the 27th Army in the Lingchuan area, this force gradually strengthened its positions and frequently raided Japanese garrison sectors.

The total strength of the enemy in this area was estimated to be approximately 24 divisions with about 168,000 personnel.

In view of these circumstances, the Japanese 1st Army decided to destroy the main force of the Kuomintang Army which was occupying the Chungtiao Range, and improve public peace in Shansi Province, by pushing the main garrison line farther to the Huang Ho. Preparations for this operation were begun in autumn 1940. In order to be able to

---

129. Details of this action are not available.

employ its strength efficiently in the main attack and not be concerned with the possibility of attacks against its flanks, the 1st Army planned to carry out the operation to destroy the 27th Army at Lingchuan and the enemy's 15th Army on the plain south of Icheng in March 1941.[130]

In order, therefore, to undertake the operation against the 27th Army in the sector west of the eastern border of Shansi Province, the 1st Army reinforced the 36th Division with elements from the 3d, 4th, 9th and 16th Independent Mixed Brigades.

The 36th Division launched an offensive against Lingchuan with elements from Chincheng and Changchih on 5 March and the main strength of the Division commenced moving from Kaoping to Lingchuan on 6 March. As the enemy withdrew into the sector southeast of Lingchuan, the Division turned to the pursuit and seized and destroyed enemy troops at various points. Then wheeling about and mopping up the remaining enemy along the way, it returned to its original station in the middle of March.

The main body of the Kuomintang Army generally held the watershed area along the northern edge of the Chungtiao Range and the 15th Army had infiltrated into the plain east of Chianghsien, south of

---

130. At first, the 1st Army planned to destroy the 15th and 27th Armies, as well as the 93d Army in the Tahangshan Range, before launching the operation against the enemy's main strength in the Chungtiao Range. However, it was later decided that as the 93d Army was inferior in composition and fighting spirit to the 15th and 27th Armies, the operation against the 93d Army could be cancelled without unduly prejudicing the outcome of the major operation.

Icheng. Here, the 15th Army engaged in guerrilla warfare, disturbing peace and order in the occupied zone. It was, therefore, considered necessary to destroy the 15th Army occupying the plain before carrying out the operation against the main body of the Kuomintang Army in the Chungtiao Range.

The Japanese 1st Army planned to advance the occupation line as far as the watershed, approximately between Henglingkuan and Changmatsun and began the attack on 10 March by employing the 37th and the 41st Divisions.

On that day, while elements of the 37th and 41st Divisions attacked the 15th Army's front and contained its main strength, the main body of both Japanese divisions started attacking from the vicinity of Henglingkuan and Changmatsun respectively. Climbing rugged mountain terrain and breaking through a series of strong enemy positions, they enveloped and destroyed the 15th Army's main strength from the rear as well as the flanks and then advanced and secured the watershed. The operation was completed in late March.

Tactical Command

When the 1st Army planned to attack the enemy in the Chungtiao Range, it referred the plan to the North China Area Army, which approved the plan and sent elements of the 35th Division, then under the direct command of the Area Army, to participate in the Lingchuan Operation. The North China Area Army wanted to increase its strength for the Chungyuan Operation[131] and asked the China Expeditionary Army to place the 33d Division (minus one infantry regiment) of the 11th Army under its command. The China Expeditionary Army agreed to do this but the arrival of the 33d Division in north China was delayed because of its participation on the Kinkiang Operation south of Fenghsin from 15 March to early April.[132] For the Chungyuan Operation, the Imperial General Headquarters on 19 April ordered the Kwantung Army to place its 32d (light bomber) and 83d (reconnaissance) Air Regiments under the command in chief of the China Expeditionary Army and four infantry battalions under the command of the North China Area Army. These units were to be returned to their original command upon completion of the operation.

The China Expeditionary Army not only placed the 33d Division (minus one infantry regiment) under the command of the North China Area Army, but also instructed the 3d Air Group to participate in the operation.

The North China Area Army attached the 33d Division (minus one

---

131. Chungyuan was the code name given this operation by General Hayao Tada, commander of the North China Area Army as he considered by this operation the enemy within the Chingyuan area would be crushed. In ancient times "Chungyuan" comprising the area along the middle of the Huang Ho (the greater part of Honan, Shansi and Shantung Provinces and some parts of Hopeh and Shansi Provinces) was considered to be the cradle of Chinese civilization. The Han Dynasty was founded within this area.
132. Monograph 179, <u>Central China Area Operations Record, Vol I.</u>

infantry regiment) to the 1st Army and also ordered the 21st and the 35th Divisions under its direct command to take part in the Chungyuan Operation.

Tactical Command by North China Area Army

The North China Area Army planned to attack the enemy by advancing the 1st Army from Shansi Province and both the 35th and the 21st Divisions, which were under the direct command of the Area Army, from Honan Province. Under this plan, the operational sector boundary between the 1st Army and the forces directly attached to the Area Army was designated as the border between Shansi and Honan Provinces, and the assembly points were the vicinity of Hsiuwu and Wuchih for the 35th Division and the sector further to the rear and south of Huochia for the 21st Division. On 7 May, together with the 1st Army, operations were to be started by the 35th Division in pursuit of the enemy toward Yuanchu and, after the 35th Division progressed in its operation, the 21st Division was to move toward Yangcheng from the Chin Ho valley.

The 3d Air Group had been cooperating in the Eastern Chekiang Province Operation from the middle of April and its main strength was deployed in the lower reaches of the Yangtzu River until late April when it was deployed at Ani and Hsinhsiang airfields by order of the China Expeditionary Army to take part in the Chungyuan Operation. Its strength and deployment were as follows:

The 3d Air Group

    The 3d Air Group Headquarters   Ani Airfield

The 1st Air Brigade

    The 1st Air Brigade Headquarters ⎫

    The 90th Air Regiment (light bomber) ⎬ Ani

    The 10th Independent Air Squadron (fighter) ⎬ Airfield

    One (reconnaissance) squadron of the 15th Air Regiment ⎭

The 3d Air Brigade

    The 3d Air Brigade Headquarters ⎫

    The 44th Air Regiment (reconnaissance and direct support) ⎬ Hsinhsiang

    The 32d Air Regiment (light bomber) ⎬ Airfield

    The 83d Air Regiment (reconnaissance) ⎭

The 1st Air Brigade was primarily assigned to support the ground operations of the 1st Army, and the 3d Air Brigade to support those of the 35th and 21st Divisions.

Tactical Command by the 1st Army

Policy: The Army planned to assemble as much strength as possible in southern Shansi Province, to employ elements to destroy and mop up the enemy in the Yangcheng area, and to dispose the main strength in the sector west of the Changmatsun - Yuanchu line in order to envelop and destroy the Kuomintang Army there, and thus advance the main front line to the Huang Ho line.

In the event the enemy 27th and 93d Armies were to take to the offensive during this operation, the 1st Army would, upon completion of the above operation, engage them at an opportune time and destroy them.

The period of the operation was scheduled to be approximately one month beginning in early June at the latest in view of the rainy season.

<u>Units Participating in the Operation</u>: The North China Area Army designated the 1st Army front as the most important sector and planned to reinforce its troop strength as much as possible. Accordingly not only did the North China Area Army reinforce the troop strength on the 1st Army front by sending the 33d Division (which had been transferred from Central China and which consisted of two infantry regiments and the main force of its supporting line units), but it also dispatched an infantry regiment which had been retained by the Area Army as a reserve unit.

A summary of the units participating in the 1st Army operation is given below:

> The 33d Division (consisting of seven infantry battalions and the main force of supporting line units)[133]
>
> The 36th Division (consisting of six infantry battalions and the main force of supporting line units)
>
> The 37th Division (consisting of nine and a half infantry battalions and the main force of supporting line units)

---

133. To reinforce the 33d Division which had left one infantry regiment in Central China, the 1st Army organized temporally a composite infantry battalion with elements from the 3d, 4th, 9th and 16th Independent Mixed Brigades and attached it to the division.

The 41st Division (consisting of 11 infantry battalions and the main force of supporting line units)

The 9th Independent Mixed Brigade (consisting of four infantry battalions as its nucleus)

The 16th Independent Mixed Brigade (consisting of three infantry battalions as its nucleus)

The Reserve Unit of the 1st Army (consisting of one battalion at first, later reinforced with another battalion)

Total: The nucleus of the total strength consisted of approximately 42½ infantry battalions.

The 1st Army published the following orders:

The operational sector shall be divided into two sectors, namely, the sector east of the line connecting Changmatsun and Yuanchu and the sector west of that line. Priority shall always be given to the west sector and, by assembling the greater part of the troop strength (35½ battalions out of the total 42½ battalions) in that sector, the supremacy of Japanese troop strength over the enemy strength[134] (fixing the ratio approximately at 0.7 to 1) shall be maintained at all costs so as to be able to envelop the hostile troops completely and annihilate them.

In order to attain this objective, the operating units shall be directed to envelop the enemy forces completely by blocking their routes of retreat with advance forces, by taking advantage of already existing positions on the front, the natural obstacles of the Huang Ho, and by swift break-through actions from both flanks. Subsequently, the Army shall engage and annihilate the enemy com-

---

134. At that time the Japanese Army considered in general that it was possible to execute an offensive successfully against the Chinese Army with its strength at one-third of the Chinese strength.

pletely by carrying out punitive and repeated mopping-up operations within the sector.

In order to make envelopment certain, inner and outer enveloping units shall be designated, and the retreat route interception line (namely, the enveloping line) shall be adjusted occasionally so as to prevent the escape of the enemy troops. The combat strength of the outer enveloping line units shall be particularly strong. The emphasis in troop disposition shall be placed upon preventing the enemy from escaping into areas south of the Huang Ho, and strong raiding units shall be rushed to occupy and secure vital areas to prevent the enemy from escaping. At the same time, every available step shall be taken to conceal our intentions, and the movement of the units shall be initiated after sunset in order to execute surprise attacks.

In order to insure that preparations for the operation would be complete, Group commanders and staff officers were assembled repeatedly to study the tactical command thoroughly so that no single point would be misinterpreted. Each unit carried out map maneuvers, war games and research of actual terrain features, and, at the same time, conducted unit training to insure that everyone would be able to meet both the demands of the terrain and battle situation in actual combat.

In consequence, the morale of officers and men was high and all were confident of victory.

The principle of tactical command of each unit was set forth as follows:

The 33d Division (consisting of seven infantry battalions as its nucleus and commanded by Lt Gen Sakurai)

The division shall mass near Yangcheng and shall prepare to attack the enemy in the sector east of the Changmatsun - Yuanchu line, separately from the main force of the 1st Army. It shall carry out a surprise attack on the enemy's first line of defense after sunset on the 7th, break through the line and rapidly advance to the sector east of Yuanchu, and, in co-operation with the force which will advance from the Honan Province, defeat and mop up the enemy in this sector.

The 16th Independent Mixed Brigade (consisting of three infantry battalions as its nucleus and commanded by Maj Gen Wakamatsu)

The brigade shall prepare near Pinglu for the attack against the main force of the 80th Army which is operating in the sector east of Pinglu. It shall initiate its movement after sunset on the 7th, and, after penetrating the enemy's first line of defense, engage and destroy the enemy in the sector. Strong raiding units shall be dispatched to river crossing points along the Huang Ho to capture these points and cut off the enemy's routes of retreat to the south of the river.

Forces on the Outer Enveloping Line in the Area of the Main Force of the Army:

The 37th Division (consisting of nine and a half infantry battalions as its nucleus and commanded by Lt Gen Adachi)

The division shall prepare for the attack near Ani. It shall initiate action after sunset on the 7th; carry out a surprise attack on the enemy's first line of defense and advance to the Huang Ho line after penetrating the defense line, where it shall establish a complete outer enveloping circle by making solid contact with the 41st Division. It shall then wheel to the north, engage and destroy the enemy within the enveloping circle, and continue its attack operations until it arrives at its position on the former first line of defense. Next, it shall engage in mopping up the enemy within the operational sector. Simultaneously with the penetration of the enemy first line of defense, the division shall dispatch strong raiding units to the river crossing points and northern key points along the Huang Ho to capture and secure the above-mentioned points and engage and destroy any escaping enemy troops. In penetrating the enemy defense line and advancing into the operational sector, the division, with its elements, shall occupy key points on the enveloping line running along its advancing route and engage and destroy escaping enemy troops.

The 41st Division (consisting of 11 infantry battalions as its nucleus and commanded by Lt Gen Shimizu)

The division shall prepare for the attack west of Changmatsun. It shall commence action after sunset on the 7th, launch a surprise attack upon the enemy's first line of defense and penetrate it, drive swiftly to the Huang Ho line, and establish a complete outer enveloping circle by making solid contact with the 37th Division. It shall then immediately wheel northward and engage and destroy the enemy within the encirclement. It shall continue its attack until it arrives in the area around the position on the former first line of defense which lies southwest of Chianghsien. Next, it shall engage in mopping up the enemy within the operational sector. Simultaneously with the penetration of the enemy's first line of defense, the division shall rush strong raiding units to the river crossing points and northern key points along the Huang Ho to occupy and secure the above-mentioned points and engage and destroy any enemy troops attempting to escape. In penetrating the enemy's defense line and advancing into the operational sector, the division, with its elements, shall occupy key points on the enveloping line running along the Chianghsien - Yuanchu road. It shall keep contact with the 9th Independent Mixed Brigade and shall engage and destroy escaping enemy troops.

Forces on the Inner Enveloping Line in the Area of the Main Force of the Army:

The 36th Division (consisting of six infantry battalions as its nucleus and commanded by Lt Gen Izeki)

The division shall prepare for the attack near Wenhsi. It shall commence action after sunset on the 7th, by launching a surprise attack upon the enemy's first line of defense and advancing deep into enemy territory, where it shall establish a complete inner enveloping circle by making solid contact with the 9th Independent Mixed Brigade. It shall then immediately wheel to the north, and, while engaging and destroying the enemy within the encirclement, shall continue its attack operations until it arrives at the area near the former first defense line position. The division shall then engage in mopping-up the enemy within the operational sector. In penetrating the enemy's first line of defense, the division shall rush part of its strength as raiding units to key points within the enemy area to capture these key points and thus facilitate the tactical command of the mopping-up operation.

The 9th Independent Mixed Brigade (consisting of four infantry battalions as its nucleus and commanded by Maj Gen Ikenoue)

The brigade shall prepare for the attack west of Chianghsien. It shall commence movement after sunset on the 7th by launching a surprise attack against the enemy's first line of defense and advancing deep into the enemy area where it shall establish a complete inner enveloping circle by making solid contact with the 36th

Division. It shall then immediately wheel to the north, and, while engaging and destroying the enemy within the encirclement, shall continue its attack operations until it arrives at the area near the former first defense line position. The brigade shall then engage in mopping up the enemy within the operational sector. In penetrating the enemy's first line of defense, the brigade shall rush part of its strength as raiding units to key points within the enemy area to capture key points and thus facilitate the tactical command for the mopping-up operation. By keeping contact with the 41st Division, the brigade shall occupy and secure with part of its strength the key points on the enveloping line along the Chianghsien - Yuanchu road and engage escaping enemy troops.

Reserve Unit of the Army

One infantry battalion (reinforced with one infantry battalion later)

The battalion shall be stationed near Chianghsien, and with the progress of the operation it shall advance to the sector north of Yuanchu.

Summary of Operational Progress by 1st Army

Preparations for the operation in the area of the main force of the 1st Army were completed by noon on 7 May and each force awaited final orders, confident of victory in the operation. However, in the 33d Division area, the arrival of the units transferred from Central China was delayed and some of them arrived just in time for the commencement of the operation. Since there was not sufficient time for these units to make thorough preparations, they joined the operation without full knowledge of the topographical conditions of the operational area and the enemy situation.

A strong northwest wind created a dust storm which continued the entire afternoon of 7 May, the day the operation began. This helped to conceal the movements of the Japanese troops.

Forces in the area of the main force of the Army commenced moving as scheduled after sunset on 7 May. The objectives of the surprise attacks were attained everywhere, penetration of enemy lines of defense was achieved and the whole operation went forward according to plan.

Yuanchu, the most important river crossing point on the Huang Ho, was captured in the evening of the second day (approximately 21½ hours after the initiation of the operation), the outer enveloping circle was established during the early morning of the third day (approximately 35 hours after the operation began), and the inner enveloping circle, around noon of the third day (approximately 40 hours after the operation began). The Army, therefore, succeeded in encircling the greater part of the enemy forces in the sector.

All units turned swiftly to the north where they engaged and destroyed from 3,000 to 5,000 enemy troops, and repeated mopping-up operations drove all enemy forces completely out of the area north of the Huang Ho.

The 33d Division commenced moving as scheduled after sunset on the 7th, and launched a surprise attack against the enemy's first line of defense. The attack was checked both by steep terrain features and by strong enemy resistance and at first did not progress as planned. However, with the favorable development of operations in the area of the main force and the progress of operations pushed from the Honan Province, the 33d Division defeated the enemy forces and subsequently engaged in mopping up operations within the sector.

The hostile 27th and 93d Armies made no move at the beginning of the operation. Later, they commenced action against the flank and rear of the Japanese forces. On the fourth day of the operation the 27th Army advanced to the area near Kaoping, and the 93d Army to the sector north of Yangcheng.

Since the objective of the operation in the area of the main force generally had been achieved, the 1st Army decided to transfer strong elements to the area endangered by this new enemy action and to destroy the enemy by taking advantage of his sorties. On 15 May, the 1st Army ordered the 33d Division, which was still fighting a stubborn enemy occupying defensive positions in depth southwest of Yangcheng, to break off the engagement and to proceed to the northwest of Tuanshihchen[135] and the following day ordered the 36th Division to proceed to the vicinity of Kaoping. On the 16th, both divisions began to move toward their designated positions arriving on the 20th and 23d respectively.[136] On the way, the 36th Division attacked the 27th Army west of Kaoping,[137] and the 27th Army retreated eastward to the mountainous area on the border of Shansi and Honan Provinces.

---

135. By 14 May, the 21st Division had arrived in the vicinity of Chuwa and had begun to attack the enemy confronting the 33d Division from the rear. Monograph No 70, *China Area Operations Record, Vol I*.
136. These dates were obtained from the Japanese *Military Magazine* issued immediately after the Chungyuan Operation.
137. Although all available sources have been explored exact date of this encounter is unknown.

The 33d and 36th Divisions attacked the 93d Army on the 20th and 23 May respectively and the Army retreated in small groups toward Lingshih. Both Japanese divisions continued mopping-up operations around Tuanshihchen and Kaoping until 15 June, when the 33d Division assembled in the Yutzu - Taiku area[138] and the 36th Division returned to its original station (Changchih - Kaoping area) (Map 33)

The Communist Army and the Shansi Army took no positive action whatsoever during this operation.

Summary of the Progress of Operation by Forces Directly Attached to the Area Army

In conformity with the Area Army orders, the 35th Division initiated its advance on 7 May. However, as the division was located far from the scene of action, it took many days of marching to reach its objective and when the division succeeded in breaking through the enemy positions, the 41st Division was already executing mopping up operations in the area. Consequently, it became unnecessary to advance the division to the Yuanchu area. Accordingly, the Area Army ordered the 35th Division to seek out and attack the enemy forces fleeing to the southeast from the Shansi Province border, and the 21st Division to advance toward Yangcheng along the Chin Ho valley to facilitate the operations of the 33d Division.[139]

---

138. Later, the North China Area Army transferred this division to the Tungshan area.
139. During the actual operation the 21st Division advanced first to Chuwa and then to Henghotsun, rather than along the Chin Ho valley toward Yangcheng as ordered by the North China Area Army as this route of advance was found to be far more helpful to the 33d Division. Monograph No 70, China Area Operations Record, Vol I.

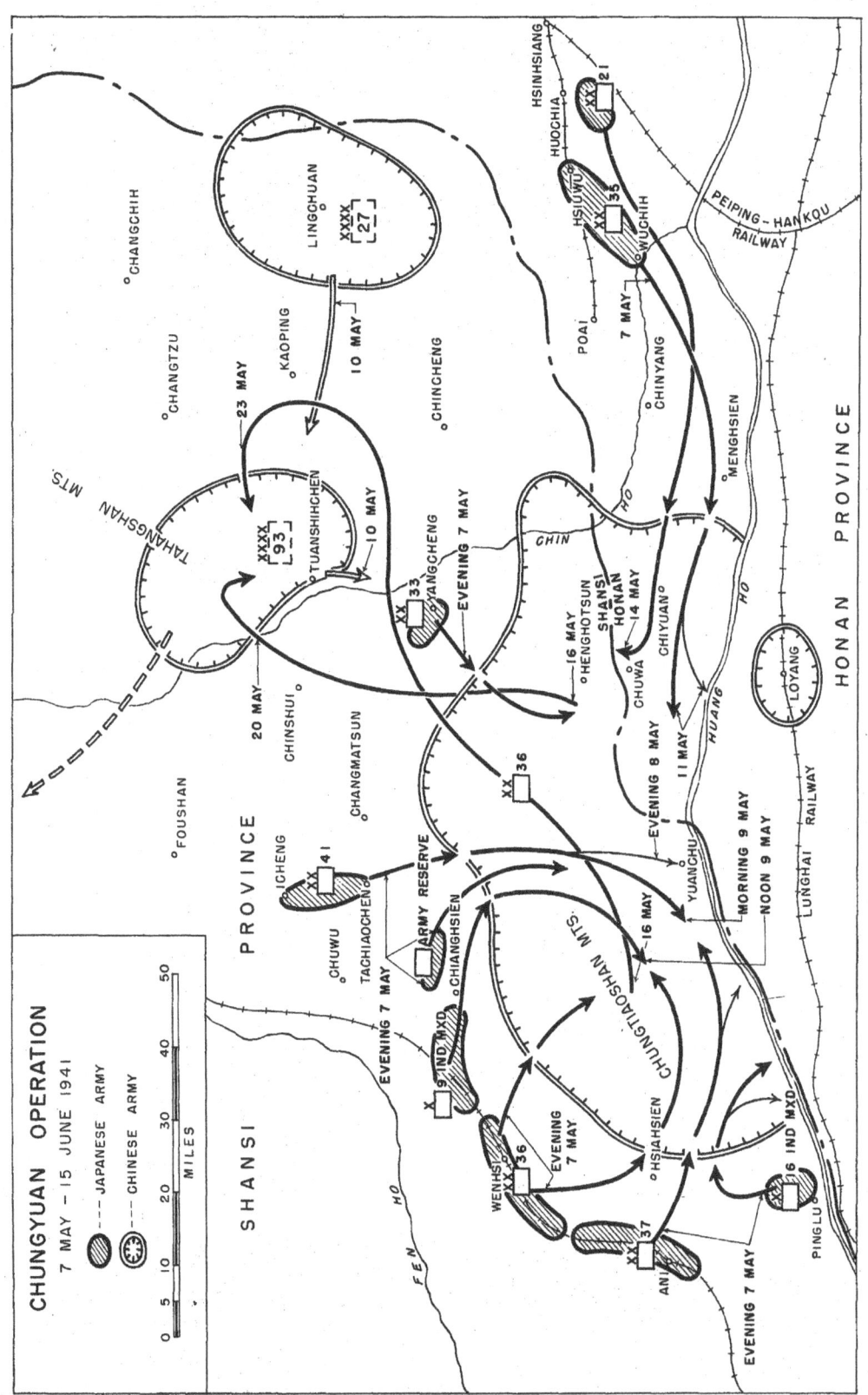

When the 35th Division penetrated the enemy's first line of defense, the enemy fled without resisting and the division thereafter engaged in mopping up the scattered enemy remnants.

The 21st Division initiated its advance around 12 May but was faced with strong resistance by the enemy in the mountain districts on the provincial border between Honan and Shansi Provinces and failed to dislodge the enemy and penetrate the line.

The Chungtiao Range occupied by the enemy was 1,000 - 2,500 meters above sea-level while the area west of the Changmatsun - Yuanchu line was a little lower, 1,000 - 1,500 meters. There were almost no inhabitants and very few roads in this area, which made it extremely difficult to carry out operations and obtain provisions.

Almost all of the enemy forces within the Chungtiao Range were destroyed by this operation, and twenty-seven mountain artillery guns and many other weapons were captured. The remaining enemy forces began to retreat in disorder, and, as a result, the main force of the Kuomintang Army, which had been threatening the peace in southern Shansi Province, was driven south of the Huang Ho, while the 93d Army gradually moved northward and retreated from the area around Lingshih to the west in order to evade further attacks by the Japanese Army. Although the hostile 27th Army was still in the southeastern part of Shansi Province it took no positive action, and peace and order in southern Shansi was substantially improved.

Containing Operation in Central China

When Lt Gen Korechika Anami, commanding officer of the 11th Army, learned that the North China Area Army was planning to launch the Chungyuan Operation in early May, in order to facilitate this operation, he decided to destroy the enemy forces operating in the key sector north of the Yangtzu River. He, therefore, published the following plan:

Basic Policy

    The 11th Army, beginning on 5 May, shall initiate attacks successively and each group shall defeat any enemy force with which it comes in contact.
    The period of time required for the operation is expected to be from seven to ten days.

Troop Strength to be Employed

    The 3d Division (consisting of 11 infantry battalions, one tank regiment and two mountain artillery battalions as its nucleus, and commanded by Lt Gen Teshima)
    The 39th Division (consisting of seven infantry battalions as its nucleus, and commanded by Lt Gen Murakami)
    The 4th Division (consisting of four infantry battalions as its nucleus, and commanded by Lt Gen Kitano)
    The 18th Independent Mixed Brigade (consisting of five infantry battalions as its nucleus, and commanded by Maj Gen Tsutsumi)

Principle of Tactical Command

    The 3d Division shall execute feint movements in the area north of Hsinyang on 22 April, and shall next initiate an attack on or about 5 May against the enemy in front of Suihsien.
    The 39th Division shall initiate an attack on or about 8 May and defeat the enemy north of Kingmen.
    The 18th Independent Mixed Brigade shall initiate an attack on or about 8 May and defeat the enemy north of Tangyang.
    The period of time for the operation of the above groups shall be from seven to ten days.
    The 4th Division shall execute a feint movement from 7 to 12 May in such areas as Loyangtien, Pingpachen and Anlu

to facilitate the operations of the 3d and 39th Divisions.

Summary of Operational Progress

On 5 May the main force of the 3d Division departed from the Hochiatien assembly points, and advanced, defeating the enemy on the way. It was estimated that the opposing enemy began to retreat from around the 7th. On the 10th, the division tightened its encirclement to the periphery of Huantanchen.

It remained at Huantanchen until the 13th, but again began moving on the evening of that day in order to engage and destroy the main force of the hostile 22d Army Group in the Tsaoyang vicinity. It penetrated Tsaoyang on the 15th and inflicted heavy damage to the enemy. Next, the division planned to destroy the hostile 29th Army in the vicinity of Hsiaopanchiao and part of the 55th Army in the Hsinyang area before it returned to its original position. It commenced movement on the 16th, and on the 17th dealt a severe blow to the 29th Army. On the 21st it attacked and defeated elements of the 55th Army in the Hsinyang area. From the 20th to the 22d, the division returned to its home base.

The main force of the 39th Division departed on 8 May from its assembly points, Kingmen and the area to the north, commenced its attack on the 9th against the strong main position of the enemy and penetrated its positions on the 10th. It then assembled at the rear of the enemy position and ordered an element to pursue the enemy to Anchiachi. The main force of the division then commenced returning to its home base.

The 18th Independent Mixed Brigade left its assembly point on the night of the 7th, advanced to the river basin of the Chiuching Ho north of Yuanan on the 9th, and changed its advance course to the east on the 10th in order to attack the enemy at Kuanyinssu. It captured Kuanyinssu on the 12th. The brigade then commenced returning to its home base.

The 4th Division, which had been ordered to carry out feint operations, advanced on the 8th toward Sanlikang and Liushuikou and achieved its mission without facing major enemy resistance. The division then carried out a feint movement on Loyangtien. An element, which was occupying Sanlikang, commenced movement on the 12th, and, after passing designated target areas, arrived at Anlu on the 14th. (Map 34)

Immediately after the commencement of the return movement of the Japanese units, enemy troops again began to occupy the areas vacated by the Japanese units. Consequently, the situation was no better than before the operation.

In this operation, although the 11th Army engaged seventeen hostile divisions, it obtained no major battle results. Also, as the area of the operation was located 300 to 400 kilometers away from the Chungyuan Operation sector it might be said that the operation had no direct effect upon the operation of the North China Area Army. However, it was believed that the operation did prove helpful to the North China Area Army's operation by preventing the Fifth War Sector Army on the north

MAP NO. 34

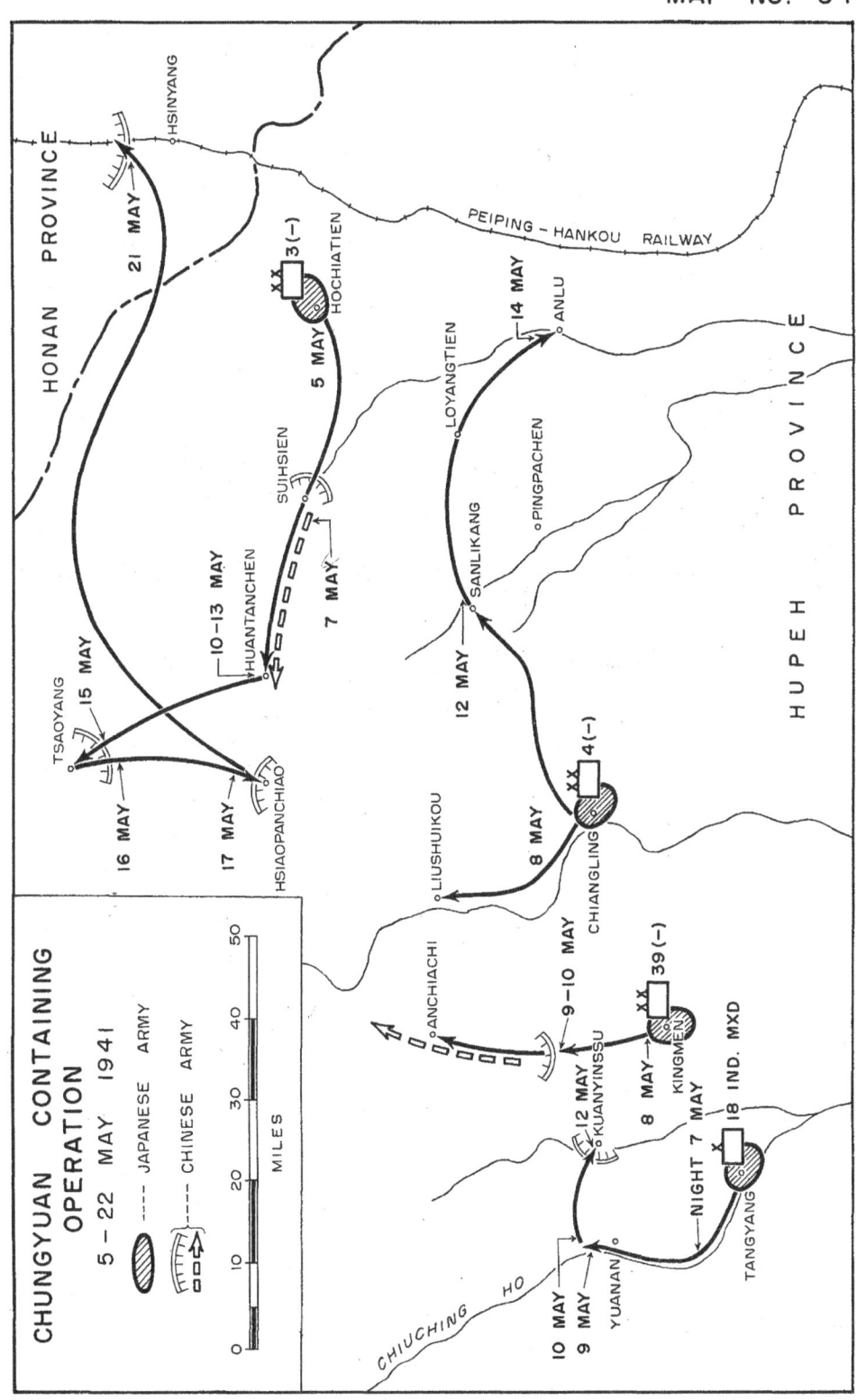

front of the 11th Army from taking part in any action in the Shansi Province area.

APPENDIX No I

The North China Area Army Order of Battle
31 August 1937

The North China Area Army Commander: General Count Hisaichi Terauchi

The North China Area Army Headquarters

The 1st Army (Commander: Lt Gen Kiyoshi Katsuki, consisting of the 6th, 14th and 20th Divisions as the nucleus)

The 2d Army (Commander: Lt Gen Toshizo Nishio, consisting of the 10th, the 16th and 108th Divisions as the nucleus)

The 5th Division

The 109th Division

China Garrison Mixed Brigade

Provisional Air Corps (see Appended Table 1)

Antiaircraft Unit directly attached to the North China Area Army (see Appended Table 2)

The 1st Independent Heavy Siege Artillery Battalion (28cm Howitzer)

The 2d Independent Heavy Siege Artillery Battalion (28cm Howitzer)

The 3d Tractor Unit (Type B)

North China Area Army Signal Unit (see Appended Table 3)

The 6th Radio Intelligence Unit

The 7th Radio Intelligence Unit

The 1st Field Meteorological Unit (mobile)

The 2d Field Meteorological Unit (fixed)

The 1st Field Survey Unit

The 3d Field Survey Unit

North China Area Army Railway Unit (see Appended Table 4)

The 1st Field Chemical Warfare Experiment Unit

Line of Communications Unit directly attached to the
   North China Area Army (see Appended Table 5)

The China Garrison Military Police Unit

Appended Table 1

Outline of the Provisional Air Corps Organization

    The Provisional Air Corps Commander: Lt Gen Baron Yoshitoshi Tokugawa

    Provisional Air Corps Headquarters

    The 1st Air Brigade Headquarters

    The 1st Air Battalion (Reconnaissance)

    The 2d Air Battalion (Reconnaissance)

    The 3d Air Battalion (Fighter)

    The 8th Air Battalion (Fighter)

    The 5th Air Battalion (Light bomber)

    The 9th Air Battalion (Light bomber)

    The 6th Air Battalion (Heavy bomber)

    The 4th Independent Air Squadron (Reconnaissance)

    The 6th Independent Air Squadron (Reconnaissance)

    The 9th Independent Air Squadron (Fighter)

    The 3d Independent Air Squadron (Heavy bomber)

Appended Table 2

Antiaircraft Units directly attached to the North China Area Army

    The 7th Field Antiaircraft Artillery Unit of the Guards Division (fixed)

    The 8th Field AAA Unit of the Guards Division (fixed)

    The 9th Field AAA Unit of the Guards Division (fixed)

    The 5th Field AAA Unit of the 1st Division (fixed)

    The 6th Field AAA Unit of the 1st Division (fixed)

    The 7th Field AAA Unit of the 1st Division (fixed)

    The 8th Field AAA Unit of the 1st Division (fixed)

    The 1st Field AAA Unit of the 4th Division (fixed)

    The 2d Field AAA Unit of the 4th Division (fixed)

    The 3d Field AAA Unit of the 4th Division (fixed)

    The 4th Field AAA Unit of the 4th Division (fixed)

    The 1st Field AAA Unit of the 5th Division (fixed)

    The 2d Field AAA Unit of the 5th Division (fixed)

    The 3d Field AAA Unit of the 5th Division (fixed)

    The 4th Field AAA Unit of the 5th Division (fixed)

    The 5th Field AAA Unit of the 5th Division (fixed)

    The 6th Field AAA Unit of the 5th Division (fixed)

    The 7th Field AAA Unit of the 5th Division (fixed)

    The 8th Field AAA Unit of the 12th Division (fixed)

    The 1st Field AAA Unit of the 20th Division (fixed)

    The 2d Field AAA Unit of the 20th Division (fixed)

The 5th Field Searchlight Unit of the Guards Division
The 6th Field Searchlight Unit of the Guards Division
The 1st Field Searchlight Unit of the 3d Division
The 2d Field Searchlight Unit of the 3d Division
The 3d Field Searchlight Unit of the 3d Division
The 4th Field Searchlight Unit of the 3d Division
The 5th Field Searchlight Unit of the 3d Division
The 6th Field Searchlight Unit of the 3d Division

Appended Table 3

North China Area Army Signal Unit Organization

    China Garrison Signal Unit

    The 22d Field Wire Communication Company

    The 23d Field Wire Communication Company

    The 2d Radio Communications Platoon (motorized)

    The 8th Radio Communications Platoon (motorized)

    The 9th Radio Communications Platoon (motorized)

    The 13th Radio Communications Platoon (motorized)

    The 53d Radio Communications Platoon (motorized)

    The 3d Fixed Radio Communications Unit

    The 9th Fixed Radio Communications Unit

    The 10th Fixed Radio Communications Unit

    The 11th Fixed Radio Communications Unit

    The 17th Field Carrier Pigeon Platoon

Appended Table 4

North China Area Army Railway Unit Organization

    The 1st Railway Inspectorate

    The 1st Railway Regiment

    The 2d Railway Regiment

    The 1st Railroad Stores Depot

    The 42d Railway Station Headquarters

    The 43d Railway Station Headquarters

    The 44th Railway Station Headquarters

    The 45th Railway Station Headquarters

    The 46th Railway Station Headquarters

    The 47th Railway Station Headquarters

    The 48th Railway Station Headquarters

    The 4th Land Duty Unit of the 3d Division

    The 5th Land Duty Unit of the 3d Division

    The 1st Land Duty Unit of the 7th Division

    The 2d Land Duty Unit of the 7th Division

    The 3d Land Duty Unit of the 7th Division

    The 4th Land Duty Unit of the 7th Division

    The 5th Land Duty Unit of the 7th Division

    The 1st Land Duty Unit of the 12th Division

    The 2d Land Duty Unit of the 12th Division

    The 3d Land Duty Unit of the 12th Division

    The 4th Land Duty Unit of the 12th Division

The 5th Land Duty Unit of the 12th Division

The 2d Construction Duty Unit of the Guards Division

The 1st Construction Duty Unit of the 11th Division

The 2d Construction Duty Unit of the 11th Division

Appended Table 5

Line of Communications Units Directly Attached to the North China Area Army

    The 1st Line of Communications Command of the North China Area Army

    The 2d Line of Communications Command of the North China Area Army

    The 3d Line of Communications Command of the North China Area Army

    The 1st Line of Communications Headquarters of the Guards Division

    The 2d Line of Communications Headquarters of the Guards Division

    The 1st Line of Communications Headquarters of the 2d Division

    The 2d Line of Communications Headquarters of the 2d Division

    The 1st Line of Communications Headquarters of the 2d Division

    The 2d Line of Communications Headquarters of the 3d Division

    The 1st Line of Communications Headquarters of the 5th Division

    The 2d Line of Communications Headquarters of the 5th Division

    The 1st Line of Communications Headquarters of the 7th Division

    The 1st Line of Communications Headquarters of the 9th Division

    The 1st Line of Communications Headquarters of the 12th Division

    The 2d Line of Communications Headquarters of the 12th Division

    The 1st Line of Communications Signal Unit Headquarters of the North China Area Army

    The 2d Line of Communications Signal Unit Headquarters of the North China Area Army

    The 3d Line of Communications' Wire Communication Company

The 4th Line of Communications' Wire Communication Company

The 7th Line of Communications' Wire Communication Company

The 9th Line of Communications' Wire Communication Company

The 12th Line of Communications' Wire Communication Company

The 15th Line of Communications' Wire Communication Company

The 1st Line of Communications Transport Battalion Headquarters

The 2d Line of Communications Transport Battalion Headquarters

The 5th Line of Communications Transport Battalion Headquarters

The 6th Line of Communications Transport Battalion Headquarters

The 7th Line of Communications Transport Battalion Headquarters

The 8th Line of Communications Transport Battalion Headquarters

The 11th Line of Communications Transport Battalion Headquarters

The 12th Line of Communications Transport Battalion Headquarters

The 1st to the 4th (inclusive) Line of Communications Transport Companies of the 2d Division

The 1st to the 4th (inclusive) Line of Communications Transport Companies of the 3d Division

The 1st and 2d Line of Communications Transport Companies of the 4th Division

The 3d and 4th Line of Communications Transport Companies of the 7th Division

The 1st and 2d Line of Communications Transport Companies of the 8th Division

The 1st and 2d Line of Communications Transport Companies of the 9th Division

The 1st to the 4th (inclusive) Line of Communications Transport Companies of the 11th Division

The 3d and 4th Line of Communications Transport Companies of the 12th Division

The 3d and 4th Line of Communications Transport Companies of the 14th Division

The 3d and 4th Line of Communications Transport Companies of the 16th Division

The 1st Line of Communications Motor Transport Unit Headquarters

The 2d Line of Communications Motor Transport Unit Headquarters

The 3d Line of Communications Motor Transport Unit Headquarters

The 4th Line of Communications Motor Transport Unit Headquarters

The 5th Line of Communications Motor Transport Unit Headquarters

The 6th Line of Communications Motor Transport Unit Headquarters

The 2d Line of Communications Motor Transport Company

The 15th to the 19th (inclusive) Line of Communications Motor Transport Companies

The 33d to the 37th (inclusive) plus the 39th Line of Communications Motor Transport Companies

The 44th to the 49th (inclusive) Line of Communications Motor Transport Companies

The 50th to the 58th (inclusive) Line of Communications Motor Transport Companies

The 71st and 72d Line of Communications Motor Transport Companies

The 78th and 79th Line of Communications Motor Transport Companies

The 80th and the 87th to the 89th (inclusive) Line of Communications Motor Transport Companies

Transport Observation Unit of the 90th and 91st Line of Communications Motor Transport Companies

The 7th and 8th Transport Observation Units of the 2d Division

The 1st to the 6th (inclusive) Transport Observation Units of the 4th Division

The 7th to the 9th (inclusive) Transport Observation Units of the 9th Division

The 1st to the 3d (inclusive) Transport Observation Units of the 10th Division

The 1st to the 3d (inclusive) plus the 7th and 8th Transport Observation Units of the 12th Division

The 7th and 8th Transport Observation Units of the 14th Division

The 1st and 2d Reserve Mount Depots of the North China Area Army

The 1st to the 3d (inclusive) Field Artillery Depots of the North China Area Army

The 1st to the 3d (inclusive) Field Engineer Depots of the North China Area Area Army

The 1st to the 3d (inclusive) Field Motor Transport Depots of the North China Area Army

The 1st and the 2d Field Gas Depots of the North China Area Army

The 1st to the 3d (inclusive) Field Rations and Clothing Depots of the North China Area Army

The 1st and 2d Field Reserve Hospital Headquarters of the North China Area Army

The 7th Section of the Field Reserve Hospital

The 10th, 11th and 19th Sections of the Field Reserve Hospital

The 22d plus the 27th to the 30th (inclusive) Sections of the Field Reserve Hospital

The 1st and 2d Casualty Clearing Units Headquarters of the North China Area Army

The 7th Section of the Casualty Clearing Unit

The 10th, 11th, 16th and 18th Sections of the Casualty Clearing Unit

The 21st and the 26th to the 28th (inclusive) plus the 30th Sections of the Casualty Clearing Unit

The 1st to the 4th (inclusive) Line of Communications Hospitals, of the North China Area Army

The 1st to the 3d (inclusive) Line of Communications Veterinary Depots of the North China Area Army

The 5th Second Reserve Infantry Battalion of the Guards Division

The 1st to the 4th (inclusive) 2d Reserve Infantry Battalions of the 6th Division

The 1st to the 6th (inclusive) 2d Reserve Infantry Battalions of the 7th Division

The 1st to the 4th (inclusive) 2d Reserve Infantry Battalions of the 11th Division

The 3d and 4th, 2d Reserve Cavalry Companies of the Guards Division

The 1st and 2d, 2d Reserve Field Artillery Batteries of the 6th Division

The 1st and 2d, 2d Reserve Field Artillery Batteries of the 8th Division

The 1st and 2d, 2d Reserve Mountain Artillery Batteries of the 2d Division

The 1st, 2d Reserve Mountain Artillery Battery of the 11th Division

The 1st, 2d Reserve Engineer Company of the Guards Division

The 1st and 2d, 2d Reserve Engineer Companies of the 2d Division

The 1st, 2d Reserve Engineer Company of the 7th Division

The 1st, 2d Reserve Engineer Company of the 12th Division

The 1st to the 4th (inclusive) Hand-car Railway Units

The 1st to the 3d (inclusive) Land Duty Units of the 3d Division

The 1st to the 5th (inclusive) Land Duty Units of the 4th Division

The 3d and 4th Land Duty Units of the 5th Division

The 1st Land Duty Unit of the 7th Division

The 1st to the 4th (inclusive) Land Duty Units of the 8th Division

The 1st and the 2d plus the 6th to the 10th (inclusive) Land Duty Units of the 9th Division

The 2d plus the 6th to the 9th (inclusive) Land Duty Units of the 10th Division

The 1st to the 5th (inclusive) Land Duty Units of the 11th Division

The 2d to the 4th (inclusive) Sea Duty Units of the 2d Division

The 1st and the 2d Sea Duty Units of the 8th Division

The 1st Sea Duty Unit of the 9th Division

The 1st and 2d Sea Duty Units of the 14th Division

The 1st and 2d Sea Duty Units of the 16th Division

The 1st Construction Duty Unit of the Guards Division

The 1st and 2d Construction Duty Units of the 2d Division

The 1st Construction Duty Unit of the 7th Division

The 1st and 2d Construction Duty Units of the 8th Division

The 2d Construction Duty Unit of the 9th Division

The 1st to the 3d (inclusive) plus the 6th and 7th Field Road Construction Units

The 1st Field Well Construction Unit Headquarters

The 4th Field Well Construction Unit Headquarters

The 1st and 2d, plus the 12th to the 15th (inclusive) Field Well Construction Companies

The 2d Field Construction Headquarters

The 1st Material Collecting Headquarters

The 1st Field Purification Unit (A)

The 2d to the 4th (inclusive) Field Purification Units (B)

The China Garrison Army Warehouse

The China Garrison Army Hospital